Intrigues

GABRIEL RIERA

Intrigues

FROM BEING TO THE OTHER

Fordham University Press

New York 2006

Library of Congress Cataloging-in-Publication Data

Riera, Gabriel.
    Intrigues : from being to the other / Gabriel Riera.
    p.   cm.
    Includes bibliographical references and index.
    ISBN-13: 978-0-8232-2671-9 (cloth : alk. paper)
    ISBN-10: 0-8232-2671-9 (cloth : alk. paper)
    1. Other (Philosophy)   2. Ethics.   I. Title.
    BD213.O85   2006
    190—dc22

                                    2006035286

Printed in the United States of America
08 07 06   5 4 3 2 1
First edition

CONTENTS

v

ACKNOWLEDGMENTS

The research for this book was made possible by the generous support of two Princeton University Research Grants.

I am also grateful for the continued support of Juliet Flower MacCannell, J. Hillis Miller, Tracy MacNulty, and Claudia Brodsky throughout the years.

Silvia Rosman was an invaluable interlocutor throughout this project. To her my most special thanks.

Portions of this book were given at the International Association of Philosophy and Literature, New York University, Cornell University, the University of Pittsburgh, and the University of Illinois.

Some parts of this book appeared in journals and edited volumes. I thank the editors and publishers for kindly granting permission to use abbreviated, expanded, or otherwise adapted versions of these articles.

"*Intrigas del otro* (Lévinas/Blanchot)," in *Etcétera* (November 2003), Fundación Descartes, Círculo de Actualización Filosófica, Buenos Aires, Argentina.

"The Possibility of 'the Poetic Said' in *Otherwise than Being* (Allusion, or Blanchot in Lévinas I)," in *Diacritics* 34, no. 2 (summer 2004), 1–22.

"'The Possibility of the Poetic Said": Between Allusion and Commentary (Ingratitude, or Blanchot in Lévinas II), in *Angelaki: Journal of the Theoretical Humanities* 9, no. 3 (December 2004), 121–35.

"Intrigue: L'Épreuve du temps chez Blanchot," in *L'Épreuve du temps dans l'écriture de Maurice Blanchot,* ed. Arthur Coors (Paris: Édition Complicités, 2006).

"Donner à lire: Le Livre et ses autres," in *Actes du Colloque International Lévinas-Blanchot,* ed. Eric Hoppenot (Paris: UNESCO, 2006).

Works frequently cited have been identified by the following abbreviations. They are arranged alphabetically under each author's name. Full citations are provided in an endnote at the first mention of the book, chapter, or article. Sources are also given in full in the alphabetical bibliography.

Maurice Blanchot

A	*L'Amitié*
AMV	*Au moment voulu*
DH	*Le Dernier homme*
DP	"Le 'Discourse Philosophique'"
ED	*L'Écriture du désastre*
EI	*L'Entretien infini*
EL	*L'Espace littéraire*
F	*Friendship*
FJ	*La Folie du jour*
FP	*Faux Pas*
IC	*The Infinite Conversation*
LV	*Le Livre à venir*
MD	*The Madness of the Day*
PAD	*Le Pas au-delà*
PF	*La Part du feu*
SH	*The Station Hill Blanchot Reader*

SL   *The Space of Literature*
SNB   *The Step Not Beyond*
SS   *The Sirens' Song*
WD   *The Writing of the Disaster*
WF   *The Work of Fire*

Gilles Deleuze

DeR   *Différence et répétition*
DR   *Difference and Repetition*

Jacques Derrida

AEL   *Adieu to Emmanuel Levinas*
D   *Demeure: Maurice Blanchot*
P   *Parages*
PA   *Politiques de l'amitié*
PoIF   *Politics of Friendship*
PSY   *Psychè: Inventions de l'autre*
WAD   *Writing and Difference*

Brian Fitch

LR   *Lire les récits de Maurice Blanchot*

Michel Foucault

LCP   *Language, Counter-Memory, Practice*
MEC   *Les Mots et les choses*
OT   *The Order of Things: An Archaeology of the Human Sciences*
PD   "La Pensée du dehors"

Martin Heidegger

BT   *Being and Time*
BW   *Martin Heidegger: Basic Writings*
CP   *Contributions to Philosophy (From Enowning)*
EGT   *Early Greek Thinking*

EHP	*Elucidations of Hölderlin's Poetry*
EM	*Einführung in die Metaphysik*
GA 2	*Gesamtausgabe 2: Sein und Zeit* [mit Randbemerkungen d. Autors]
GA 30	*Gesamtausgabe 30: Die Grundbegriffe der Metaphysik*
GA 39	*Gesamtausgabe 39: Hölderlins Hymnen "Germanien" und "Der Rhein"*
GA 55	*Gesamtausgabe 55: Heraklit 2. Logik: Heraklit Lehre vom Logos*
HHI	*Hölderlin's Hymn "The Ister"*
HW	*Holzwege*
IM	*An Introduction to Metaphysics*
KPM	*Kant and the Problem of Metaphysics*
LH	"Letter on Humanism"
N	*Nietzsche*
OWL	*On the Way to Language*
PATH	*Pathmarks*
PLT	*Poetry, Language, Thought*
QCT	"The Question Concerning Technology"
SZ	*Sein und Zeit*
TK	*Die Technik und die Kehre*
US	*Unterwegs sur Sprache*
VA	*Vorträge und Aufsätze*
WHD	*Was heißt Denken?*
WM	"What Is Metaphysics?"
WT	*What Is Called Thinking?*

Edmund Husserl

| CM | *Cartesian Meditations* |
| IP | *The Idea of Phenomenology: A Translation of 'Die idee der Phaënomeno-logie,' Husserliana II* |

Emmanuel Levinas

AE	*Autrement qu'être; ou, Au-delà de l'essence*
AT	*Altérité et transcendance*
CPP	*Collected Philosophical Papers*

DQV	*De Dieu qui vient à l'idée*
DEE	*De l'existence à l'existant*
DL	*Difficile Liberté: Essais sur le judaisme*
EDEHH	*En dècouvrant l'existence avec Husserl and Heidegger*
EE	*Existence and Existents*
EeI	*Éthique et infini*
EN	*Entre nous: Essais sur le penser-à-l'autre*
GCM	*Of God Who Comes to Mind*
HAH	*Humanisme de l'autre homme*
HGN	"Heidegger, Gagarin et nous"
HGU	"Heidegger, Gagarin and Us"
HS	*Hors sujet*
NP	*Noms propres*
O	*De l'oblitération: Entretien avec Françoise Armengaud à propos de l'œuvre de Sosno*
OB	*Otherwise than Being: or, Beyond Essence*
PN	*Proper Names*
RPH	"Quelques réflexions sur la philosophie de l'hitlerisme"
RS	"Reality and Its Shadow"
SMB	*Sur Maurice Blanchot*
TeI	*Totalité et infini: Essai sur l'extériorité*
TI	*Totality and Infinity: An Essay on Exteriority*

Stéphane Mallarmé

| OC | *Œuvres complètes* |
| SP | *Mallarmé: Selected Prose Poems, Essays, Letters* |

Jean-Paul Sartre

I	*L'Imaginaire*
PI	*The Psychology of Imagination*
QL	*Qu'est-ce que la littérature?*
WL	"*What is Literature?*" *and Other Essays*

Paul Valéry

| OCV | *Œuvres complètes* |

Intrigues

Introduction

The unnarratable other loses his face as a neighbor in narration. The relationship with him is *indescribable* in the literal sense of the term, unconvertible into a history, irreducible to the simultaneousness of writing, the eternal present of a writing that records or presents results.

—*Emmanuel Levinas*, Otherwise than Being

Passive: the un-story (*non-récit*), that which escapes quotation and which memory does not recall.

—*Maurice Blanchot*, The Writing of the Disaster

Thinking otherwise than he thinks, he thinks in such a way that the Other might come to thought, as approach and response.

—*Maurice Blanchot*, The Writing of the Disaster

The encounter: what comes without advent, what approaches face-on, and nonetheless always by surprise, what requires waiting and what waiting awaits but does not attain. Even at the innermost heart of interiority, it is always irruption of the outside, exteriority shaking everything.

The encounter pierces the world, pierces the self; and this piercing, everything that happens, without happening (coming about with the status of what has not arrived), is the reverse side that cannot be lived of what on the right side cannot be written: a double impossibility that by a supplementary act—a fraud, a kind of falsehood, also a madness—must be transformed in order to adapt it to living and writing "reality."

—*Maurice Blanchot*, The Infinite Conversation

Writing the Other

Intrigues: From Being to the Other examines the possibility of writing the other. It explores whether an ethical writing that preserves the other as such is possible and discusses what the implications are for an ethically inflected literary criticism. Emmanuel Levinas and Maurice Blanchot, whose works constitute the most thorough contemporary exploration of the question of the other and of its relation to writing, are the main focus of this study. The book's horizon is ethics in the Levinasian sense: the question of the other that, on the hither side of language understood as a system of signs and of representation, must be welcomed by language and preserved in its alterity. However, Martin Heidegger is an unavoidable reference. While it is true that for the German philosopher being is an immanent production, his elucidation of a more essential understanding of being entails a deconstruction of onto-theology, of the sign, the grammatical and logical determinations of language, all decisive starting points for both Levinas and Blanchot.

For Heidegger, ethics, as a region of philosophical questioning, comes after metaphysics (knowledge and theory) and is determined by the effect of oblivion that Plato's philosophy institutes. Heidegger's thinking marks a departure from an intellectualist tradition for which theoretical comprehension is the starting point of thinking. According to Heidegger, being is primarily determined in noncognitive ways, by modes of existence that are more basic than the intellectual grasp of the concept. In "Letter on Humanism" Heidegger seeks to define an ethics prior to any ethics, an "original ethics" understood as dwelling or sojourn, as the preserving of the open in its opening and mystery.[1] This is what the structure of care or concern (*Sorge*) means in *Being and Time*, in which the proximity of being to *Dasein* (being-there) is already in view.

The world is for Heidegger part of a structure proper to existence (*ek-sistence*: since the prefix *ek-* marks the exposition at play in being-in-the-world, throwness and facticity, a form of being that goes beyond the classical opposition inside/outside) called being-in-the-world (*In-der-Welt-Sein*). *Dasein* is a being for whom its being is a matter of concern and in which being-in-the-world reveals itself as a unifying structure. It is the structure of care that determines how entities come into presence, but inasmuch as the structure of care presupposes a unique relation to being, it is being that conditions the structure of our making-present. Later on Heidegger will say that being "gives or sends," but soon after he abandons the schema of the history of being to think what gives being—the Event of Appropriation or Enowning (*Ereignis*).

In an existential sense the "in" of being-in-the-world means a "being-alongside" (*bei*), *dwelling*, a relation of familiarity or proximity that is irreducible to spatial contiguity (BT 80/54).[2] But in a more essential way, dwelling names the responsibility that certain forms of existence (the thinker's, the poet's, the founder of a people) contract with being's unconcealing—its preservation. In the conferences and courses on Hölderlin, "The Origin of the Work of Art," and "Building Dwelling Thinking," Heidegger defines the fundamental feature of dwelling as the act of preserving and spearing, "saving" the world "by setting it free into its own presencing" (PLT).[3]

If for Heidegger being is an immanent event that originates in itself, its relation must be secured in accordance with its modality of manifestation. Poetry and thinking must be up to the task of preserving the incommensurable advent of being; they must expose themselves to what is without measure and without object; that is, they must become ek-static responses that leap (origin, or *Ursprung*) into the uncanny or unfamiliar par excellence. This entails a radical redefinition of language, beyond its classical metaphysical determination and beyond its modern determination as the correlation of represented contents and the mind. In order to retrieve both the truth of ontology and the truth of being, Heidegger proposes to take a "step back" beyond the Platonic determination of the being of entities, and to approach what being "was" in its first opening. If being cannot be captured in a single word, but is rather "the word for every word" (GA 55),[4] its opening is nonetheless felt throughout language. The enigma of being sustains language; it is the essence of language and can only unfold itself in language as the language of being.

What is decisive then are the modes in which being grants or gives itself and, above all, that there is a forgetting of being, its withdrawal as the privileged mode of granting itself. Heidegger privileges certain forms of unconcealment, like poetic language and thinking, to preserve being from the totalizing hold of the essence of technology and its monotonously dangerous way of manifesting beings. The essence of dwelling or sojourn reveals itself as a relation of sense (*Sinn*). The *there* is the open, the site from which things can have a place and a sense. Sense, therefore, is the very structure of the opening. Being is fundamentally what "gives sense" (*es gibt*), but this giving entails a production (*technē*) whose essence has been forgotten and endangered by technology, the dominant, albeit partial, way of uncovering beings.

Therefore, Heidegger's project revolves around *technē*s Janus face, between *poíesis* understood as the initial opening of being as a whole (*phusis*) and technology as its partial uncovering. This explains why Heidegger's meditation on the work of art is the site for thinking a more originary ethics and why it unfolds in a context dominated by the question of nihilism and its "abandonment of being" in its double determination as

Platonism and, in its "final stage," as technology. The work of art provides Heidegger not only with an occasion to accomplish the "step back," the "leap," but also with a schema to think this relation in terms of truth—the *schematism* of truth as (un)-veiling, or a way of radically rethinking figuration. This entails a redefinition of figuration that prepares the ground for tracing the "topology of being."

In seeking to establish a more essential dwelling, Heidegger aims to make explicit *Dasein*'s historiality, destiny (*Geshicht*), inasmuch as *Dasein* is understood as the site in which the question and meaning of being is put into play and, consequently, the question of the foundation of the destiny of a people. Poetic language understood as the listening and responding to the poem can constitute itself as the true *ethos*, inasmuch as "what remains is founded by the poets" (EHP).[5] The poet thus assumes the figure of a founder of being (*des Begründer des Seyns*), although this soon changes into a witness of being, someone who responds in accordance with the tenor of being's call. The poet finally becomes the figure of serenity (*Gelassenheit*), of the essential relation to language as a renunciation of mastery. Inasmuch as *Dasein* is understood as the guardian of the open or, rather, of the opening, only thinking and poetizing can guard it by bringing being to language.

However, and given the immanent essence of being, questions remains about whether this dialogue between thinking and poetry simply amounts to the surrendering of philosophy's own possibilities, a suture of sorts that deposes the philosophical *lógos*, making it succumb to the prestige of the poem. Does this dialogue open a path (*Weg*) to an "*anderen denken*" (other thinking) that could shield us from the violence of non-aletheiophanic modes of (un)concealment that unfold within the space of being's oblivion (*mimesis*, representation, technology)? It is a violence to which, it should be remembered, Heidegger himself surrendered by committing himself to the politics of National Socialism. Does the "original ethics" that is at the heart of Heidegger's "step back" think the responsibility of its own exposition to the other sufficiently? These are the questions that Levinas and Blanchot posit to Heidegger. In so doing they breach the immanence of being and thus open the possibility of an ethical writing of the other.

Throughout the book ethics bears no relationship to a set of principles or values but, rather, points to a profound mutation of thinking that by subordinating the order of knowledge and representation finds other significations beyond the order of discourse, or what Blanchot will call "dis-course."[6] By inflecting the word "discourse" with a discrete hyphen, Blanchot signals a nondiscursive supplement, something that "escapes systems, order, possibility, including the possibility of language, and that writing, perhaps—writing, where totality has let itself be exceeded—puts it in play" (WD 204/134).[7] It is writing that brings about this mutation of thinking. At stake for both Levinas and Blanchot then is how to mark a nondiscursive excess within discourse without erasing or reducing it. How should one read and write the other in the same without having the other return to the same?

Critics in recent years have discussed an "ethical moment or turn" characterized by the other's irruption in the order of discourse. The other becomes a true crossroads of disciplines since it affects several aspects of discourse: the constitution of the subject, the status of knowledge, the nature of representation and what (gender, power) that representation represses. However, there has been a tendency to graft the other to paradigms whose main purpose is to reassess questions of identity, fundamentally in terms of representation; the other thus loses some of its most crucial features.[8]

This does not mean that the sway of the other has had no positive effects.[9] Given that the other has made discourses and narratives possible, to claim that the other is "unnarratable" and "unrepresentable" may appear scandalous, if this claim were made by someone who is neither committed to a rational philosophy nor to justice, as Levinas clearly is. There is something else at stake in Levinas's claim: an indication that the proliferation of the other, its recurrence in current debates, is a sign of its exhaustion, or of its final demise. Because of knowledge's drive to make an inventory of its main features and to put them at the service of communicative action and representation, little seems to remain of what the other meant to convey—what escapes the principle of identity and identification. It is as if, paradoxically, the more we speak about the other the more we yield to the same.

Discourse regulates the other by anticipating its differences, by reducing its surprising arrival, reinvesting its excessive features and localizing its provenance. It calculates and anticipates the other by transforming it into the measure of possibility. Philosophy fares no better when it comes to the other, refusing, as it has, anything that could put in question the privilege of a self-centered consciousness. Philosophy cannot welcome the other because it is grounded in a conception of the self who constructs itself by subtraction from the other. It is in the subject that questions and answers originate since Descartes. Metaphysics endows the subject with the faculty of questioning itself, a power through which it appropriates anything foreign, transforming the other into the object of its own question. Philosophy, therefore, also transforms the other into an object of knowledge and representation; there is no "question of the other" because philosophical discourse posits a correlation between the question and the answer.

This is the case in Kantian morality, where the other is another reasonable being to whom I do not need to listen in order to know what I owe him. It is the subject's reason that tells me what is his or her due. "I owe something" to the other means that no sharing is constitutive of that relation. The question of responsibility thus consists neither in an exposure to nor in an encounter with the other. Inasmuch as the light of self's consciousness founds Kant's ethics, the self does not need to hear the other's demand. Obligation here concerns the relationship of the subject to itself and the form of its will. The only demand made by practical reason is that the will become universal and without contradiction. Kant's imperative is therefore logical rather than ethical, since I do not need to appeal to the other in order to confirm my judgment.

Classical philosophical inquiry cannot open itself to the question of the other, except by reducing it to the same: an alter ego, subject, man, or even *Dasein*. In each of these determinations the question takes place in the relationship of consciousness with itself. As a questioning instance, consciousness erases any "before" to itself. The self's freedom to be reasonable a priori rules its relation to the other according to its own measure, and not to that of the other.

A metaphysical position separates consciousness from a number of events (the body, the other human being, language, community) in order to guarantee a pure relationship to itself and define the a priori conditions of any possible coexistence among free subjects. The subject's legislative reason ignores the alterity of the other, its singularity, and can only know the universality of the law. It has already decided who the other is—another reasonable autonomous subject about whom it can determine beforehand what it has the right to demand.

In the works of Levinas and Blanchot it is possible to read another experience of the other; a question comes from the "other shore" (Levinas) or outside (Blanchot), a call the subject cannot anticipate, a murmur lurking behind language's propositional structure, or the constitutive duplicity of the image. The "approach and the response" (Blanchot) are "experiences" that force thinking to undergo a radical transformation and to "think otherwise than [it] thinks." These modalities can be grouped together under the term *encounter*, which points to a relationship with what is absolutely exterior. In the encounter thinking enters into a relationship with what no longer depends upon it and, in this sense, entails a "writing of the outside."[10]

Blanchot characterizes the type of relationship that thinking establishes with the outside as "relationship without relationship," since the terms involved absolve themselves from any reciprocity. All the features of this nonrelationship must, nevertheless, be thought and written as a "relationship." To encounter the other cannot be conceived as a form of recognition, but rather as the very "experience" of what is not recognizable and thus short-circuits the mechanism of recognition. By "outside" it is necessary to understand what cannot be represented or remains outside of representation, but also the very density of what cannot be represented. Only in this sense is it possible to speak of the question *of* the other. This is much different from the self-questioning subject who reduces the question of the other by failing to hear the other's call or by anticipating what the contents of this call will be.

Is it possible to write the other without assimilating it or without reducing it to the same, to an object or a thing, to concepts or categories, to constative (theoretical) or to performative (praxic) statements, to descriptions, and even to narratives? What kind of writing would be up to this challenge, if language unavoidably brings things into presence and reduces singularities to generalities?

Intrigues of the Other

The purpose of this book is to interrogate the other's persistence and its insistence as the knot of an *intrigue* that takes place at the margins of discourse and that can be considered the impossible condition of its possibility. Contemporary thinking is sensible of the other's difference and to the resistance it poses to discourse. It has invented a number of protocols to both welcome its approach and preserve the other in its singularity, which can be summarized according to two dominant modalities.

The first understands the other in terms of difference, of a multiplicity and plurality of intensities or forces. Here the other is an immanent and autonomous field of forces; and in order to be up to its proliferating diversity, a multiple array of forms is demanded from the thinker or writer. The second modality understands the other not as *heteros* but as *alter*—the other singular one that overtakes the same by surprise, divesting it of its autonomy and power.[11] The other either fascinates the self, occupying it with an unending and infinite demand (Blanchot), or reveals its vulnerability, sensibility, or radical passivity (Levinas).

The focus of this book will be this second modality of thinking the other. However, as we will see, this distinction between heteromorphic and heteronomic approaches does not hold neatly. In spite of their commonality there are decisive differences within the so-called heteronomic thinkers. Blanchot shares with Levinas his understanding of the other as what presents all the features of a nonrelationship (infinite removal, demand of an unending attention and responsiveness, asymmetry, excessive form of its approach), but nevertheless he parts ways with him when it comes to the pious and religious dimension of ethics. No other contemporary writer has been able to sustain an atheistic position in such a rigorous manner and to convey it so thoroughly in writing.

While Levinas does not grant any privilege to Nietzsche, Blanchot's atheism takes root in a reading of Nietzsche that does not simply liberate a proliferation of masks and forms, as in Gilles Deleuze, but produces a dissolution of forms and of their imaginary hold. Blanchot combines a fidelity to multiplicity and heterogeneity with an unending and infinite responsiveness to the other. He also takes Nietzsche's eternal return of the same as a point of departure for a different understanding of temporality, whose implications for writing the other are decisive. Therefore, within heteronomic thinking, it is possible to distinguish between a writing of ethics as *religo*, in which the other is the origin and end of signification, and an ethics of writing that keeps watch on the anarchic and unending absence of meaning.[12]

In spite of this crucial difference, Levinas and Blanchot share a basic premise—the other escapes both the order of discourse and the framework of narration, but must nevertheless be written. The exigency of the other both allows and disavows a response; this is the paradox that the writers I study confront in their texts, one that will allow them to elaborate a poetics of otherness and to rethink the relations between writing and ethics. Faced with the assimilating grasp of the concept, if the other must be preserved as such, writing has to abandon a series of guarantees and pass tangentially through the scene of knowledge and the order of representation so as to become its welcoming. Writing and ethics are the hinge of an "*intrigue* of the other," and the reason why Levinas and Blanchot constitute the focus of this book.

Levinas deploys the question of the other beyond Hegel and any possible dialectical recuperation, beyond even the horizon of fundamental ontology (Heidegger) and of a phenomenology of shame (Sartre). This "beyond" is in reality a movement of retraction towards more primary determinations of subjectivity and language. From the other's face (*visage*) to psychism (*psychisme*), from the "straightforwardness of prose" to the saying (*le dire*) that subtracts itself from the order of discourse (not without leaving the marks of its subtraction in the very texture of discourse), Levinas accomplishes a reduction of philosophical language that makes an ethical writing possible. He moves away from the ontological plot of *Totality and Infinity* (TI),[13] dominated by a metaphysics of the subject, to a "clandestine *intrigue*" that in *Otherwise than Being* (OB)[14] writes the mode of the approach of the other—its "*otherwise than Being.*"

Throughout this book the term *intrigue* denotes a mode of writing, an "invention of the other" against calculation, anticipation, identification and assimilation. Levinas displaces the term *intrigue* from its literary and narratological contexts. After reinscribing it within the context of "first philosophy," he refers to a dimension of language not assimilable to fables, narratives and aesthetic representations.[15] On the hither side of any semiotic or hermeneutic adventure, *intrigue* names the inextricable pre-originary implication of the other in the same. But Levinas is not the only one who privileges this term.

Maurice Blanchot conjugates the different meanings of *intrigue* in the sense of *intricare*, to entangle or perplex and also in the archaic sense of to embarrass.[16] He also puts into play the topic of essentiality, a room, or the interval separating two "characters" as a framework from which the encounter with the other can take place. Even though Blanchot deploys the *"intrigue* of the other" in "the space of literature," as well as in a reflection that refuses to give philosophy the last word, *intrigue* here, as well as in Levinas, refers to what subtracts itself from aesthetic representations. In this term it is possible to read the inextricable coimplication of philosophy and literature that takes these two concepts to their very limits. In this sense, both Levinas and Blanchot must be set apart from forms of ethical criticism that privilege narratives as the domain in which to best investigate human conflicts, American moral philosophy being one example.

Blanchot's trajectory can be divided into three periods. The first goes from *Faux Pas* (FP)[17] to *The Space of Literature* (SL)[18] and is dominated by a Hegelo-Kojèvian conceptuality and an understanding of language influenced by Mallarmé. Blanchot brings together the experience of the night that literary writing liberates with an excessive negativity that cannot be put at the service of comprehension. This nothing is, as in Mallarmé, constitutive of language and, as in Kojève's reading of Hegel, constitutive of the world. Blanchot is interested in a form of negativity that is at play in literary language and that resists dialectical sublation. Language makes things appear and brings them into presence by naming them, but it can only do so in substituting the thing for its absence (PF 46).[19]

In *The Space of Literature* Blanchot grafts Heidegger's schema of ontological difference as well as his understanding of the nothing (*das Nichts*) to this still-Hegelian negativity. Hegel's negativity thus becomes a concealed origin—the condition of all presence and truth that language is unable to gather, since in literary language the object gives way to its "vibratory disappearing" (PF 46). Things can only come into presence because language presupposes a constitutive absence and dissimulates the nothingness that is its very condition. Language bears witness to this absence but forbids access to what it cannot apprehend; therein is its ambiguity. By the same token, language invites a transgression of this limit because the writer desires the absence which makes language possible and that resists nomination. At this stage of Blanchot's work, it is possible to detect a shift from "the night" as object of thinking to what eludes thinking, the absence of meaning, which then becomes his main concern.

The Infinite Conversation (IC)[20] marks a second period in which Blanchot, through a radical reduction, evacuates Heidegger's nothing of any trace of presence. Grafting this Heideggerian matrix to excessive negativity, Blanchot elucidates a form of "negativity" he calls the neuter (*le neutre*), which belongs neither to presence nor to absence. The thinking and writing of the neuter can only take place by presupposing that it does not constitute any form of opening (Heidegger) and that the working of totality has already been accomplished (Hegel). The neuter marks a turning point and opens a third period in which the question of writing is also conceived as the question of the other, in the ethical sense of the term. This period closes with *The Step Not Beyond* (SNB)[21] and *The Writing of the Disaster*.

Blanchot dispels the reassuring and misleading idea that literary language is simply self-referential. In literature language becomes image, the ghostly glimmer of a dissimulated absence eroding any form of identity. Inasmuch as an opacity lurks in its very center whose pressure is felt as if coming from an outside, language cannot be a transparent medium of idealization. A desire for the impossible nonlinguistic origin of language and an ensuing exigency to respond to this absence of meaning unfolds in literary language. This exigency evinces an ethics of writing that interrupts the homogenizing grasp of narratives. To narration Blanchot's writing thus juxtaposes what he calls "un-narrative supplement," a "passive relation," that breaches the circular movement of recognition, representation and comprehension. One of the modalities of this supplement is the *récit*, where language welcomes the approach of the other and responds to it. However, the temporality of this response is not the belated discursive retelling of a set of incidents making up a story. It is rather the encounter with the other itself: "this event upsets relations in time, and yet affirms time, the particular way *time happens* . . . and the time of the metamorphoses where the different temporal ecstasies coincide in an imaginary simultaneity."[22]

Intrigue thus names a para-discursive and counter-narrative mode of writing. It is para-discursive because, while employing all the resources of the order of discourse and occupying all of its emplacements, it does not aim to fix, represent, synchronize or police the other. And it is a counter-narrative, not in the sense of an alternative story, even if Levinas privileges the subaltern figures of the orphan, the widow and the stranger, but rather as what evades any story. There is no place here for a question such as "can the subaltern speak?" Indeed, the other is the first to speak and by speaking either commands the self and gives direction to meaning (Levinas), or disaffects meaning from any imaginary compromise when encountering the real, thus exposing us to the absence of meaning (Blanchot). No counter-narrative would do justice to the *intrigue* of the other, even if it is necessary to write against narrative's simultaneity, inasmuch as it reduces the other's diachrony to the plot of a homogenous timeline. If alternative narratives or counter-narratives have a symbolic function of restitution, this comes from the forceful interruption that the "*intrigues* of the other" weave on the hither side of the order of discourse.

Narratives are instruments of knowledge and comprehension and are underwritten by *mimesis* and plot. A narrative text represents a sequence of incidents tied together by chronology, causality, and equivalence, some of which create an action structure or plot.[23] Within the context of narrative theory, where Aristotelian conceptions prevail, plot not only names this action structure but also becomes an overall organizing principle—an aesthetic structure that turns a random sequence of facts into a significant structure.[24] It is the episodic dimension of narrative that draws narrative time in the direction of a linear representation, since chronology accomplishes a synchronization of time sanctioned by a preunderstanding of death and finitude as possibility. In the words of Walter Benjamin, "Death is the sanction of everything that the storyteller can tell,"[25] because plots produce a representation of time as a whole bounded by death. This bounding of time's heterogeneity and of the diachrony of the other's approach is the product of the privilege the present tense enjoys in narratives, even if they are told in the past. The repetition at play in storytelling, the rephrasing of the story by discourse or narration, secures the bounding of time.

Once death ceases to be a possibility, as in Levinas and Blanchot, and repetition ceases to have a constructive and semiotic role in order to become a disseminating force, the present is no longer the dominant temporal dimension, and the bounding of plots reveals itself as a coercive mechanism. This becomes evident in Levinas's use of Blanchot's *The Madness of the Day (La Folie du jour)*, where the demand for storytelling comes from the figures of the ophthalmologist and the psychiatrist, pillars of the order of discourse and the state. This requisition for narratives already presupposes a given order of telling (beginning, middle and end) that guarantees coherence and intelligibility. For Levinas it is precisely this coercive order that prevents the interruptions of discourse "found again and recounted in the immanence of the said." These interruptions would reveal the trace of a diachrony "that does not enter into the present, that refuses simultaneity (OB)."

In order to render the inextricable relation to the other, the *intrigues* I study loosen up "the grip of being" (Levinas) and accomplish a breaching of mimesis and plot. By so doing, these *intrigues* unfold in a space adjacent to literature, or at least to "literature" as philosophy traditionally defines it. Further, since philosophical writing has produced a homogenizing representation of the other through its emplotment in ontological narratives, the *intrigues* also unfold in a space adjacent to philosophy. The poetics of otherness I examine throughout this book posit a demand to both philosophy and literature. The former must face the impossible even if it only speaks the language of what is possible; the latter must face the absence of meaning, even if it can never succeed in fully evacuating meaning.

The "*intrigues* of the other" cannot be made to fit into an "either . . . or" equation (discourse/narration or nondiscourse/nonnarration), because it is a writing that holds together the interruption of discourse and the marks left by these interruptions, as in Levinas's ethical writing. This holding-together maintains the two series unbounded and relegates plot to a secondary dimension. In Blanchot, it is a writing of the "neither . . . nor" (neuter) whose discrete markings inflect discourse with the "density" of what precedes it. *Intrigue* thus provides a syntax for Blanchot to think both the difference at play in writing and the question of the other as an ethical demand. It also provides a syntax for Levinas's barbarism of the "otherwise than being," the manner in which the other approaches and comes into language. The rhythmic scansion of *Otherwise than Being* is the "passive relation" of a "clandestine *intrigue*" with the other, and the book's "spiraling movement" also finds its justification in the *intrigue's* syntax.

Thinking can encounter the "unnarratable other" (Levinas) in the "unnarrative" (Blanchot) modality of the *intrigue*. It is here that one can read an inextricable co-implication of the other in the same in a time that escapes both memory and the recovery of the past as recollection (past present). The temporality of the *intrigue* is the future anterior whose scope is best illustrated by Derrida's phrase, "he will have obliged (*il aura obligé*)," with which he opens one of his essays on Levinas. The future anterior is a tense that evades the time of the present since it simultaneously points towards a future and a past. Because this tense eludes the present, the subject of the phrase (he-it [*il*]) is not copresent to himself; the subject contracts an obligation that comes from a past, but his response does not assimilate this past to the present of consciousness. The response unfolds in a future that bypasses presence.

"Substitution" (Levinas) and "relation of the third type" (Blanchot) are the two modalities of a heteronomic understanding of the other that have implications for writing and reading. The fact that both Levinas and Blanchot read and write copiously about each other's work makes an elucidation of these modalities even more difficult because this heteronomy also inflects writing and reading. Although they reserve idiosyncratic terms to refer to the form of this relationship, "friendship," "ingratitude," the two share features of the relation to the other that require asymmetry and lack of reciprocity. Consequently, their texts have to be understood according to the schema of the *intrigue*. As a way of responding to this heteronomic configuration of reading, my argument moves back and forth between philosophy and literature in an effort to make explicit why the question of the other (ethics) concerns writing, and why the question of writing concerns ethics.

The book moves back and forth between philosophy and literature and confronts two sets of texts whose scope touches the very core of our

time. My way of proceeding is philological and situates the main concepts and issues within the context of two philosophical continental traditions: phenomenology and post-Hegelian approaches. Works by
Husserl, Heidegger, Fink, Sartre, Merleau-Ponty, as well as Kojève, Bataille and Nietzsche are therefore made to dialogue with Levinas and
Blanchot. Levinas's aesthetic categories belong to a French tradition that,
although popularized by Sartre, has its point of origin in Alain and
Valéry, while Mallarmé and Kafka shape Blanchot's understanding of
literary language. These connections are made explicit in my book. *Intrigues: From Being to the Other* aims to contribute to contemporary debates
on the "ethical turn" of literary criticism, and to bring to the domain of
narrative theory what Blanchot calls the un-narrative supplement that is
not only crucial for an ethics of writing, but also for an ethically inflected
literary criticism.

The Passion of Time: *Au moment voulu* (Nietzsche-Heidegger-Blanchot)

> To see the Moment (*Augenblick*) means to stand in it.
>
> —*Martin Heidegger*, Nietzsche

> And now? Now, the evidence had been shattered; the broken pillars of time were holding up their own ruins.
>
> —*Maurice Blanchot*, When the Time Comes

For Blanchot *intrigue* names an inextricable relation between at least two human beings and the not-assimilable strangeness that language harbors. The "relation of the third type" is "without horizon," by which Blanchot means that neither a positive structure (disclosure, manifestation, transcendence), nor a negative principle (the working of the negative, death), could manage to deneutralize it, to fill it with a content capable of containing the neuter's disruptive paucity.[1]

Blanchot, not unlike Levinas, employs the term *intrigue* to refer to the "relation of the third type" and to the "exigency of speech" when faced with the strangeness of language. *Intrigue* is not only a descriptive term, but also what unfolds in and as "le moment voulu." However, given that Blanchot deploys the temporality of the eternal return of the same, "the moment" is suspended between an anarchic past and a future to come. *Intrigue* names the temporalizing of the approach of the other, the event of the other, but also the temporality of the "responsive speech" that is writing.

In Blanchot *intrigue* names the modality of the relation of the third kind as *topos* in which the exigency of speech triggers the scene of responsibility when faced with the strangeness of language. This scene is always a sudden and unexpected encounter in a space devoid of qualities—usually a room whose only feature is its typicality—and inhabited by a limited number of characters that function as points of passage for the circulation of the nonlinguistic rustle of language. This configuration speaks of the event-character of the relation of the third kind, which is neither a given nor a fact, but something proper to literary language. The literary mode of this encounter is the *récit*, a narrative modality interrupted by a sudden caesura that short-circuits the relationship between narrative discourse and narration. Moreover, this caesura disturbs the temporal markers of narrative and introduces an un-narrative supplement that in *Au moment voulu* (AMV)[2] Blanchot designates with the term *intrigue*.

In *Au moment voulu*, *intrigue* is not only a descriptive term but also what unfolds in and as *"le moment voulu."* The purpose of this chapter is to read how the *récit* responds to the other, to the strange par excellence, once it deploys a configuration deprived of a horizon. This configuration presents three features: the outside interrupts the order of meaning, the order of the world ceases to be the guarantor of intelligibility, and the present is not the ruling temporal instance.

While following in detail the experience of writing in Mallarmé, Kafka, and Rilke, *The Space of Literature* (1955) focuses on the moment when the writer forgets that "the ultimate demand that his movement makes" is not the fact of having a work, but that "someone (*quelqu'un*) faces this point" (SL 171/EL 226, 228): what eludes language and representation. *The Space of Literature* brings the experience of the "other night" to the order of discourse and thus repeats the writer's Orphic gesture; the "other night" is what escapes the order of discourse but, at the same time, makes writing possible. Years earlier, in a "fictional" text titled *Au moment voulu* (1951), Blanchot explored the features of what later became "the space of literature." In this *récit* language undergoes an experience of fidelity to the event *of* writing and follows a path that is the opposite of *The Space of Literature*. The *récit*'s language decomposes the spatio-temporal coordinates that make up the order of the world in such a way as to respond to "the ultimate demand" of writing.

Au moment voulu belongs to an important period in Blanchot's fictional and critical production; it is part of a set of texts in which several issues intersect: the impossible possibility of writing, the status of the *récit* and the other as what is strange.[3] These unfold within a context punctuated by a productive reading of Nietzsche that takes Blanchot to a radical exploration of the event's temporality. Anticipating the reflections Blanchot will develop in later texts, *Au moment voulu* engages "the inaugural thought of our contemporary history,"[4] Nietzsche's eternal return of the same. No other contemporary writer repeats this thought so thoroughly.

In Blanchot, writing maps out the contours of the outside and obliquely approaches what thinking has refused to face but, in the end, is revealed to have been the determining question of our time. For this reason, Blanchot's "refusal of philosophy" (Bruns) can be equated neither with philosophy's refusal to think the other (if there is refusal it is not philosophical) nor with relinquishing a thinking of the epoch. Indeed, Blanchot's writing unfolds within a space framed by a series of figures that mark the end of philosophy, but that nevertheless demand that one face "what calls to thinking" in a space adjacent to philosophy's closure.[5] Blanchot's "refusal" is the expression of an ethical demand to think the impossible and to remain faithful to this experience Therefore, his "extreme contemporaneity"[6] lies precisely in his way of welcoming "the most profound question": that of the event *of* the other. That is, of the other as the event breaching totality, the system of knowledge, and the framework of philosophical discourse.[7]

It is not enough to claim that Blanchot's writing fragments time, that it dislocates space and reduces characters to a ghostly human semblance. Blanchot's approach to the question of time cannot be easily or simply accommodated to the modern drive for fragmentation, dispersion, and reversion of timelines. To state that Blanchot's *récits* accomplish a fragmentation of time presupposes an intra-temporal understanding of time as a continuum. If this were the case it would be possible to rearrange the fragments of time in a chronological pattern, an operation that Blanchot's *récits* systematically resist.

Finally, to claim that Blanchot's characters are a ghostly semblance of humanity presupposes that the human being should be considered the source and final term of the relation to the other. However, doing so implies overlooking that this relation involves a term that introduces a distance between human beings, the neuter, and that this term is the impossible possibility of the relation to the other. The metamorphosis that literary signs undergo in Blanchot must go hand in hand with a mutation of thinking. What is at stake in Blanchot's repetition of Nietzsche's eternal return of the same? What does it tell us about our "epoch" and about time? What operations does it unfold in order to produce a mutation of thinking? How does it manage to preserve the other in its strangeness?

Time—Of the Other: Eternal Return, Ecstatic Temporality and the Event

"Behold this gateway, dwarf!" I continued. "It has two faces. Two paths meet here; no one has yet followed either to its end. This long lane stretches back for an eternity. And the long lane out there, that is another eternity. They contradict each other, these paths; they offend each other face to face; and it is here at this gateway that they come together. The name of the gateway is inscribed above 'Moment'" (*Augenblick*).

—*Nietzsche,* Thus Spake Zarathustra

The eternal return of the same, "the supreme and most burdensome thought," according to Nietzsche, who suffered its sudden revelation. Although Heidegger stresses that the eternal return is not a doctrine but, rather, an experience *of* thinking, he seems to attenuate its impact. He does so by characterizing Nietzsche as "the last metaphysical thinker of Western history"(N 1, 15)[8] and by subordinating this experience of thinking to the "guiding question" (the question of being). Heidegger thus contains Nietzsche within the web of metaphysics by deploying a highly overdetermined gesture.

On the one hand, he diminishes the proximity of Nietzsche's thinking to crucial aspects of *Being and Time* (ecstatic temporality, anticipatory resoluteness in the moment of decision, *Ereignis*). On the other, he strikes a blow against the abyssal force of the eternal return of the same, since Heidegger injects being into becoming, transforming the latter into a consistent impermanence. In this movement of appropriation (*Being and Time*) and expropriation (*Nietzsche*), much is cast aside so that Nietzsche can easily fit within Heidegger's narrative of the possibility of a new commencement of thinking. In spite of his painstaking philological reconstruction of the *Nachlass*, Heidegger suppresses the implications of some crucial aspects in Nietzsche: Dionysos and the redefinition of the sensuous, woman and, fundamentally, the "now" (*Augenblick*) as moment of eternity.[9] Although this philological reconstruction goes hand in hand with a reading that retrieves some of the figural aspects of *Thus Spake Zarathustra*, it nevertheless remains blind to (the) *writing* (of) "moment" on the gateway, and to what the eternal return brings to "the question of writing."

In *Being and Time* Heidegger conceives "the eternity" of the eternal return as the moment (*der Augenblick*) of decision and insight *proper* to a *Dasein* who temporalizes time by a resolute anticipation of its possibilities. These possibilities are set forth in the horizon of death; by anticipating death *Dasein* projects itself in advance into the possibility that *Dasein* is itself. By existing, by taking over its own facticity, *Dasein* alone makes possible its own possibilities. Further, *Dasein*'s ecstatic temporality delimits the scope of its presence to itself and to the world inasmuch as it opens, from the direction of the anticipation of its *being-for-death*, the different ecstasies of time by which entities can appear as "having been," "present" or "to come." However, the ecstasies of time articulating *Dasein*'s being "'outside-of-itself' in and for itself" (SZ[10]/BT § 65) and its transcendence in the direction of being can only give access to a series of represented "to comes" and "pasts." These series refer only to this self-present futurity that *Dasein* deploys throughout time, since care (*Sorge*) is the unifying structure of being-in-the-world.[11] It is hard to see then how the abyssal force of the eternal return, its event-character, could ever be preserved within the structure of care. Is it possible to integrate the event-character of the "moment" into the framework of representation? Can one gather together the "moment" as a totalization of time in the *Augenblik* of the instant? Can this gathering be simply the property of *Dasein*?[12]

If Heidegger's analytic of *Dasein* fails to do justice to the event-character of the eternal return, other phenomenological approaches appear to be more attuned to the altering irruption of the event. Henry

Maldiney claims that "the event affects us by shattering both the world's ground where we have our anchoring and the world's horizon under which we find signification."[13] The feature defining the event is, for Maldiney, its irreducible character, its not taking place in the world. Likewise, by opposing events to facts, Claude Romano stresses the former's irreducible nature. While facts always take place within the horizon of meaning a world supposes, the event transcends its own effectuation as fact and appears as something irreducible to its own context. The temporality of the event is inaugural, retrospective, and prospective, while the fact's temporality is an opening, always past and future.

While facts suppose a chronological temporality, the temporalization of the event is not a process; it is more accurate to refer to it, with Romano, as dramaturgy (*dramatique*): in it nothing changes in the present, but everything has already changed. This change becomes accessible as such only belatedly. The event is *at the same time* absolutely to come, coming from a future inaccessible to any awaiting, and always already past or without any possible contemporaneity; the event puts into motion a present in perpetual delay with itself.[14] Anticipating our argument, it is possible to claim that the present of the event is, as Blanchot puts it, "un instant toujours en instance."[15]

In claiming that the event is incommensurable to the modalities of presence, it is as if phenomenology were catching up with the implications that Blanchot's writing of the event already anticipated in the 1950s. However, while Blanchot reaches a point of no return—"a relation without horizon," "an absence of the world," "a time without time," "the other death or dying,"—phenomenology reinscribes this irreducible dimension of the event within the context of the world. For this reason, the event becomes the possibility of an adventure of meaning. Further, phenomenology also loses its ability to respond to the impossible demand (the demand of the impossible) of preserving the "absence of meaning" as such, the "piercing" that the event's irruption produces in the fabric of meaning, according to Blanchot:

The encounter: what comes without advent, what approaches faces-on, and nonetheless always by surprise, what requires waiting and what waiting awaits but does not attain. Even at the innermost heart of interiority, it is always irruption of the outside, exteriority shaking everything. The encounter pierces the world, pierces the self; and this piercing, everything that happens, without happening (coming about with the status of what has not arrived) is the reverse side that cannot be lived of what on the right side cannot be written: a double impossibility that by a supplementary act—a fraud, a kind of falsehood, also a madness—must be transformed in order to adapt it to living and writing "reality." (EI[16] 608/IC 414, translation modified)

The encounter is the event par excellence which brings together all the features a phenomenology of the event only recently began to elucidate: the surprise of its coming, its eluding any form of anticipation, its disruption of the order of the world and of consciousness, and its peculiar way of manifesting itself. But unlike phenomenological approaches, for Blanchot the event can be neither lived nor written.

How can the event be preserved as such if it eludes presence and the horizon of the world? Blanchot introduces the "madness" of the eternal return of the same (the matrix of a ghostly time) as the "supplementary act" needed to approach its "unlivable" side or "reverse." He also grafts this "madness" to the "fraudulence" of a "literary" writing that transgresses the impossibility of writing the event.

Blanchot's writing deploys and repeats Nietzsche's eternal return as a way of responding to the alterity of the event. In what follows I read the inscription of the most abyssal (*abgründlich*) thought as a way of undermining a logic of appropriation and the value of the proper (*eigen*), as well as attempts to appropriate what comes as the absolute other. Blanchot's *Au moment voulu* is a way into this problematic.[17] First, because this text reenacts the thought of the eternal return of the same and does so as a *pensée d'écriture*. Blanchot thus imprints an unprecedented dimension upon "the inaugural thought of our contemporary history" (Nancy). Second, because the graphics of the eternal return undermine any form of presence and point to a dimension of the being-event of the event. Although the question "what 'exactly' had happened" hints at the event of *Au moment voulu*, one will not be able to tell what happens, happened, is happening or will happen exactly. There is no measure for facing the irreducible and the incommensurable—what is simply alluded to as "what had just happened"—but one must nevertheless approach it in an affirmative way. In *Au moment voulu* the reader faces the vertiginous movement of the eternal return, its disruption of the proper or same. In Blanchot's repetition of Nietzsche's eternal return, it is possible to read a thinking of the otherness of time as the necessary and impossible condition for thinking the other.

In *Au moment voulu* there is a series of temporal markers that concern the nature of the event's irruption: "what 'exactly' had happened," "has it taken place?" "once?" These markers call attention to the impossibility of using any chronological or chronometrical criteria. The imminent and evident nature of "what had just happened" is not that of facts, and so this modality subtracts itself from any objective apprehension of time. In *Au moment voulu* the modality of the event's temporalizing is that of an *intrigue*: un-narrative "supplement" that weaves together the "madness" of the eternal return and the "fraudulence" of fictional writing.

Intrigue: The Un-Narratable Supplement

Au moment voulu cites and recites itself as an *intrigue*: "I know I am mixed up in a profound, static *intrigue*, one that I mustn't look at, or even notice, that I mustn't be occupied by and that nevertheless requires all my strength and all my time"(SH).[18] This is a strange *intrigue* that does not ask for the subject's receptive faculties but still demands his time, that involves but, at the same time, expels the "I" as a source of power and decision; an *intrigue* then of what exposes the subject to a passivity more original than any intentionality, as well as to a demand that turns subjectivity inside out. It should be noted that the French word *exigence* derives from the Latin *ex-agere*, to push outside. *Intrigue* here does not designate a rationally plotted situation, purposively aimed at some goal, a mystery decipherable through clues or a dialectical or hermeneutic adventure, but an *intricateness*—in the sense of *intricare*, to entangle or perplex, and also in the archaic sense of to embarrass. No other word could better indicate the peculiar status of the event of narration, of the narration of the event and of the event of the narration of the event. As in *La Folie du jour, Au moment voulu* entangles all and each of these borders and folds them in the bottomless (double) ring of the eternal return:

"Claudia came back shortly afterwards. I did not know her." (AMV 25/SH 209);

"Claudia came back shortly after I did. I could add that these words, that, in my eyes, had once ushered in Claudia's life and made her the person who comes after, came back too, and drew me toward the same truth: I didn't know her. In this way, the whole cycle began again." (AMV 136/SH 249);

"Claudia came back shortly after I did. . . . And yet even though the circle is already drawing me along, and even if I had to write this eternally, I would write it in order to obliterate eternity: Now, the end." (AMV 137, 166/SH 250, 260)

These are the main "dimensions" of the *intrigue* called *Au moment voulu.*[19] To the folding of the first and third cycles into the second, a supplementary turn can be added to this *intrigue*, which is its anarchic character. It alludes to an irretrievable past to which the double ring of *Au moment voulu* responds. However, given the peculiar temporality of this anarchic event, the response does not come after the call but in an "other" time. This is what Blanchot calls "the time without time" (*le temps sans temps*): "time had passed, and yet it was not past; that was a truth that I should not have wanted to place in my presence" (AMV 8/SH 203).

The matrix of the eternal return allows Blanchot to deploy this "time without time." What remains to be seen is how Heidegger's conception of the instant or moment is affected by this deployment. In his reading of Nietzsche, Heidegger claims, "To see the Moment (*Augenblick*) means to stand in it."[20] *Au moment voulu* therefore helps us to understand what is at stake in both "seeing the moment" and "standing in it." It also allows us to think whether it is possible to ascertain these two claims in such a way, given the peculiar temporality of the eternal return.

Intrigue inflects itself all throughout *Au moment voulu*, especially in opposition to story/history (*histoire*): "No one here wants to be connected to a story (*histoire*)!" (AMV 108/SH 239). It does not refer to a factual situation nor allow the story/history (*histoire*) to constitute itself in a principle of narrative intelligibility based on the causal unfolding of sequences.

Intrigue points to a mood expressing itself in "a cruelly complex move-ment," of which the reader is not able to retrieve any cause, origin or motive. Faced with the disseminating effect of an entangled movement— anarchic, atopic, without purpose—one of comings and goings, a story/ history (*histoire*) would have been the promise of a resting-place or at least the promise of a reduction of the other to the same. But a story/history would have been possible only if there was a present destined to pass and to be retained in the past; in other words, a present retrieved from the past by a consciousness able to relate these moments from the privileged point of the present (in the *Augenblick* of a synthetic instant).

However, the eternal return withdraws any right to presence. The de-mand of the return "excluding any present from time, would never release a now in which the same would return to the same, to the self" (SNB 27). The return's exigency is that of a time without a present, the time of writing or dying (*mourir*): "Death! But in order to die, one had to write—The end! And to do that, one had to write up to the end" (AMV 86–87/SH 232). A story/history (*histoire*) would have stopped the differ-ing and deferring of the return and reduced its ring to the circle of a *récit odysséique* in which neither a decisive distancing or separation (*é-loignement, Ent-fernung*) nor a true exposure to the outside as demanded by the other's approach takes place (LV).[21]

What goes by the name of *intrigue* cannot be translated as the narration of an experience or as the story/history of a subject affirming itself through the incorporation of a strange experience. This intrigue reads, rather, like the reciting of what interrupts the communication between narration and story: "I also have the feeling that I am not staying in my place—yes, with a certain absurd obstinacy, in my place, on my feet—but even more: *I have become a little unstable, I move from spot to spot*" (AMV 157–58/ SH 257, my emphasis).

Intrigue separates or distances (*é-loigne*): a. the *incidents* one from another, but also from what leaves ghostly traces of presence upon the texture of *Au moment voulu,* "what had been figured was inscribed on an infinitely thin film" (AMV 113/SH 148)[22]; b. the *incidents* from the possibility of determining "what had 'just' happened"; c. the voice from the narrative agency; d. the voice from the *incidents*; e. the subject from the order of "the normal life"; and finally, f. the *récit* from its re-citing.

This strange event that is *Au moment voulu*, as well as what is narrated as "*le* moment voulu," weaves its textuality with threads of a Heideggerian provenance, the graphics of *Ent-fernung* and *Ereignis*. According to Derrida:

> le disjoint du proche et du présent produit, engendre et décèle à la fois une fissure sans limite: dans le savoir ou le discours philosophique. . . . Cette loi sans loi de l'é-loignement n'est pas l'essence, mais la topique impossible de l'essentialité. Elle croisse un schéma discursif de Heidegger et nous prépare à penser à la fois la proximité, le chiasme éloignant puissamment l'une de l'autre ces deux pensées: *l'Ent-fernung* ("é-loignement"), *l'Ereignis* ("l'événement"), en cette collusion sans identité du proche et du lointain que nous abordons de ce pas. (P)[23]

While Derrida is correct in emphasizing Blanchot's proximity to Heidegger, it is not only a matter of intersecting Heidegger's two graphics with Blanchot's idiomatic writing, an intersection that would suppose a certain exteriority of one to the other. Against Heidegger's deployment of a history/story (of metaphysics), intended to preserve his discourse from the abyssal menace of the eternal return, it is possible to read *Au moment voulu* as its affirmation. This affirmation ties together the graphics of *Ent-fernung* and *Ereignis* to the abyssal ring of the return. The distancing of immediacy interrupts the proper *Ereignis* gives or sends. Indeed, Blanchot's *récit* interrupts any possible derivation of an "epochal history of being" from *Ereignis*. While for Heidegger the eternal return liberates the possibility of anticipating the meaning of the event ("To see the Moment [*Augenblick*] means to stand in it"), in *Au moment voulu* the encounter of the moment entails no anticipation of the event, and the stability of any position thus gives way to an entangled and dispersing movement.

Time's Aporia

Au moment voulu can be called a text of the aporia, since it intensifies the gap between saying and showing and plays one against the other to its maximum possibilities. The text thus annuls what most other fiction manages to get away with, its dissimulation.[24] However, one can go a step further and say that in *Au moment voulu* the text of the aporia's law takes the form of a breaching of essence and of each of its figures. Blanchot's *récit* is a text of the aporia because it is the text *of* time's aporia. After entering the room, after scanning its space, the narrative voice states:

What I did not see, why I saw only at the last . . . but I would like to be able to pass over all that quickly. . . . As for this young woman who had opened the door for me, to whom I had talked, who had been real enough, from the past to the present, during an inestimable length of time, to remain constantly visible to me—I would like to let nothing be understood about her, ever. (AMV 16–17/SH 206)

No logical explanation can resist the nature of this asymmetrical encounter in a realm that exceeds the visible. However, one cannot make use of its opposite pole, the irrational and the invisible, in order to ground an explanation. Underlying the scene of the encounter is a generalized metalepsis that subverts both binary logic and dialectics. The resemblance of the young woman, whom the narrator names Judith, "resembling herself" (AMV 8) is a resemblance without antecedent and without a theme; it is the *ressemblance cadaverique*. In the corpse and in the work of art, according to Blanchot, we have access to what images itself, a return of the image to itself prior to its being an "image of. . . ." What Blanchot calls the other version of the imaginary is the image's eternal return to itself. The image is "the same" as itself in its very alterity. This resemblance is the repetition of the real, a repetition that is without present.[25]

Judith, whose most notorious feature is her visibility (a visibility that exceeds the appropriating gaze and demands *inattention* as a response), "was ahead of me *(en avant de moi)*" (AMV 150/ SH 254). Hers is the name for what cannot be fixed in the epiphany of a face, but through which the *intrigue's* saying unfolds because she is entangled with an anarchic past: "she had bound herself furiously to the infinite" (AMV 148/SH 254). In contrast, Claudia's main narrative predicate is "she came back shortly after I did" (AMV 25/SH 248). Claudia evolves in the same way that the image comes after the object, according to both the temporality and hierarchy of the classical economy of representation. Claudia's name marks a lapse of being-in-common's time with respect to that of the face-à-face, that is, with the time of what exceeds representation. If there is "Claudia's side," the everyday, the economy of the home (AMV 54/ SH 220), there is no such thing as "Judith's side," since her name points to what breaches the economy of the same and what opens onto forgetting and to an anarchic past.

The *intrigue* that is both *Au moment voulu* and *the* "moment voulu" has already begun. We are already in it, but it is brought about by an *encounter*: "because the friend who lived with her was not there, the door was opened by Judith. I was extremely, *inextricably* surprised, certainly much more so than if I had met her by chance" (AMV 7/SH 203). This encounter precipitates what Blanchot calls a "passive relation," a type of rapport exceeding the frames of narrative intelligibility: "passive: the *un-story*, that which escapes quotation and which memory does not recall, forgetfulness as thought. That which, in other words, cannot be forgotten, because it has always already fallen outside memory" (ED[26] 49/WD 28).

This *hors mémoire*, which transpires as a contact with a proximity exceeding all presence, transports the one touched by it to both a dimension where the dialectics of the visible and invisible is no longer operative and to a time without present. This contact is not a contact with a factual past but with what Blanchot will later call disaster (*désastre*): "the immemorial past which returns, dispersing by its returning the present, where, ghostly, it would be experienced as a return (*où il serait vécu comme revenant*)" (ED 34/WD 16).

As could not be otherwise, this contact is narrated after the fact, takes the form of a devastating affection upon the "I," and is reported by Judith to him who suffers it without this affection being "his": "Well, according to what she told me, she saw me. . . . No, she wasn't surprised to see me paying so little attention to the fact that she was present" (AMV19–20/SH, 207). Judith is thus the witness to a contact that takes the form of a rather peculiar face-à-face:

she [Judith] was young in a way that made her strangely resemble herself. I kept looking at her, I said to myself: So this is why I was so surprised. Her face . . . reawakened in *me a terribly distant memory, and it was this deeply buried, very ancient memory* that she seemed to be copying in order to appear so young . . . now that I could look at her from the depths of my memory, I was uplifted, taken back to another life. (AMV 9–10/SH 203–4, my emphasis)

The narrator points to the asymmetry of the encounter. He stresses that he did not see her looking at him because of his total absorption in looking at her. He also points to his inability to find reasons for not seeing her imminent proximity and thus activates the topology of the *é-loignement*:

Why didn't I see her? As I said, I don't really know. It's hard to go back over an impossible thing when it has been surmounted, even harder when one isn't sure the impossibility isn't still there. . . . What is strange about not seeing something distant when nearby things are still invisible? (*Qu'y a-t-il d' étrange à ne pas voir ce qui est loin, quand le proche est encore invisible?*) (AMV 20–21/SH 208)

As with the chronological markers above, this set of questions indicates that the topology of *é-loignement* transgresses the criteria of objective knowledge. The unlivable dimension of the event cancels out the prerogatives of knowledge and perception and gives way to fascination. In Blanchot, fascination always marks the disappearance of the subject as the basis of "experience":

This was, I must say, a discovery so disastrous physically that it took complete control of me. As I was thinking that, *I was fascinated by my thought, and overshadowed by it.* Well, it was an idea (*pensée*)! And not just any idea but one that was proportional to me, exactly equal to me, and if it allowed itself to be thought, I had to *disappear.* (AMV 12/SH 204)

This becoming idea (*pensée*) of the narrator erases his presence, since the provenance of this thought is the outside (*dehors*) that no interiority can assimilate. The status of this disappearance as the "effect" of a "discovery physically disastrous" is not that of a fact, as there is no one to support or suffer it. This disappearance is punctuated rather by the narrator's "coming back to his senses" after collapsing and "I had no doubt about what had just happened (*ce qui venait de ce passer*) (AMV 12/SH 205)." However, the attempt to clarify the contents of this event is interrupted by his comings and goings in the restricted *topos* of the hallway: "I was simply penetrated by a feeling of horror, and by these words, which I still believe: '*Oh no, is this beginning again? Again! Again!*' I was stopped short, in any case" (AMV 13–14/SH 205, my emphasis).

"I," who suffers and bears this superlative violence, can only be "I" as the effect of a repetition of a singular idea (*pensée*). Consequently, the equating of thought and "I" in the expression "my idea" (*ma pensée*) can amount to neither identification nor interiorization. This affection (effect of the *intrigue*) is said as *achrony*, a disjunction in identity that, by opening a rift (or by opening identity as a rift) interrupts any egology. The encounter "takes place" in the hallway leading to the room. "I's" displacements, his steps (*pas*), being "the steps (*les pas*) of immobility," do not connote the image of a physical displacement, of a progressive movement leading to the accomplishment of actions or goals (AMV 15/SH 205). The encounter does not belong to the economy of power, action or decision: "I went in more or less without knowing . . . I couldn't see, I was miles from realizing I couldn't see" (AMV 15/SH 206).

Another scene, the one referred to as the "terrible scene," is also localized "at the point where the hallway forked" (AMV 130/SH 246). And although at the "close" of the *récit* the hallway will be referred to as "the road," it leads nowhere. When alluding to "the absolutely dark moment of this intrigue," the narrator states:

I can recall that, however long this *road* may be and whatever may be its detours through the futile repetition of days and of moments, nothing can prevent it from being once again and yet again the *hallway* that separated the two small rooms and that I happened to enter. (AMV 165/SH 259)

The hall is the *topos* of a static coming and going (*parcours immobile*), of a pulsating intensification without displacement and of a leaving of traces without marks or markers. What one would improperly call narrative sequences cannot be integrated into a progressive and unified narrative because of the return of the same's temporality. The narrator's allusions to scene, incident, and situation are aspects that the plural insistence

of the outside takes. This insistence and punctuation elicit the reverberations of a forgetting understood neither in a negative way nor as a
deficiency.

The ring of the return closes itself off. The hallway is "the road,"
but the narrator has no steps (*pas*) for this road. There is no trajectory,
progression, development, nor resolution. The two movements organizing the encounter are a "stationary falling down," which is at odds with
the vulgar way of understanding time as flux or as a circular unifying
cycle and a recoiling, which is a reversal of manifestation. They constitute
the two nonvisible axes of nocturnal comings and goings that are interrupted by intensities of violence, shock, cry, and shudder.

These intensities interrupt the narrative intelligibility of *Au moment
voulu*, since they disrupt the reader's ability to synchronize the hiatuses.
For example, it is very difficult to situate the narrator's first encounter
with Claudia in relation to the one with Judith, which is said to "take
place" at midday (AMV 37). Here the border between "normal life"
(*l'ordre du jour, la vie gaie*) and "nocturnal space," a distinction that, to a
certain extent, organizes the "un-narrative," is blurred. Nevertheless, the
remarked interruptions not only in the story, but also by the narrator,
that affect the status of the event are decisive; has it taken place, once?
When referring to the "terrible scene" and to its "figure," the narrator
affirms that it "had the strangest relations with time" (AMV 135/SH
249). Because of the effraction of time, this event, this "sovereign instant," does not belong to time but nevertheless concerns time in that
peculiar modality of "concerning without concerning," so insistent in
Blanchot's writing.[27] Time's effraction takes the figure of a point whose
pressure is felt all throughout the *récit*. The linguistic rendering of this
pressure is a "something is happening" expressing the "extraordinary
pressure" of a point which is not alien to time, "but [which] represented
as well the pure *passion of time*" (AMV 144/SH 252).

The interplay between everyday life and the nocturnal "experiences"
opening to the gateway called "moment" is problematic. For this reason,
and especially if one takes into account Blanchot's own analysis of the
quotidian in *The Infinite Conversation*, one cannot make of the everyday a
ground for the "passion and excess" of *Au moment voulu*. The everyday is
neither a ground nor a necessary frame of reference.[28] If the quotidian

is "what is most difficult to discover," it is because its essential feature is its "absence of meaning" (EL 355/IC 238). It is precisely this feature that makes the quotidian germane to the "experience of writing," understood as a "rapport neutre" (EL 355).

Blanchot takes issue with the analysis of the quotidian by Pascal, and by Lukács in *Soul and Form*,[29] because they deploy a dialectics of opacity redeemed by an extraordinary event that illuminates the insignificant monotony of everyday life. Blanchot argues instead that what is decisive about the quotidian is that it designates "a region or a level of speech" beyond the adventure of meaning—the opposition true and false—and beyond dialectics: "a neuter speech" (EL 361/IC 242). Being the interruption of what is endless, the interruption at play here is the imminence of the event felt as a "misfortune that already occurred without being able to present itself" (ED 93). In *Au moment voulu*, as in other texts by Blanchot, this is *achrony*'s interruption, a disruption of the mechanisms of synchronization proper to narration that cannot be reabsorbed by the continuity of discourse and that leaves the syntactical, sequential, semantic, and pragmatic connectors of the narrative in disarray.

The reverberations of the forgetting and the pressures of the point are condensed in a "terrible scene," a nocturnal scene involving Judith's dictum "*Nescio Vos*," "two words howled by Judith from the depths of her memory" (AMV 137/SH 249). It is important to mention that Judith is asleep and that the narrator refers to her as "this dream body (*ce corps de rêve*)" (AMV 134/SH 249). This amounts to saying that this scene is "closer to the nocturnal region," since "notwithstanding events that seem to belong to time, and even though it is peopled with beings that seem to be those of the world, this interminable 'day' is the approach of time's absence, the threat of the outside where the world lacks" (EL 361/SL 267). Judith sleeps, but her body is made of a dream or is possessed by a dream. In other words, between the one who sleeps and the one who dreams there is an absolute difference; the latter being "the premonition of the other, of that which cannot say 'I' anymore, which recognizes itself neither in itself nor in others" (EL 361/SL 267). Therefore, "*Nescio Vos*" comes from far beyond Judith's memory or from a topology of consciousness/unconsciousness.

The other's foreboding, however, is not a theme and does not belong to the discourse of the day, the language shared by a group. Uttered in a foreign language and in a dead one as well, the saying (*dire*) of the other's premonition evades communication. It signals without signifying, and its saying says the immemorial in a language that, for a man of letters, as the narrator seems to be, belongs to the region of an impersonal memory (AMV 137/SH 250).

However, the provenance of this saying remains indeterminate, exceeding the frame of a personal or metaphysically bound remembering/forgetting. Beyond their codified transmission as a possible example of grammar,[30] what counts in the generality and anonymity of these words is the fact that they were "thrown back at me by the immensity, after great labor on the part of the shadows, thrown back into my face as the benediction and malediction of the night" (AMV 137/SH 250). "*Nescio Vos*" is a stumbling block for the principle of identity and a monument to the asymmetry of the "other relation," "the greatest and truest utterance, for me, the radiant heart, the expression of the familiarity and the jealousy of the night" (AMV 137/SH 250). If "*Nescio Vos*" is an "echo of another time," its reverberations mark the return and the return's return: "I didn't know her." This expression could pass for one of indifference, ignorance and carelessness or a lack of power regarding identity. Nevertheless, it signifies "the exaltation of this return, the fact that it was a monumental event elevated to its own glory" (AMV 136/SH 249) and resonates as an extra-ordinary event, as "*le* moment voulu":

Claudia came back shortly after I did. Everything was quiet and I think she rested then. And yet, later, I saw *her** looking at me through the open door of the hall (I was opposite, in the studio). . . . It had happened to me in the past, when I lived alone in the South. . . . The night, when I would open the door and I would look tranquilly down at the bottom of the stairway: it was a completely tranquil and intentionless movement, purely nocturnal, as they say. *At this instant*, across the immense space, she gave me the impression that she too was sitting down at a bottom of a stairway, on the large step where the stairs turn; having opened the door, I looked at her, she was not looking at me, and all the tranquility of this movement, which was so perfectly silent, today had the truth of this body slightly stooped in an attitude that was not one of expectation, nor of resignation, but of a profound and melancholy dignity). . . . *This instant* was never disturbed, or prolonged, or deferred, and maybe she didn't know me, and maybe, she was unknown to me, but it didn't matter, because for one and for the other this instant really was the awaited moment (*le moment voulu*), for both of us the time had come. (AMV 138–9: *"je *la*" in italics in the text/SH 250)

The figure ("when the face [*figure*] of this moment shows itself") of this instant, "*le* moment voulu," can be read as a version of "Orpheus's Gaze," which is not only a reflection on what activates writing, but also the *"point d'attrait"* of *The Space of Literature* (SL 1). However, between Orpheus's descent in "Orpheus's Gaze" and the "figure of the moment" in *Au moment voulu* there are some important differences.

In the Orphic adventure related by Blanchot, Eurydice is a figure that dissimulates both "the profoundly obscure point toward which art and desire, death and night, seem to tend," as well as "the *instant* when the essence of night approaches as the *other night*" (EL 225/SL 171). Orpheus's task (*œuvre*) is to "bring it back to the light of day and to give it form, shape, and reality in the day," not by direct optical contact, but by a detour (EL 225/SL 171). We know that in Blanchot's reading of this myth, Orpheus forgets the work because "the ultimate demand that his movement makes" is not the fact of having a work, but that "someone (*quelqu'un*) faces this *point*" (EL 226, 228/SL 171). It is as if *Au moment voulu* favored the exigency that was forgotten by Orpheus's impatience (a necessary and positive moment in Orpheus's movement), and by the inspiration compromising the work's existence.[31] Here we come across one of those moments in Blanchot where the interrelation between his essays and his fictional writing becomes manifest. In this particular case, the sign of this relation is the feminine object pronoun (*la*) that appears in italics and, more importantly, within two scenes that bear structural and functional similarities. The interplay between *Au moment voulu* and "Le Régard d'Orphée" confirms that they belong to the same textual cluster.

The typographical emphasis put on the pronoun adds a surplus of indeterminacy to its deictic function, thus marking what could not be marked without demarcating itself. Orpheus is in the predicament of looking at Eurydice, but she is not all there is to be seen. He is also faced with "what night dissimulates, the other night, the dissimulation that appears" (EL 227/SL 172). It is precisely this dissimulation that is seemingly (*simul-simil*) indicated by the feminine object pronoun (*la*) in italics. The syntagm, "Je ne *la* connais pas," is placed under Judith's dictum *"Nescio Vos,"* since Judith can be read as a figure of dissimulation.

"*Le* moment voulu" is the moment of an asymmetrical encounter whose "figure" is recited as repetition. What is "figured," however, involves an "immense extension" (AMV 138), although Claudia's apartment is a studio and "the only aspect that made it seem roomy was the hallway that divided it into two areas (*deux regions*)" (AMV 30/SH 211). The encounter in proximity unfolds at an infinite distance; the topological configuration, however, disrupts the synchronicity of an encounter between equals for which the other will simply be an alter ego. This distancing is the distance of the approach of the other as other (as otherwise than being and not as being-other) and not the distance of physical displacement. However, no grasping or optical co-optation is at play here. This is, rather, the inattentive gaze that "exposes I to the passion of the utterly passive where, with eyes that are open but that do not look (*les yeux ouverts sans regard*), I become infinite absence" (ED 90–1/WD 54), as in the encounter with Judith where what shows itself is the figure of a supreme apparition (*apparition souveraine*) (AMV 140/SH 250).[32] In this asymmetrical encounter the feminine object pronoun (*la*) does not indicate one of its terms (Claudia), but rather what circulates in that encounter as well as what it dissimulates: "the point unknown . . . and the even more unknown relationship of this point to me," a relation that "did not make everyday life easy" (AMV 141/SH 251).

We can now return to Heidegger's statement, "To see the Moment (*Augenblick*) means to stand in it" and assess its validity in light of *Au moment voulu*'s insights. Placed in the proximity of Heidegger's reading of the eternal return in Nietzsche, Blanchot's *récit* engages the philosophical horizon from the perspective of the question of writing. He is thus able to make explicit another thinking (writing) of time at play in Nietzsche, something that Heidegger's reading neutralizes.

One cannot easily assimilate the exposure of this "apparition souveraine" (*le moment voulu*) to the "standing in the moment," because to be "on the same level as this beautiful instant" (AMV 105/SH 238) entails disrupting the economy of the day, all the parameters of intelligibility and all of its mechanisms of permanence and presence—all that the word *histoire* condenses. But what does "to stand *in* the moment" mean for *Au moment voulu*, especially if the moment comes without coming, comes by not coming, or comes by a coming whose localization is displaced according to the temporality of the *intrigue*, of temporality as *intrigue*? In addition, what does one have to understand by "standing in the moment" in *Au moment voulu*, especially if the stance of this "standing" is a question *of* writing and, therefore, "toujours en instance?":

> I can recall that, however long this road may be and whatever may be its detours through the futile repetition of days and moments, nothing can prevent it from being once again the hallway that separated the two small rooms and that I happened to enter. . . . I can recall all that, and to recall it is no doubt one more step into the same space, where to go farther is already to bind myself to the return. And yet, even though the circle is already drawing me along, and even if I had to write this eternally, I would write it in order to obliterate eternity: Now, the end (*Maintenant, la fin*). (AMV 166/SH 259)

In order to "stand in the moment," "I" has to write the *"Maintenant, la fin,"* and by doing so "I" never leaves the circle, since, by attempting to put an end to the unending dispersal of the writing of "La fin" and the fact of writing to the end, "I" keeps exposing himself to the time of writing as dying (*mourir*), as the oracular form shows: "Death! But in order to die, one had to write—The end! And to do that, one had to write up to the end" (AMV 86–87).

When writing is not oriented towards immortalizing, nor functions within an economy in which death is either a possibility (Hegel) or the possibility of the radical impossibility of being-there (Heidegger), it results in an unending movement. It is time's aporia that makes an alternative reading of Heidegger possible. To "stand in the moment," "I" has to write the "Maintenant, la fin," but by writing it, "I" never leaves the circle, since the attempt to put an end to the unending dispersal keeps exposing him to the time of writing as dying (*mourir*). Moreover, one cannot make "seeing the moment" and "standing in it" homologous. If the same returns, it does not return to the same.

The return alters, differs, and undermines any ground from which to erect a position, post, or site in which to anchor oneself. No substantial "I" remains when faced with the *nonexperience*[33] of "seeing the moment" in the absence of any horizon, not even a resolute *Dasein*, but what "remains" is a *quelqu'un*;[34] it is a presence differed and differing from itself by its anarchic engagement in an *intrigue* to which it must respond before any knowledge or comprehension of the call's tenor. It is a trace attesting to the response in a fugitive erring "in the manner of an image, even though it is absolutely present" (AMV 155/SH 256).

Therefore, the copula between the statement "to see the moment" and the utterance "to stand in the moment" dissimulates their incommensurability. It is the time of this incommensurability to which Blanchot's writing exposes us, the time of an encounter, of the event that responds to the other with an "initial speech" (writing) (EL).

Dwelling: Between *Poiēsis* and *Technē*

We have not busied ourselves in the foregoing with the transformation of word meanings. Rather, we have stumbled upon an event whose *immensity* still lies concealed in its long unnoticed *simplicity*.

— Martin Heidegger, *"Logos (Heraclitus, Fragment B)"*

Thinking is itself the proper acting insofar as to act means to comply with the essential unfolding of being.

— Martin Heidegger, *"Die Technik und die Kehre"*

On Dwelling

Although aberrant from the point of view of conventional literary scholarship and no less debatable from literary theory,[1] Heidegger's discourse on poetry and the work of art throws some light on why the project of a "metaphysics of *Dasein*," sketched out after *Being and Time* and developed in the Marburg courses, veers radically into the "thinking of the Turn (*Kehre*)."[2] Heidegger's series of courses and conferences on Hölderlin and the "origin" of the work of art have his disastrous engagement with National Socialism, as well as his attempt to disentangle himself from it, as a background. However, they reveal themselves as ideal materials to think the problematic articulation or dialogue between poetic saying (*Dichtung*) and thinking (*Denken*). Thinking here becomes a letting be (*sein lassen*), a bringing of being to language, understood as the dwelling or sojourn, since in being-there men "let [the world and truth] spring forth (*Ursprung as entspringen lassen*)" (KPM 136/148).[3] Thinking as act becomes a "compliance with being" (TK 47), an "ethics" in the sense of guarding or keeping watch of the Open site.

If in *Being and Time* the being-there of man (of its being or *Da*sein) constitutes this disclosure (*Erschlossenheit*), during the 1930s the work of art and poetic language (*Dichtung, Ursprache*) become the privileged site of disclosure. Disclosure is an *Ursprung*, the groundless event of coming into presence (grounding) that simultaneously withdraws itself from it, an *anarchic* origination that throws men into the Open. In the work of art, understood as essential language, beings as a whole (*phusis*) open (PLT 55); and thinking must secure this gathering in its historical and linguistic character, which in turn entails that thinking must become the recollection of the origin (PLT 74).

While the question of poetic language (of essential language) is well documented in Heidegger's critical bibliography, this is not the case with the question of ethics.[4] Heidegger alludes implicitly to ethics in *Being and Time*, and more explicitly in the "Letter on Humanism" (LH/PATH);[5] but these have been totally obscured by his abject political engagement.[6] In the latter Heidegger seeks to define an "ethics" prior to any ethics, an "original ethics" understood as dwelling or sojourn, as the preserving of the Open in its opening. This is what the structure of care or concern (*Sorge*) meant in *Being and Time* (¶ 44), in which the proximity of being to *Dasein* was already in view.

Unlike Husserl, for whom the world is constituted by a transcendental ego, the world is for Heidegger part of a structure proper to existence called being-in-the-world (*In-der-Welt-Sein*). In Heidegger's notation *ek-sistence*, the prefix *ek* marks the exposition at play in being-in-the-world, throwness and facticity, a form of being that goes beyond the classical opposition inside/outside. *Dasein* is a being for whom its being is a matter of concern and in which being-in-the-world reveals itself as a unifying structure. It is the structure of care that determines how entities come into presence, but inasmuch as the structure of care presupposes a unique relation to being, it is being that conditions the structure of our making-present. Later on Heidegger will say that being "gives or sends," but soon after he abandons the schema of the history of being to think what "gives" being (*Ereignis*). In an existential sense the "in" of being-in-the-world means a "being-alongside" (*bei*) or *dwelling*, a relation of familiarity or proximity that is irreducible to spatial contiguity (BT 80/54). But in a more essential way, dwelling names the responsibility that certain forms of existence—the thinker's, the poet's, that of the founder of a people—contract with being's unconcealing: its preservation. Later on, in "Building Dwelling Thinking" (1951), Heidegger defines the fundamental feature of dwelling as the act of preserving and sparing, "saving" the world "by setting it free into its own presencing" (PLT 150).

Although Heidegger abandons the language of fundamental ontology gradually, the schema I just outlined above organizes the series of texts that will be focus of this chapter: "Art as Will to Power" (the 1934–35 Nietzsche course), the conferences and courses on Hölderlin, and "The Origin of the Work of Art."[7] If for Heidegger being is an immanent event that originates in itself, its relation must be secured in accordance with its modality of manifestation; poetry and thinking must be up to the task of preserving the incommensurable advent of being. They must expose themselves to what is without measure and without object; that is, they must become ek-static responses that leap (*Sprung*) into the uncanny or unfamiliar par excellence. This entails a radical redefinition of language beyond its classical metaphysical determination and beyond its modern determination as the correlation of represented contents and the mind.

There is an inextricable relation between being and *Dasein*, a relation of *uncanny familiarity*—a forgotten familiarity, it is true, that has to be brought back to its "originality" by a process of estrangement. Witness the energy Heidegger invests in articulating the question of being as the essential question of thinking, not to render it more familiar, but to preserve its unfamiliar essence as such. We should not forget that in Heidegger "to bring (something) into (its) essence, into its own (*das eigenet*)," is the task of a thinking that never unfolds under the principle of identity. Moreover, since the bringing into essence is never a grounding onto predefined transcendental principles, the "in" of being-in-the-world is not a basis, but the different directions in which the *ek-* of ek-sistence throws man's being into its facticity. It is always an exposition or expropriation. A becoming-familiar, homely, always supposes the exposition to the foreign or unfamiliar, and this is why man is "the uncanniest of the uncanny" (HHI 51–79),[8] which means that the ground itself "is" uncanny (*Ungeheure*) or self-revealing in its withdrawing, *abyssal.*[9]

In the "Letter on Humanism," when glossing from paragraph 44 of *Being and Time*, Heidegger states: "Being is essentially farther than all beings and is yet nearer to the human being than every being. . . . Being is the nearest. Yet the nearest, the truth of being, remains the farthest from the human being" (LH 252). These dimensions of the near and the distant are not intra-worldly spatial determinations; they point rather to what will become the *Gegen* (region), the "topology of being" that the "dialogue" with poetry and the work of art can only expose once the "step back" from metaphysics takes place. Nearness occurs or unfolds as language itself, "the house of being in which the human being ek-sists by dwelling, in that he belongs to the truth of being, guarding it" (LH 254). This gloss signals a shift from *Dasein* understood as the ground of being to being as such. From 1935 onward one thesis underlies Heidegger's thinking: that language is "*onto*-logical" or,· in other words, the essence (*Wesen*) of language (nothing onto-*logical*) is the language of being, which may help to explain the double interrogation of the being of language *and* of the language of being. What matters here is being itself (*Se-yn*). This odd archaic spelling suggests that Heidegger thinks it from a non-metaphysical determination, understood according to the history of its own self-disclosure and withdrawal, a history that comes into the Saying of language.

However, ontology cannot elaborate the question of being, as it belongs to a determined figure of being. Ontology is derived; it plunges its roots in a previous saying of being that it covers up in its very constitution as a discourse, but without totally effacing it. It is precisely this derived discourse that has been received throughout the history of philosophy as *initial* (*Anfang*), and from which the Greek essence of being issues or *begins*. The confusion (substitution) between the derived and the initial has two consequences. First, it produces a covering up of the inaugural essence of being that cannot simply be reduced to its ontological derived formulation, but that in turn leads to a complete misunderstanding of the first Greek thinkers, "pre-Socratics." Second, it makes a full comprehension of ontology in its true essence impossible and produces a partial interpretation of the Platonic-Aristotelian philosophy, mistakenly conceived as the absolute beginning (IM 137/184).[10]

In order to retrieve both the truth of ontology and the truth of being, Heidegger proposes to take a "step back" beyond the Platonic determination of the being of entities and try to approach what being "was" in its first opening. If "being" cannot be captured in a single word but is rather "the word for every word" (GA 55, 82), its opening is nonetheless felt throughout language. The enigma of being sustains language; it is the essence of language and can only unfold itself in language as the language of being. We can thus distinguish three stages in Heidegger's path of thinking.

The first covers the period from *Being and Time* to the late 1930s. This is the period of fundamental ontology that stems from the double frame of an existential analytic and from the temporality of a privileged entity (*Dasein*). Because, as we saw above, *Dasein* is an entity for which "in its very Being, that Being is an issue for it" (BT 32),[11] its existential structure can illuminate the analysis of the "question of being" whose meaning is the heart of this whole period. The "question of the meaning" of being is posited within the horizon of the forgetting of being, *Verhesenheit* in the active sense of repression, and of the ensuing appropriation of the history of ontology, whose goal is to make this question once again "transparent" (BT 44/23). This appropriation calls forth a *destruction* "of the traditional content of ancient ontology until we arrive at those primordial experiences in which we achieved our first ways of determining the experience of being—the ways which have guided us ever since" (BT 44/23). This destruction is a genealogical enterprise that aims to prepare the conditions for a creative appropriation of the tradition, but it is also a critique of the dominant way of treating ontology.

In the second period Heidegger subordinates the horizon of *Dasein* to the question of how being unfolds itself in history. What is decisive now are the modes in which being grants or "gives" itself and, above all, that there is a forgetting of being, that is, its withdrawal as the privileged mode of granting itself. Here the privileging of certain forms of unconcealment, like poetic language and thinking, are mobilized to preserve being from the totalizing hold of the essence of technology and its monotonously dangerous way of manifesting beings. Being's withdrawal implies that for the whole of Western thought, being is understood as presence in its different historical configurations. Finally, we can speak of a third period whose guiding thought is *Ereignis*. Here Heidegger thinks what has been suppressed by the determination of being as presence, which concerns time as well as the relation determining time and being. As an unthought, though, it can only unfold as language, once the latter is conceived as "the relation of all relations" (OWL 107).[12]

How can this essence of language be made explicit? How can one speak of language in such a way that it is not simply reduced to a system of signs, to an object, to an instrument of communication and calculation? It will take Heidegger several years to "bring language to language" (OWL 59), since what is finally at stake in thinking is the possibility of undergoing an "experience with language" (OWL 58–59), a mutation in our habitual way of treating language as an entity or object that the subject can master at will, and even a mutation in how fundamental ontology has understood language.

Two threads weave Heidegger's writing. On the one hand it is the language of metaphysics (its lexicon and syntax), which unfolds in terms of the principle of reason and from which he retrieves more primary configurations. On the other hand it is a language that has no precedent in the metaphysical tradition, which no longer operates under the principle of reason, as Angelus Silesius's rose is "without reason" (*Abgrund*), and attempts to say what cannot be said in the order of metaphysical reason.[13] Heidegger "hears/listens" this language in the proximity of the poets. He "re-says" it, one of the "originary" meanings of *Dichtung* as we will see below, although this re-saying is not a repetition. Finally, he deploys it in a space that is neither "poetic" (literary), nor conceptual.[14]

This language can only speak from the situation of what Heidegger calls the "end of philosophy" (*Ende der Philosophie*).[15] However, by such a formula he is neither expressing a nihilistic judgment nor declaring the surrender of thinking. By referring to a situation in which metaphysics has exhausted its essential possibilities, he instead points to a space in which thinking, once delivered from the adherences of a derivative way of understanding being (metaphysics of subjectivity and representation, the partial unconcealment at play in the essence of technology), can give way to an other thinking (*anderen Denken*), an understanding of the "history of being" from the perspective of being's own sending and, beyond it, to what "gives being" (*es gibt Sein*): *Ereignis*. It is in this space, on "this side" of the metaphysical closure, that this unheard-of language can speak in its strangeness, although it was already lurking all throughout, as the *Beiträge* bears witness.[16]

In the margins of his copy of *Being and Time*, the so-called *Hüttenexemplar*, Heidegger writes, "language is not shared, it is rather the originary essence of truth as *there*" (GA 2, 117). It is because the essence of dwelling or sojourn reveals itself as a relation of sense (*Sinn*): the *there* is the Open, the site from which things can have a place and a sense. Sense, therefore, is the very structure of the opening; being is fundamentally what "gives sense" (*es gibt*). But this giving entails a production (*technē*) whose essence has been forgotten and endangered by technology, the dominant, albeit partial, way of uncovering beings. "Enframing (*Gestell*), (the essence of technology), comes to pass for its part in the granting that lets man endure . . . that he may be the one who is needed and used for the preserving and keeping watch (*Wahrnis*) of the coming to presence of truth" (QCT 33).[17] Heidegger speaks of this dwelling, of the language of being as the being of language, in the proximity of Hölderlin, thus indicating that the "dialogue" between the poet and the thinker is of decisive importance for an elucidation of the question of ethics, and that its insights go well into the "late Heidegger," in particular in[18] *On the Way to Language* (1959).[19]

Hölderlin provides directives for thinking the relation between being and man or mortals in the "time of distress" (*dürftiger Zeit*) (PLT 91), the time of the god's departure or flight, which is one of the two events that mark Heidegger's thinking on dwelling. The second is the devaluation of all values in which Nietzsche signals a provisional understanding of nihilism that must be brought back to its essence. In a sense, Nietzsche points backward, in the direction of something accomplished, while Hölderlin points forward, in the direction of something yet to come. Another way of putting it is to say that Nietzsche points in the direction of danger (the essence of technology), while Hölderlin points in the direction of what can save (*Retten*) us—dwelling as the preserving of the pure *phuein*.

Does this dialogue between thinking and poetry simply amount to the surrender of philosophy's "own possibilities," a suture of sorts that deposes the philosophical *lógos*, making it succumb to the prestige of the poem?[20] Does this dialogue open a path (*Weg*) to an "*anderen denken*" that could shield us from the violence of non-aletheiophanic modes of (un) concealment that unfold within the space of being's oblivion (mimesis, representation, technology)? It should be remembered that Heidegger himself surrendered to such violence by committing himself to the politics of National Socialism. Does the "original ethics" that is at the heart of Heidegger's "step back" think the responsibility of its own exposition to the other sufficiently?[21] The stakes are high and we must tread a thin line. This is the line that separates a discourse determined by a voluntarism whose lexicon derives from certain misreadings of Nietzsche and of Jünger, even when Heidegger tries to undermine them both, and in which *Kamp*, strife, destiny, foundation and decision prevail, from a discourse that seeks to secure an exposition to and of the other of reason (*Gelassenheit*).[22]

We are therefore faced with a triple knot that involves politics, a certain way of both succumbing and taking a stance against a metaphysical determination of politics, thinking, poetry (their dialogue), and ethics. Politics, because after the 1930s Heidegger seeks to make explicit *Dasein's* historiality, destiny (*Geshicht*), inasmuch as *Dasein* is understood as the site in which the question and meaning of being is put into play and, consequently, the question of the foundation "of the destiny of a people."[23] Poetic language, thinking understood as the listening and responding to the poem, can only constitute itself as the true *ethos*, inasmuch as "what remains is founded by the poets" (EHP 97). The poet thus assumes the figure of a founder of being (*des Begründer des Seyns*), although this soon changes into a witness of being, someone who responds in accordance with the tenor of being's call. The poet finally becomes the figure of serenity (*Gelassenheit*), of the essential relation to language as a renunciation of mastery.[24] Ethics, because inasmuch as *Dasein* is understood as the guardian of the Open or, rather, of the Opening, only thinking and poetizing can guard it by bringing being to language.

This is a strange knot, though, since Heidegger does not think politics as a political emplacement,[25] but rather in the site of the poem: Hölderlin's poetry and Sophocles's tragedy. In the course on *Hölderlins Hymnen "Germanien" und "Der Rhein"* the concept of the national (*das Nationell*) does not refer to the community of blood and soil as in the 1933 "Rectoral Address," but rather to the site of historical dwelling.[26] In the course on *Hölderlin's Hymn "The Ister"* the essence of the *polis* is not political, but a mode of ek-sistence, the *Da* of *Dasein*: exposition to the unconcealment of being as such (GA 39).[27]

Heidegger also does not think the poem (*Dichtung*), "the essential determination of art" (PLT 72), as an aesthetic emplacement, but rather as an aletheiophanic site, as *technē*, that is, as a mode of unconcealment or *poiêin* in accordance with the essential unfolding of the truth of being (*phusis*). He approaches the poem as the site in which the initial essence of being, that from which everything that is can come into presence, gathers as a whole. Poetic language (essential language) thus becomes the eminent way out of the oblivion of being.[28]

Regarding ethics, finally, Heidegger does not think this concept in the traditional domain of subjectivity, values, norms and principles, but as the site of language itself, a language that is no longer "the expression of thinking, feeling and willing" (OWL 34–36), the communication of speaking subjects (OWL 59/P 96–97), nor a possession or faculty of the human being (OWL 107, 114–15/P 221). What is at issue is thus a change in attitude toward language. We must pay some heed to these displacements, to the reinscriptions they configure and to the topology they trace, since it is nothing other than the "topology of being." In the end everything hangs on the "experience with language," on the possibility of "bringing language to language," in which the *poetics* of dwelling and the thought of the truth of being are one and the same: a *Sage* or Saying.

In this chapter I will unpack the complex articulation in which Heidegger's meditation on the work of art takes place. I will show that it unfolds in a context dominated by the question of nihilism, its "abandonment of being" in its double determination as Platonism and in its "final stage" as technology. That is, in a context in which the very question of dwelling is most at risk. Most importantly, the question of nihilism is guided by Heidegger's realization that its overcoming is impossible, and that thinking must take a "step back" if it wishes to secure a more originary relation with being or dwelling. The work of art provides Heidegger not only with an occasion to accomplish the "step back," the "leap," but also with a schema to think this relation in terms of truth—the *schematism* of truth as (un)-veiling, or a way of radically re-thinking figuration, which will be the object of the chapter 3. This entails a redefinition of figuration that prepares the ground for tracing the "topology of being."

My reading highlights the intertextual implication of a constellation of texts: the Niezsche course, the essays and conferences on Hölderlin, the essay "The Origin of the Work of Art," and the conference "The Question Concerning Technology." I will move from one to the other as a way of layering the question of poetic language as the question of being (*Seinsfrage*) and will devote a whole section to "The Origin of the Work of Art." Although the goal is to unfold the Heideggerian conceptual landscape in detail, I will also highlight the relevant articulations for our reading of Levinas and Blanchot, especially what these writers take as points of departure or plainly reject.

Poiēsis and Technē

What in truth is decided in the apparently extrinsic and, according to the usual view, even misguided designation of art as *technē* never comes to light, neither with the Greeks nor in later times.

Martin Heidegger, Nietzsche

In "The Origin of the Work of Art" Heidegger seeks to accomplish a metamorphosis in our understanding of the work of art. At stake is an "overcoming (*Uberwindung*) of aesthetics" that would enable us to think *technē* as the original mode of the unconcealment of beings, in the face of the obfuscation at play in nihilism.[29] At first Heidegger's reading of Nietzsche seems to favor the possibility of a way out of nihilism through art, which explains why the work of art becomes the strategic entry point into Nietzsche's conception of being as a whole and into his reversal of Platonism through the "revaluation of all values." At stake in this revaluation is the relation of truth and art, which would be able to preserve the unveiling of the whole of beings (*phusis*), as well as the irreducible opacity that this exposition allows. Nihilism in its double configuration, as the accomplishment of Platonism and as the essence of technology and its peculiar way of unveiling entities, threatens this form of manifestation Heidegger calls *poiēsis*.

Platonism, the metaphysical expression of Western nihilism, is grounded in the abandonment of being (*die Seinsverlassenheit*), according to Heidegger. By opposing revaluation to the devaluation of all values, Nietzsche fails to "overcome" nihilism. He remains caught within a logics of valuation in which the will to power, the expression of being as a whole, becomes the supreme value. As long as one moves within the schema of valuation and goals, Heidegger's problematic reading of Nietzsche claims, one is bound to a moralistic and idealistic interpretation of nihilism, provisional at best, since it fails to grasp its fundamental determination: the abandonment of being (CP 96).[30]

Heidegger shows that the essence of technology as *technē* is coemergent with the birth of metaphysics as "idealism" (Platonism). In the positing of the idea as the beingness of being, the *einai, ousia,* the presence of presencing, the being of beings as a whole is lost. The essence of nihilism is the history of the abandonment of being, (CP 139). In its completed form as technology, however, nihilism rules as will to power; the essence of European nihilism has to be thought in terms of the essence of technology. This is what Heidegger will call *Ge-stell* or *En-framing* and it is first thematized in the *Beiträge* (1936–38) as machination (*Machenschaft*) or "the preponderance of the makeable," or the "self-making" (*technē*) that orients the interpretation of *phusis* (CP 11, 88). That culminates in a metaphysics of lived experience (*Erlebnisse*) and worldviews (*Welltanschaungen*), which are the two main targets of Heidegger's "overcoming of aesthetics" in the Nietzsche course.[31]

When in "The Question Concerning Technology" (1953–54) Heidegger states that the essence of technology is anything technological, he signals that his strategy aims to leave behind both an anthropological conception for which instrumentality is the defining feature, and a humanistic one that sees in technology either a saving or destructive power. Heidegger's way of approaching the essence of technology is destining (*Geschickhaft*); he envisions it as a modality of the unconcealment or unveiling of being, a coming into presence under the form of production (*Hervorbringen*) or *poiēsis* (QCT 14–15/GA 55, 201). The essence of technology is not man's will to power, but rather being's granting. It is being that sends (*Schicken*) this configuration and is thus essentially an "ordering revealing," or an "ordaining of destining" (QCT 19, 24) exceeding any human doing.

The question of the essence of technology thus unfolds in the proximity of *poiēsis*, understood as the bringing forth of an entity, as for example the erecting of a statue of a god in the temple's enclosure. I will discuss this example below, but for now it is important to note that "The Origin of the Work of Art" (1935–36) is inextricably implicated in "The Question Concerning Technology," in the same way that the latter is implicated in "The Origin of the Work of Art," as the 1956 Addendum bears witness.

There are good reasons for this, since there is an *inextricable* relation between *poiēsis* and *technē* that took Heidegger several years to explicate. The self-reading Heidegger introduces in the Addendum to the 1935–36 essay seeks to reorient our reading and to bring this relation to the forefront. In "The Origin of the Work of Art" Heidegger claims that *technē* denotes a mode of knowing in which what is present as such is experienced; it is an essential mode of knowing consisting in *alētheia* or the uncovering of beings. But there is more; the essence of *technē* "supports and guides all comportment towards beings" (PLT 59). It is the unveiling of beings in the sense that "it *brings forth* present beings as such beings *out of* concealedness and specifically *into* the unconcealedness of their appearance" and consequently *technē* "never signifies the act of making" (PLT 59).

In *technē*'s essence Heidegger thus ciphers the *intrigue* of the *simple* as fold, not only because *poiēsis* and *technē* are the two faces of *Stellen*, of the modes of the unveiling of *alētheia* (truth), but also and fundamentally because they are "destining (*Geschickhaft*) modes of unveiling." They say the simple, *phusis* understood as *"the originary mode of appearing,"* one by *preserving* it, the other by *challenging* and *enframing* it. There is an archi-original split of *Stellen* between *poiēsis* and *technē* that opens up the two paths of unconcealment. The ambiguity of the essence of *technē* points to the secret of unveiling, of truth. *Poiēsis* preserves the archi-originary, the *polemos*, the strife that *phusis* is, inasmuch as *"phusis kruptesthai philein,"* disclosure in self-withdrawal.[32] It is more originary than *technē*, since the latter forgets all about it. The essence of technology represses or hides this other mode of unveiling. This "deficiency" is due neither to the implementation of machinery and tools nor to the preponderance of calculation or representation, but rather to technology's fidelity to its *destining* granting essence. One can see that what is at stake in the question of technology is precisely the question of "the constellation in which revealing and concealing, the coming to presence (*Wesende*) of truth, comes to pass" (QCT 33) which is the forgotten mystery of being.

By positing the whole of being as standing reserve (*Bestand*), technology mutates into a particular mode of production Heidegger calls provocation or challenging (*Herausforden*), which entails that technology does not let things come into their presence. It is a form of interpellation that challenges forth things into an order (*Stellen*) and thus blinds us to the withdrawal that is constitutive of truth's coming forth (QT 27). Nature (*phusis*) as a whole is summoned forth to answer in terms of the directions established by this order. It ceases being the original opening and thus becomes a standing reserve (*Bestand*) of forces from which technology can draw as it pleases.

This dominant form of unconcealment that commands the essence of technology receives the name of *Ge-Stell* (QCT 19), a name condensing all the *Stellungen* that throughout the history of metaphysics have been deployed to think presenting and producing and whose function is central in "The Origin of the Work of Art." There is nothing incidental in it since *Gestell*'s essential feature is that of being "a destining (*Geschick*) that gathers together into the revealing that challenges forth" (QCT 31). However, the destining (*Geschick*) of unveiling entails a danger: the possibility of losing sight of a more original unveiling. If the destining challenges *exclusively* in the mode of *Gestell*, we face the "extreme" danger of losing the irretrievable opacity at the heart of manifestation. No matter how much *Gestell* can gather in its destining interpellation, it cannot *grant*; it cannot encounter what endures and what withdraws in its bringing together, because "only what is granted endures. That which endures primarily out of the *originary origin* (*das anfänglich*) is what grants."[33]

If *Gestell*'s unveiling is dangerous, it is the other path that can save us by reestablishing man's dignity, one that consists in "keeping watch (*wahren*) over the unconcealment—and with it, from the first, the concealment—of all coming to presence on this earth" (QCT 32). Once again we come across the question of dwelling, since in its origin *technē* meant the unveiling that produces the truth of being in the radiance of what comes into presence, that is *poiēsis*. By unequivocally placing *poiēsis* under Hölderlin's maxim "poetically dwells man upon this earth," Heidegger indicates that it is the only stance able to respond to the enigma of the "pure manifestation" (*phusis*). The task of the poet "in destitute times" is the recollection or remembrance (*Andenken*) of being. Poetic saying accomplishes a turning or reversal (*Umkehr*) of thinking from forgetfulness that enables the history of being (*Seinsgeshichte*) to emerge for the thinker as the history of forgetting, but also as the promise—the remembering-awaiting—of the not yet to come. *Poíesis* is pious (*promos*), as it yields to "the holding-sway and the safe-keeping of truth" (QCT 34).[34] The poet becomes someone who "hints," not in the direction of the presence of things, but in their withdrawal, thus announcing not what withdraws, but the very movement of withdrawal (WHD 27).[35]

In this context, punctuated by nihilism and the danger that the essence of technology harbors, Heidegger's turn toward the work of art and the poem functions as a hinge between an "overcoming" that becomes more and more problematic, and a "step back" that seeks to secure an appropriation (*Verwindung*) of the repressed and suppressed essence of truth and open a path to the other beginning, or *inceptual* thinking. Heidegger posits the question of the origin (*Ursprung*) of the work in the horizon of the overcoming of aesthetics, that is, "simultaneously with overcoming a certain conception of beings as what is objectively representable" (CP 354/502). To overcome aesthetics (metaphysics) means freeing the question of the truth of being's priority from ideal, causal, transcendental, and dialectical explanations of entities as "a leap into [philosophy's] first beginning" (CP 354/504). This leap can only be enacted if thinking secures a *schematism* of the pure setting up and setting forth of truth in the work of art, in its *createdness* (*Geschaffensein*) or "ek-static" *Ursprung*—a schematism in accordance with being's pure origination of which it must also be a response.

The overcoming of aesthetics therefore aims to conceive the work of art as no longer issuing from the autonomous creative activity of an artistic subject. The work itself would therefore not be an object at the disposal of a creative or receptive subject. Further, to be able to think the essence of the work as such supposes that one leaves behind the determination of art as the cipher (symbol or allegory) of a spiritual content, along with its implicit metaphysics of representation in which imagination is equated with the subject's productive power, and the work with its symbol.

Uberwindung is a term with a Nietzschean provenance. This is not surprising given that the first version of "The Origin of the Work of Art"
was drafted during the time Heidegger dictated the first part of his course
on Nietzsche,[36] "Art as Will to Power," in 1934–35. There are a series of
elements in the course's text that not only indicate that Heidegger had
already acquired a different conception of the work of art (of its relationship with truth) than the one he finds throughout the history of aesthetics (metaphysics) and in Nietzsche's "aesthetics in the extreme," but also
that this different conception is presupposed throughout his interpretation of Nietzsche:

Nietzsche speaks only of the "artist phenomenon," not about art. Although it is difficult to say *what art "as such" is, and how it is*, still it is
clear that works of art belong to the reality of art, and furthermore so
do those who, as we say, "experience" such works. The artist is but
one of those things that together make up the actuality of art as a
whole. Certainly, but this is precisely what is decisive in Nietzsche's
conception of art, that he sees it in its essential entirety in terms of
the artist. (N 1, 70, my emphasis)

What art "as such" is, and "how it is," these are things that, according
to Heidegger, Nietzsche does not say, cannot say. Neither does Heidegger in an explicit manner, but at crucial junctions in the course, when he
makes explicit the original meaning of *technē* as the eminent mode of
unconcealment, as the "letting of what is already coming to presence
arrive" (N 1, 81–82), or when he defines "great art" as the preserving
(*Bewahrung*) of "being's manifestation as a whole" (N 1, 84), we do see
that the essence of the work and of its working are everywhere present in
the course.[37]

Inasmuch as Heidegger's confrontation (*Auseinandersetzung*) with National Socialism overdetermines the course on Nietzsche, its effects are
also felt throughout "The Origin of the Work of Art."[38] In the course
it is a question of subtracting Nietzsche from the National Socialist
appropriation and, in particular, from biologistic and axiological interpretations that were at the basis of the "philosophy of Hitlerism," as well
as from the romantic impetus of a Wagnerism that provided the Nazi
regime with the schema of its aesthetic representation.[39]

One can see that the stakes of the course are high and that they are behind the radical rethinking of the concept of work in the conference and the essay. In both cases it is the destiny of the German people that is of central concern. When he reopens the question of Nietzsche's "artistic states," the opposition of the Dionysian and the Apollonian, under the heading of rapture (*Rausch*), Hölderlin's name is mentioned for the first time. After quoting from his letter to Böhlendorff of 4 December 1801, Heidegger states:

The opposition is not to be understood as an indifferent historical finding. Rather, it becomes manifest to direct meditation on the destiny and determination of the German people. Here we must be satisfied with a mere reference, since Hölderlin's way of knowing could receive adequate definition only by means of an interpretation of his work. It is enough if we gather from the reference that the variously named conflict of the Dionysian and the Apollonian, of holy passion and sober representation, is a hidden stylistic law of the historical determination of the German people, and that one day we must find ourselves ready and able to give it shape. The opposition is not a formula with the help of which we should be content to describe "culture." *By recognizing this antagonism Hölderlin and Nietzsche early on placed a question mark after the task of the German people to find their essence historically. We will understand this cipher? One thing is certain: history will wreak vengeance on us if we do not.* (N 1, 104, my emphasis; see also GA 39, 290–94)

Nietzsche *and* Hölderlin: the thinker who thinks after the event of the "death of God" and the ensuing nihilism, the poet who attests before the thinker the departure of the gods "in a destitute time" (PLT 91–96) eliciting a suspension of time, a time without time, in which the "not yet to come" could have its chance. But in the end, it is the poet who provides the directions for an alternative path to the thinker who is faced with the completion of metaphysics ("Nietzsche"—that is, the Nietzsche who, once subtracted from the reductive interpretations of the time, can be brought back to his "own truth," that of being the last metaphysical thinker) and the nihilism embodied by the "philosophy of Hitlerism" and its aesthetics provided by Wagnerian collective work (*Gesamtkunstwerk*). For Heidegger, "to be a poet in a *destitute* time (a time of *distress*) means: to attend, singing, to the trace of the fugitive gods. This is why the poet in the time of the world's night utters the holy (*das Heilige*). This is why in Hölderlin's language the world's night is the holy night" (PLT 94).

If the thinker must follow the poet's directives, this is because in this situation it is a matter of paying heed to the echo of the abandonment of being, of bringing it forth from its forgetting. Letting it resound amounts to recognizing the distress, which is not a mere feeling (a psychological or anthropological determination), but rather the "attunement of the reservedness" (CP 50). *Distress* is the grounding attunement of the "step back," of the leap into *inceptual* thinking or the other beginning, which Heidegger contrasts to wonder (*thaumazein*), the grounding attunement of the first beginning: "[in] reservedness . . . *Dasein* attunes itself to the stillness of the passing of the last god. Situated creatively in this grounding-attunement of *Dasein*, man becomes the guardian and caretaker of this stillness" (CP 13).[40] Reservedness thus thinks the structure of care (*Sorge*) in a more original way. It becomes the "ground of care" (CP 25) and explains why its recovery from the poet's path "in the direction of the truth of be-ing (*Seyn*)" (CP 10) becomes the implicit program of the course on Hölderlin, as if the grounding of fundamental ontology were not sufficiently fundamental. Everything unfolds then between Nietzsche and Hölderlin, between nihilism and poetic saying. What is at issue is a destining ciphered in the form of an antagonism. How does Heidegger cope with the principle of the antagonism between "the Dionysian and the Apollonian"?

THREE

The Enigma of Manifestation
(Figuration in Heidegger)

From the "Overcoming of Aesthetics" to the "Step Back";
or, From Nietzsche to Hölderlin

Heidegger's detour through Hölderlin's poetry leaves the project of the "overcoming of aesthetics" in disarray and opens the path to a "step back" from metaphysics and a radical redefinition of language. This detour does not amount to making Heidegger's a poetic thinking, a conceptual retranslation of poetry's findings—whatever they may be—nor the model of Heidegger's *Kehre*. Not without a certain interpretative violence on Heidegger's part, Hölderlin the poet acts much like a "chemical agent" that captures metaphysics's "unthought," the dimension in which metaphysics finds its proper site. If the philosopher institutes being, the poet is the one who says be-ing (*Seyn*) by bringing it to language as sacred. Poetry is not simply the arbitrary product of imagination and a function of the unreal (Sartre). It is the setting up according to a schema that will recur throughout "The Origin of the Work of Art,"[1] and which I will refer to in detail below, of what is effectively real (*das Wirkliche*) in language. The poet's song sets up being; it is the enigma of being that sings in Hölderlin's poetry.

The singular task of poetry is to institute being in language. Poetry is the poetry *of* being; it is being that in poetry says the first and last word. In its essential determination language is, for Heidegger, *Urdichtung* or primordial *poiēsis*, previous to any poetic work but also to any poetry or to the poetic that any form of work of art entails. *Poiēsis*, as "The Origin of the Work of Art" defines it, is the unconcealment or setting forth of truth. Language is the *poiēsis* of truth because in it being manifests itself in the open, because it opens the space of a world in which entities come into presence and in which they are preserved as such. This understanding of language yields a rather astonishing conception of poetry as a founding saying that subtracts itself from the grounds of metaphysics and particularly from a metaphysics of representation.

At what price, though? Heidegger's attempt to hear in the poem the poetizing previous to the poem (*das Gedichte*) compels him to bracket or even suppress the subjective dimension of poetry, as well as its materiality; for the most part, he tends to disregard Hölderlin's theoretical essays. Further, Heidegger's approach to the poem bypasses the materiality of writing as if it were simply an obstacle, something *Vorhandenheit* (present-at-hand). Here, as with the most recalcitrant forms of logocentrism, writing must be left behind if a true understanding is to be obtained, an understanding that is inseparable from hearing. Listening to the poem means hearing the resonance and vibration of a saying (*Schwingubgsgetüge eines sagen*) (GA 39, 15); this is the echo of the abandonment of being. This resonance determines the syntax and the semantics of the poem and not the other way around, as would normally be expected.

In *Being and Time* hearing is defined as an essential possibility of discourse (BT ¶ 34, 206/163). By hearing Heidegger does not refer to a mere acoustical perception but to an existential possibility, the understanding's condition of possibility (*Verstehen*). Hearing supposes a particular relation to the other human being, since it inscribes the dimension of alterity at the heart of existence. It also expresses the discursive modality of being-with and understanding: "lending an ear to, listening to . . . (*hören auf. . .*) is *Dasein*'s existential way of being-open as being-with towards the other (*den Anderen*)" (BT 206/163, translation modified). There is no being-with without hearing, which explains why Heidegger states: "Indeed, hearing constitutes the primary and authentic way in which *Dasein* is open for its ownmost potentiality-for-being—as in hearing the voice of the friend whom every *Dasein* carries with it" (BT 206/163). Without engaging with the rather baffling appearance of the "voice of the friend" in this context, it is important to stress that the first figure of alterity that is at the origin of hearing is friendship.[2]

If Ricouer is right in reading the passage as an allusion to Aristotle's *Nicomachean Ethics*, if what is at issue is a question of responsibility as the hearing of a voice, Heidegger's point of departure is different from Levinas's. For him hearing is also an essential component of responsibility, but obedience (*Gehorchen*) has an "ethical" priority over this dispositional hearing (*hören*). Unlike Levinas, for whom the saying of the other, which is contact and proximity, cannot become the object of knowledge, Heidegger stresses the interdependence between understanding and hearing: "Dasein hears because it understands" (*Das Dasein hört, weil es versteht*) (BT 206/163); this interdependence or submission to the other founds a belonging (*Zuggehörigkeit*), which means that hearing is at the heart of being-with.[3]

It is not until Heidegger engages with the hearing of the poem, the elucidation (*Erläuterung*) that brings to light the pure saying of the poem in each word (US 38–39), that he begins to unfold its essential dimension.[4] Man is a conversation (*Gespräch*), however not in the sense of a true conversation between a subjectivity and the other human being who faces me "in the straightforwardness of discourse" (Levinas), nor in the sense of a "being-for-the-other" (*être-pour-autrui*), the existence of an ego for another ego (Sartre).[5] For Heidegger conversation means to hear "in the essential word [the] one and the same on which we agree," that which speaks "in a single and same voice" (EHP 56–57). The gathering of the speaking of language in a single saying that the prefix *Ge-* connotes means that in its essence *Dasein* is enrooted in language as "onto-logy." This conversation opens as the possibility of its existence; it happens inasmuch as conversation, "once the calling of the gods occurs, when they place us under their call, bring[s] us to the language (*Sprache*) that questions whether and how we are, how we respond and correspond (*zusagen*) or refuse (*versagen*) our being" (GA 39, 71).[6]

Because being installs the poet in this conversation, both an authentic saying and hearing can unfold in poetry; the poet becomes the "spokesman" of the voice's call that, in turn, convokes him to the task of preserving and sharing it with men. The poet is the only one who can safeguard this conversation in which "what is said and heard are the 'same' (HS)" (EHP 55). Man must respond to the call of a language issuing from the gods for an authentic conversation to unfold, "but the gods can come to expression only if they themselves address us and place us under their claim. A word which names the gods is always an answer to such a claim" (EHP 58). An authentic conversation thus consists in naming the gods and in setting forth a world.

Hearing/understanding the poem amounts to listening to the resonance and the echo of its saying:

It is thus above all the totality of the poetic saying's rhythmic configuration that "expresses" the so-called meaning. . . . Yet it is the fundamental tone of a poetry that creates its own form in the inner draft of the totality that from the start determines the saying's rhythmic configuration. The fundamental tone in turn comes each time from the metaphysical site proper to each particular poetry. (GA 39, 15)

The poem's saying is rooted in a poem *before* the poem, what Heidegger calls a fundamental tone that is tuned to a fundamental mood, or state of mind (*Stimmung*) (GA 39, 77–78), and which the commentary must identify. In *On the Way to Language* Heidegger speaks in terms of the site (*Ort*) of the poem as the wave that puts the saying into motion and that carries it back to the source of its saying (OWL 160/38), a movement that the word *rhythm* best captures, although not in the sense of a series of sounds that flow in time (*fluss, fliessen*) but rather as an harmonious gathering (*Fügung*) (127/230). For Heidegger, rhythm does not entail a hypnotic or entrancing movement, as is the case for Levinas, but a movement that leads to abatement and peace (*Ruhe*), far removed, as we will see below, from the rapture and exaltation of Wagnerian aesthetics.

One should recall that the word *Stimmung* can refer both to an objective reality, "this restaurant has no ambiance," and to a subjective one, "the chef is in a terrible mood today." In its existential sense *Stimmung* is more fundamental than the distinction between subject and object (BT ¶39). There is a link between *Stimmung* and voice, *Stimme*. The former suggests a certain music of things with which we are in (dis) accord, while the latter refers to what attunes us to it.[7] The *Stimmung* is a fundamental existential in which the discovery of *Dasein*'s being-thrown, its facticity, occurs. Mood therefore can be reduced neither to a simple act of perception nor to an act of reflection (BT 174/136). *Stimmung* is thus the condition of possibility of a "sich-richten auf," an exposition to the world and the other, and the condition of possibility of affection, of the everyday dealings with the environment (*Umwelt*). This is the schema that commands Heidegger's use of *Stimmung* in his courses on Hölderlin and explains why poetic saying can reveal *Dasein*'s being as much, if not more, than theoretical knowledge. An existential determination of mood and affection, *Stimmung* is more original than representational thinking.

So what is the *Stimmung* that the poem exposes and how is it attuned? The fundamental mood or *Grundstimmung* is what determines the relation to being, "what brings forth the appearing of beings in its opening" (GA 39, 86) and thus has a metaphysical signification and not an aesthetic, psychological, or anthropological one. Heidegger calls "sacred mourning" (*Trauer*) the *Grundstimmung* that "sets forth in an essential way another opening of being in its totality" (GA 39, 83).[8]

The path to the essence of language passes through the poem, but to follow this path means to undergo an experience with language. We must be prepared to acknowledge that we do not own language. In its essence, language is not in principle the expression of a conscious content, but what opens the space of a play within which man can become a speaking and a thinking subject, the echo or respondent to being's claim (WM 44–45/81). The path to the essence of poetry thus supposes the identification of a *Dichtung* in the poem. Heidegger identifies it through a lesson (*lectio*) that language carries within its fold:

Dichten . . . derives from the Old High German *tithôn*, which is related to the Latin *dictare*, a frequentative form of *dicere* = saying. *Dictare*, to re-saying something, to say it aloud, to "dictate," to expose something through language . . . Poetic comes from the Greek ποιεῖν, ποίησις—to produce something. . . . We can take advantage of an indication that contains the original signification of the word *tithôn-dicere*. This word has the same root as the Greek word δείχνυμι. The latter means to show, to make something visible, manifest, not in a general sense, but under the guise of a particular showing. (GA 30, 290)

Dichten as an act of poetizing in language is a saying or a dictation, something that suggests a prescriptive regime, under the form of a sign that makes the thing thus said manifest. In its essential diction the poem is the manifestation of what appears as being, the unending and repeated manifestation of being. What defines the poem is a specific way of showing (*weisendes offembarmachen*). Because the task of Hölderlin's poetry is both to think and to poetically say the essence of poetry, his poetry being language's *lectio* or being's *diktat*, he is the "poet of poetry." But Hölderlin is also the poet of "a destitute time," that is, he bears witness to the event that has marked the time to which we still belong, the abandonment of being and the forgetting that characterizes the epoch of the end of metaphysics.

Poetic enunciation is a "hinting," a "showing" which presupposes a way of being in which *Dasein* is already exposed to being. In the Hölderlin courses a new dimension of language, absent from *Being and Time*, appears for the first time: the *Wink*. In *Being and Time* language is still a founded phenomenon, derivative with respect to *Rede*, discourse in the sense of both manifestation and articulation:

The existential ontological foundation of language is discourse or talk (*Rede*). . . . Discourse is existentially equiprimordial with state-of-mind and understanding. . . . Discourse is the articulation of intelligibility. . . . The way in which discourse is expressed is language (*Sprache*). Language is a totality of words—a totality in which discourse has a "worldly" being of its own. . . . Discourse is existentially language, because the entity whose disclosedness it articulates according to signification, has, as its kind of Being-in-the-world (*in-der-Welt-sein*)—a Being which has been thrown and submitted to the "world."(BT 204–5)

In *Being and Time*, then, the essential determination of language is discourse that, in turn, is defined by the articulation of *Dasein*'s intelligibility.

Any other form of communication appears as deriving from this articulation. However, in the courses and conferences on Hölderlin, language as a system of signs and as signifyingness refers to a more original determination, the *Winke*, the language of the gods: "poetry—enduring the signs (*der Winke*) of the gods, the setting forth of being" (GA 39, 48). Poetry is a type of showing through which the gods become manifest "not as the object of thinking or contemplation, but in the very act of hinting (*Winken*)" (GA 39, 42/32). Heidegger distinguishes between the hint (*Wink*) as a gesture (*Gebarde*) that lets the sense of the gesture appear in the hint itself, the sense of being, from the sign (*Zeichen*) as index of signification (OWL 24–6). As a gesture that hints, the *Wink* lets something appear, it is an "act without words" in the sense that what is shown does not exhaust itself in the meaning of words.

In the poem Heidegger reads the accomplishment of the projective essence of ontology: "being is what demands in us creation so that we can have the experience" (EHP 251). This setting forth can only occur as an exposition to the holy as the whole or "originary wholeness" (*das Heilige, heil*) (EHP 85). For this reason, the poet becomes a semi-god whose particular way of being Heidegger makes explicit in his interpretation of Hölderlin's poem "Der Rhein." The semi-god occupies an intermediary place between men and the gods, the earth and the sky. In its fundamental mood or tonality (*Grundstimmung*), the poetic saying frees this originary interval that Heidegger thinks as the double fold of being, as the difference (*Unterschied*) between being and beings. Heidegger thinks the semi-gods in terms of destiny (*Shicksaal*), the *milieu* (*die mitt*) where men and gods find their place and face each other.[9]

This unheard-of conception of the poem entails the idea of a setting forth without performance and as the extreme exposition to being or *Ursprung*, whose essence will be the object of "The Origin of the Work of Art." Poetic saying becomes the site of an ontological exasperation, as it is the expression of the vehemence of its exposition to being (GA 39, 66).

In *Being and Time* poetry amounts to a naïve and spontaneous preontological clarification of being and consequently to *Dasein's* preontological self-clarification. It thus has a more traditional philosophical function; it belongs to a set of documents (*Zeugnisse*) that the philosopher incorporates in the context of the existential analytic to show that what he claims is not his invention but instead has a concrete grounding. Philosophical discourse is the existential revelation of these concrete spontaneous contents (BT 241/197). In ¶ 34, however, poetry possesses a proper ontological dignity since "in 'poetical' discourse (*Dichtung*), the communication of the existential possibilities of one's state-of-mind (*Befindlichkeit*) can become an aim in itself, and this amounts to a disclosing of existence" (BT 205/192). The disclosing potentiality that Heidegger privileges in the series of texts and courses that are the focus of this chapter also entails a redefinition of poetic language.

Three statements best define this new approach to language that differs from the one Heidegger introduced in *Being and Time*: Hölderlin enables an understanding of poetry's essence; poetry is the essence of language; and *Dasein*'s foundation takes place in poetic language, since it is thanks to language that *Dasein* becomes the "witness of being" (GA 39, 62). In poetic language a world opens up, but where there is a world there is also danger, the menace of being by nonbeing in its double modality—the leveling down of everything brought about by the essence of technology, and the proximity to the gods (GA 39, 64). Heiddeger ciphers all the features of this new understanding of language in Hölderlin's verses: "much has man experienced. / Named many of the heavenly ones, / since we have been a conversation / and able to hear from one another."[10] *Dasein* is here an event of language; the conversation "we are" opens up the time of human history. It is the poem that enables *Dasein* to dwell in the world as poet and the gods' initiative that bring us to language.

Heidegger understands the essence of poetry, language, as a creative or installing process (*stiftender Entwurf*) (GA 39, 164), a bringing forth, as he puts it in "The Origin of the Work of Art." As a semi-god the poet makes the distinction between mortals and gods possible, which in turn brings forth the domain of being as such. The semi-god marks the site from which to think the essence of both mortals and gods; his essence is thus defined as "destiny," a creative passion that invites the other men to participate (GA 39, 178). The setting forth of being founds a fidelity to being as the final presupposition of any other form of belonging and, at the same time, compels one to a decision whose stake is the hearing of being's "origin." *Dasein*'s opening to being, an opening which is both reserved and destined to *Dasein*, occurs as a hearing, but unlike the hearing of mortals (*Ueberhören*) that turns away from the origin into forgetting, the poet hears the origin in its origination (*Ursprung*) and opens the possibility for thinking.

The figure of the poet as semi-god is at the heart of a thinking of being as *pure origin* and *origination*: "to being's essence corresponds the being's inaugural repercussion on being. Being brings forth poetry to originally find itself in it and thus, by withdrawing into poetry, to have its secret opening" (GA 39, 219/238). Being is its origination; it is an absolute immanence, and it is all that "there is" (*il y a*). No exteriority or exposition to an "otherwise than being" is ever involved in this *Ursprung*. We should not lose sight of the fact that poetic language is the matrix that allows Heidegger to elaborate the pure origination of being since, as we will see in the next chapters, it marks the site of a profound *differend* between Heidegger and Levinas. If for the former being is all "there is" (*il y a*) in its pure percussive opening, for the latter "*il y a*" equals pure being, a restricted economy or totality whose origination is not immanent, as it comes from the Other. While for Heidegger *poíesis* names the opening of being, for Levinas, infinity's revelation in the face of the concrete other names the separation from being, the instantiation of the "*otherwise than* being" that, in turn, is the signification of being. Levinas reads Heidegger's *onto-poiesis of being* (its sending itself to itself in the element of the poem and its opening to itself in its secretive exposition) as a myth that fixes subjectivity in a time without hope. Blanchot feels the need to accentuate the unfolding of essential language in slightly different terms. To Hölderlin's song celebrating the pure appearing, Blanchot will oppose Orpheus's song and its disconcerting fascination with the movement of withdrawal. Hölderlin-Orpheus does not sing the holy but rather the "other night," which is not "the sheltering profusion of the day" (EHP 133) but an irreducible heterogeneity. If for Heidegger art and the poem, two modes of essential language, safeguard the truth of being, Levinas and Blanchot, for different reasons, "let go the prey for the shadow."

In "the pure appearing" lies the enigma of being for Heidegger. As soon as the space of the poem opens itself to this enigma, the initial difference between the appearing and what appears unfolds. In this difference lies the secret which poetry unveils: the secret of the double fold of being, of the ontological difference. Moreover, the enigma of this unveiling compels the poet and the thinker to respond in accordance with this immanent manifestation by leaping to this pure origin and by exposing themselves to an activity without object: "if the essence of poetry is to be determined, it is always necessary, as in the case of any essential creation of history, that it be starting from its extreme limits. . . . At these limits the creators know, as do the poets, that for them there is no object (*Gegenstand*: that nothing faces them). They must set forth being" (GA 39, 231/251).

It is not until his 1943 "Post-face" added to "What Is Metaphysics?" that Heidegger for the first time posits the idea of a dialogue between thinking and poetry, where the thinker's task consists in saying being and the poet's in naming the sacred. Heidegger defines thinking as the loyal hearing to being's mysterious call, that is, to the saying in which the truth of being comes to language (WM 46). For Heidegger, Hölderlin's poetry is hymn because "the song bears witness to the holy—to the ground of the belonging together of men and gods" (EHP 85, 91). In the poem the sacred (*das Heilige*) itself "bestows the word and itself comes into this word" (EHP 98); the poet's native land is the region between men and gods where he experiences both the exile of the sacred and the dreadful power of the sacred word he must endure: "the holy is the awesome (*Ungeheure*) itself" (EHP 85); "for the essential condition of the poet is grounded not in the reception of the god, but in the embrace by the holy" (EHP 91).

Heidegger transports Hölderlin to the primal scene of thinking, to the sudden bursting of being in its inaugural guise (*phusis*). Poetic saying responds to the essential determination of *logos* as the "laying that gathers, what lets lay before" (EGT 66). The poem thus sings the coming of the gods "as when on a holiday" (*Feiertag*), the day when men can open to the luminosity of the day and when the encounter with the gods can take place: "the holiday, first sent by the holy, remains the origin of history. History is the 'collected gatherings of all such sendings of destiny'. . . . The poet becomes the founder of the history of a humanity. He prepares the poetic upon which a historical community dwells as upon its own ground" (EHP 129–30). The poet is neither a visionary nor a foreteller;

the sacred he announces opens the interval of a suspension of time. It indicates the region in which men's dwelling can unfold.

In the end the poem is the hymn *of* the sacred which it names only by effacing itself before it; it is the silent saying that leads to god's word, a god that speaks through a nonexpressive and wordless language. The bringing forth of the poem encloses the silence of god in its language, exposing it by concealing it as well. The poem is at the same time the veil of the absent god's presence and, due to the darkness and absence of god, its hinting. The poem is the language of the gods that went silent; it is this resounding silence. The poet thus speaks in the poem but at the price of a terrible mutilation, since he gives his voice to what cannot speak, to what is unnamable.

If the essence of technology entails the supreme danger of losing sight of this mystery (the mystery of the sacred, of being/language), the poet in "times of distress" is *dichterberuf*).[11] Because he stands without fear or trembling in face of the absence of the gods, the poem is the remembrance (*Andenken*) of the sacred. The poet is faced with a double infidelity, the gods' who have fled and men's who have forgotten the source.

What is the status of this *phenomenopoiesis*? Does it lead to religious thinking? For Heidegger god is the product of a metaphysics that translates its essence and provenance in onto-theological terms. It is the manifestation of being as sacred that can only grant its divine essence to a positive god: "the divine is divine because it is sacred" (EHP 58/77). God and men find their reciprocal mediation in the sacred, which is "the divinity's only essential place that in turn can grant the dimension to the gods and to God" (HW 248).[12] It is from the essence of the sacred that one can think the essence of the divinity, and from the essence of being, the sacred. Does this way of putting things entail a form of idolatry? Levinas would answer in the affirmative. Is Heidegger asking the poet for the impossible? Blanchot would also answer in the affirmative. Heidegger wants to come up with a form of ontological foundation of being in an abyssal structure, a foundation for an age without fundaments and from which the gods have fled.

Moreover, he wants to preserve a saying of the origins as what subtracts itself from the predicative structure of language, even from the words of the poem. Poetry is a saying without a said (utterance); one cannot translate its saying (*Gedichtete des Gedischtes*) into the said of poetic language (*Gesagte*). The poetic saying is a pre-diction of what has never been before and that announces itself in this saying in which what is destined to us manifests itself in defiance of our conceptual grasp and the economy of representation. If it is true that Levinas and Blanchot dispute many of these ideas, their conceptions of language derive from Heidegger's understanding of poetic language as what can subtract itself from the order of discourse.

The poet is the thinker's ancestor; he prepares the condition for the coming of the sacred by showing men how to "lend an ear" to hearing and thus to refrain from reducing beings to a "standing reserve." Heidegger's way of handling *techne*'s Janus face is by articulating a myth—the myth of being—older than the metaphysically determined opposition between *mythos* and *logos*, unless this anteriority were not already part of the myth in question and consequently a myth of *logos*—a Saying (*Sage*).

This detour through Hölderlin has enabled us to clearly see what is at stake in the "overcoming of aesthetics." We have seen the decisions that determine Heidegger's argumentative gestures and the turns in his path of thinking, in what at first sight could simply have passed for an overrated valorization of poetry and language, an aberrant discourse, a mystical pathos. We can now go back to the course on Nietzsche and reframe Hölderin's contributions to the initial question of the "overcoming of aesthetics."

Even if the goal of the Nietzsche course is to extract his thinking from the ideological grasp of National Socialism—"*We need the ability to see beyond everything that is fatally contemporary in Nietzsche*" (N 1, 127, my emphasis)— Heidegger must also settle an account with him. At issue is the aesthetic interpretation of art, as well as the conception of truth or being as a whole as will to power. In order to weigh the radicalism of Heidegger's determination of the work of art, of its *working*, it is necessary to keep in mind the limitations of Nietzsche's "metaphysical" conception of art and the limits Heidegger establishes to circumscribe it. These limits concern the essence of the work of art and the essence of truth:

If we ask what the essence of creation is, then on the basis of what has gone before we can answer that it is the rapturous bringing-forth of the beautiful in the work. Only in and through the creation is the work realized. But because that is so, the essence of creation for its part remains dependent upon the essence of the work; therefore it can be grasped only from the Being of the work. Creation creates the work. But the essence of the work is the origin of the essence of creation. *If we ask how Nietzsche defines the work, we receive no answer.* For Nietzsche's meditation on art—and precisely this meditation, as aesthetics in the extreme—does not inquire into the work as such, at least not in the first place. *For that reason we hear little, and nothing essential, about the essence of creation as bringing-forth.* (N 1, 115, my emphasis)

With regard to createdness (*Geschaffensein*) and unlike Hölderlin, Nietzsche does not think the work's essence, the exposition of the work to truth or being, or the opening and leap to what is without object. Heidegger establishes another limit in Nietzsche's inability to grasp the work *as such* and the *working* at play in the work. This limit touches "what . . . in the essence of art [in its working] calls forth the question concerning truth" (N 1, 143): "*Was Heisst das Kunsterwerk?*" This is the question that Nietzsche's meditation on art "as aesthetics in the extreme" can neither respond to nor, more importantly, posit. After a long excursus on the apophantical (*apophantisch*) essence of truth, Heidegger's own most enduring thought, he states that Nietzsche "does not pose the question of truth proper" (N 1, 148). That he fails to do so is not a simple oversight, but rather the failure to circumscribe the "domain of the question," as his understanding of truth unfolds within a positivist discourse, within a domain that is still epistemologically determined.

Heidegger circumscribes Nietzsche's definition of art within the limits of aesthetics (metaphysics), a delimitation that does not bar him from using Nietzsche against the most dangerous manifestations of aestheticism—Wagnerism. In fact, Heidegger subscribes to the Nietzschean indictment of Wagner. However, what is most important is how Heidegger interprets the decline of "great art" that coincides with the formation of aesthetics, "the relationship of man's state of being," which ends with the "forfeiting of [art's] essence, [with its] losing its immediate relation to the basic task of representing the absolute" (N 1, 84). It becomes in the end, in Hegel's terms, "a thing of the past." It is important to remember here that "The Origin of the Work of Art" deals precisely with "the enigma of art" as a way of reopening the question of Hegel's "end of art."

We should not lose sight of the knot that Heidegger establishes in what he calls the "third basic development for the history of knowledge about art." On the one hand art relinquishes its essence, on the other, and "parallel to the formation of aesthetics," something else unfolds:

> Great art and its works are great in their historical emergence and
> Being because in man's historical existence they accomplish a decisive
> task: they make manifest, in the way appropriate to works, what beings
> as a whole are, preserving such manifestation in the work. Art and its
> works are necessary only as an itinerary and sojourn for man in which
> the truth of beings as a whole, i.e., the unconditioned, the absolute,
> opens itself up to him. (N 1, 84)

This double development marks the moment of decision; it commands the deconstruction of the solidarity of a subjectivist aesthetic with a nihilist worldview necessary to retrieve the working of the work of art from "great art." There is a historical need for the work of art, but this has nothing to do with "spiritual needs," or *almost* nothing, but it is the extent of this *almost* that is decisive. In the shadow of Nietzsche's criticism of Wagner, we saw how Heidegger walks the inverse path from Hegel to Hölderlin. But to repeat Hölderin's path entails a displacement, especially in light of what is deemed to be Nietzsche's failed "overturning of Platonism," the "death of God," and nihilism. Wagnerism transforms the work of art into "a collective work" and constitutes itself as a regressive conception of the work of art, since after the "end of art," once art ceases to be an "absolute need," it conceives "the artwork as a celebration of the national community. It should be *the* religion" (N 1, 84).

We must pay some heed to Heidegger's critique of Wagnerian aesthetics, as it paves the way for an understanding of the work of art, of its origin as the "great work." It does constitute one of the two axes of Heidegger's deconstruction of aesthetics, along with the determination of the idea as *eidolon* and the Platonic determination of art as *mimesis*. Not only is the "collective work's" goal reactive when viewed within the sequence of the "History of Aesthetics" (N 1, 77–91), but it also suffers from an essential limitation: its subordination of language to music and "theatrical arrangement." In "The Origin of the Work of Art," even when it is a question of tragedy as the example of linguistic work (*Sprachwerk*), nothing is *theatrically* displayed, staged, presented, or represented. Tragedy as *Sprachwerk* is the site of an installing that transforms the account of a conflict into a conflict fought by each essential word. In "The Origin of the Work of Art," poetry (*Dichtung*) and language understood as poetry "in the essential sense" (PLT 74) "projects the Open," "lets the Open" be. The subordination of language to music is an obfuscation of the Open. Instead of a "letting be" or "preserving," Wagnerism strives for a "domination" of art and the "pure state of feeling," language yielding to "lived experience." Subscribing to Nietzsche's critique of Wagner and after quoting *The Will to Power*, Heidegger sums up what is at stake in the conception of the "collective work," in a language that brings to mind Levinas's harsh criticism of art in "Reality and Its Shadow":

Here the essential character of the conception "collective artwork" comes to unequivocal expression: the dissolution of everything solid into a fluid, flexible, malleable state, into a swimming and floundering: the unmeasured, without laws or borders, clarity or definiteness; *the boundless night of sheer submergence*. In other words, art is once again to become an absolute need. But now the absolute is experience as *sheer indeterminacy*, total dissolution into sheer feeling, a hovering that *sinks into nothingness*. (N 1, 87, my emphasis)

We are faced here with rapture (*Rausch*) but devoid of the "in-forming" force of figuration (language, poetry), "the unalloyed state of feeling and the growing barbarization of the very state to the point where it becomes the sheer bubbling and boiling of feeling abandoned to itself" (N 1, 88).

Much has happened between Hölderlin and Nietzsche. Heidegger turns the former against the latter, but he also uses Nietzsche against the most reactive configuration of an aesthetic conception of art. Even if Nietzsche had the merit of rediscovering the destinal law at play in the conflict of the Dionysian and Apollonian, he lacks "the purity and simplicity that are ever present in Hölderlin" (N 1, 88). This means that Hölderin "sees the essence of the historical *Dasein*, the agonistic nonadversity of heritage and mission" in a more essential way than Nietzsche

(GA 39, 293–94). The "overcoming of aesthetics," the explicit program of the 1934–35 Nietzsche course, mutates through Hölderlin into a "step back" from metaphysics and aesthetics.

For Hölderlin, Greece and Germany are two examples of the bringing forth of being to nature. As Hölderlin puts it in his essay "On Religion," human language is the site where nature experiences itself as something divine, which is only possible because human language is itself an expression of nature.[13] For Heidegger, even though Hölderlin does not know the force and scope of the word *phusis*, understood as "die Lichtung des Offenen," the opening/clearing of the open (EHP 79), he points in the direction of something that remains in "a concealed relation with what was once called *phusis*" (EHP 80).

It is this "other thing" that, in Heidegger's reading of the letter Hölderlin wrote on 4 December 1801 to Böhlendorff, defines the Greek and the German essences in terms of their relation to the whole of being: the free use of the proper or national, the possibility of naming the sacred in "the time of distress" that characterizes the German essence. However, this nomination entails a danger—its reduction to something mediated, to an entity. The danger Heidegger detects in the mystic entrance of Wagnerism and the mastering drive of the essence of technology contrasts with Hölderlin's sobriety, his relinquishing of any mastery over the sacred through the act of nomination.

If Hölderlin marks the path to a different understanding of being beyond metaphysics, it is because in his poetry there is no valuation, no will to power, no imposing mastery, but rather a measuring: "to be a poet, is to measure" (VA 196/235).[14] Poetic saying is a measuring (*massnahme*) in which *Dasein* receives the measure that appropriates its being. Poetry is the measuring that installs man's dwelling; however, this measure comes from what is measureless.

Preserving the Unfamiliar

L'Origine de l'œuvre d'art appartient à un grand discours sur le lieu et sur la vérité.

　　　　　　　　　　　　　　　—*Jacques Derrida*, La Vérité en peinture

Except that the work of art never presents anything (*stellt nie etwas dar*), and this is so for the simple reason that it has nothing to present, being precisely itself what creates in the first place that which enters for the first time and thanks to it in the open.

　　　　　　　　　　　　—*Martin Heidegger*, "The Origin of the Work of Art"

The ontological difference is the 'not' between beings and Being. Yet such as Being, as the 'not' in relation to beings, is by no means a nothing in the sense of a *nihil negativum*, so too the difference, as the 'not' between beings and Being, is in no way merely the figment of a distinction made by our understanding (*ens rationis*).

—Martin Heidegger, Pathmarks

If, as I have detailed above, Heidegger aims to rescue Nietzsche from a series of reductive interpretations, his reading also seeks to settle accounts with a still "aesthetic" conception of art. Where Nietzsche begins with the most "perspicuous" and familiar phenomenon, the artist, Heidegger starts with the most opaque and *unfamiliar*—the work. Once conceived outside traditional schemas, the fundamental determinations of the work of art belong to the *Un-geheure* (the unfamiliar, uncanny, extraordinary, enormous, terrible, excessive, and even monstrous).[15] There is something that Heidegger wants to *restitute*, but since it is not a thing— nothing *like* a thing—it resists the grasp of aesthetic conceptuality.[16] "The Origin of the Work of Art" is a text that by maintaining a fidelity to this resistance exposes it and exposes itself to the *Un-geheure*. This is so because its stake is to think what the aesthetic tradition, as examined in "The Six Basic Developments in the History of Aesthetics" (N 1, 77–91), has left unthought. It is around this unthought that the work, the *uncanny* essence of its working, and truth are knotted together; "The Origin of the Work of Art" says the *uncanny* as the bringing forth of truth.[17]

Although it is possible to recognize philosophemes that belong to the speculative aesthetic tradition (Kant, Romanticism, Hegel), "The Origin of the Work of Art" goes beyond this frame.[18] The text is itself *uncanny*, not only because the *uncanny* is its thesis (*Setzung*), but also because it *preserves* the *uncanny* that only the work of art as the eminent mode of truth's unveiling brings into the open.

"Art is truth setting itself to work" (*Die Kunst ist das Sich-ins-Werk-Setzen der Wahrheit*) (PLT 39/24); "The setting-into-work-of truth thrusts up the unfamiliar and extraordinary and at the same time thrusts down the ordinary and what we believe to be such" (*Das Ins-Werk-Setzen der Wahrheit stösst das Un-geheure auf und stösst zugleich das Geheure, und das, was man dafür halt, um*) (PLT 75/61).

In "The Origin of the Work of Art," the *uncanny* (*Un-geheure*) makes its first appearance in the section "The Work and Truth," which is de-

voted to the elucidation of truth's concealment. In this context, it signals
that a transformation of the ordinary, the "immediate (reliable) circle of
beings" or "clearing" in which "we believe we are *at home*" (PLT 54/41)
is at stake: "Nevertheless, the clearing is pervaded by a constant concealment in the double form of refusal and dissembling. At bottom, the
ordinary (Geheuer) is not ordinary (nicht geheuer); it is *extraordinary, uncanny (Das
Geheuer ist im Gründe nicht geheuer; es ist un-geheuer)*" (PLT 54/41), as if the
structure of *Verweisung* (assignment or reference), the phenomenon that
marks the entrance into the order of meaning and thus announces the
familiar world in *Being and Time*, had to be submitted to a more originary
determination.[19] What is *uncanny* in truth's unconcealment is that, by
exceeding the logical and grammatical determinations imposed by the
Greek beginning of philosophy, the hegemonic position that judgment
plays in modern metaphysics, and the quantitative drive of modern scien-
tific discourse, the essence of truth is "the *primal conflict* in which the open
center is won within which what is, stands and from which it sets itself
back to itself" (PLT 55). The *uncanny* in question therefore has to do
with strife (*pólemos*).[20]

The second appearance of *Un-geheure* in "The Origin of the Work of
Art," this time in the section "Truth and Art," concerns the work's "fac-
tum est," the "thrust" (*Stoss*) of createdness (*Geschaffensein*), what characterizes the being work of the work of art. The "that it *is* of (the work's)
createdness" distinguishes itself from the "it *is*" of "everything present to
us," in that it (the "is") does not fall *immediately* into oblivion: "in a work,
by contrast, this fact that it *is* as a work, is just what is *unusual*" (PLT
65/53). What is extraordinary about the work of art is its "offering"—
"that it be" (*Dass es sei*) (PLT 66/53).[21] The enormity and extra-ordinari-
ness of the work's thrust transforms our ordinary outlook of beings. In
other words, the essential mode of createdness (*Geschaffensein*) is the work's
preserving (*Bewahrin*). Preserving the bringing forth of truth is the work's
Un-geheure. Preserving the work as knowing, says Heidegger, "is a *sober*
[and here we must understand this term in opposition to the *rapture* of
the "national aestheticism" represented by Wagnerism][22] standing within
the *extraordinary awesomeness* of the truth that is happening in the work"
(PLT 74).

It is the happening of truth that is extraordinary, but since the work of art is the eminent way of truth, it produces a mutation of our "everyday being-in-the-world." If truth, as conceived by Heidegger, overflows the logical and grammatical frameworks imposed by philosophy, the founding or instituting of the work of art is also "an overflow" (*Überfluß*): "an endowing, a bestowal" (PLT 75/63). "The Origin of the Work of Art" is not only a discourse "on the site and on truth" (Derrida) but also one on what exceeds the place and truth itself, a discourse on *spacing*. That this site and this truth "is" language and that language in its basic determination is poetry (*Dichtung*) indicates that the *uncanny* that works and un-works throughout the essay points to what cannot be figured—*das Ereignis* (the *Event of Appropriation, Enowning*),[23] something that is only hinted at in "The Origin of the Work of Art" and remarked in the Addendum written a posteriori, but that the belated publication of the *Beiträge* confirms:

For this reason there is the note of caution on page 61 of "The Origin of the Work of Art," "In referring to this self-establishing of openness in the Open, thinking touches on a region that cannot yet be explicated here." The whole essay deliberately yet tacitly moves on the path of the question of Being. . . . Art belongs to the *disclosure of appropriation* (*sie gehört in das Ereignis*) by way of which the "meaning of Being" can alone be defined. (PLT 86/73)

In Heidegger's belated self-reading, there is a re-traction of the work of art one step back from the question of being into what belongs to the thinking of *Ereignis*. As in any self-reading, one must tread with care, as the essay is massively invested by an argument that revolves around foundation (*Gründen*)—the foundation of being and the foundation that being grants to a historical people. "The Origin of the Work of Art" is an essay that contains two sets of premises, one that belongs to the confrontation (*Auseinandersetzung*) with National Socialism and that is still invested by a problematic ontology of historicity. The other, the more daring, points to the thinking of *Ereignis* and the "topology of being" (the section that introduces the *Riss* and the *Geviert*), which Heidegger wants to privilege in the Addendum. This is so not only because it puts the essay in line with what by the 1950s has become Heidegger's main concern, but also to disinvest the essay from its militant tone.

How does the uncanny overflow of the work of art happen? "It is due to art's poetic essence that, in the midst of what it is art breaks open an open place, in whose openness everything is *other* than usual (*alles anders ist als sonst*). By virtue of the projected sketch set into the work of the unconcealedness of what is, which casts itself towards us, everything ordinary and hitherto existing becomes an *unbeing*."(PLT 72/ 59–60)

If the *uncanny* "overflows" the framework of our everyday behavior toward entities, determined as they are by derivative logical and grammatical assumptions that obfuscate our attitude toward being; if the work of art as the eminent manifestation of truth exceeds the frames of aesthetic representation; and if the "expert" way of dealing with the work of art neutralizes the force of what it preserves, Heidegger's own discourse has to account for this overflowing, for this "exasperation" of the *uncanny*. Heidegger's text must mark and remark this crescendo, and he does so in two instances: one in the famous passage on the peasant's shoes, the other in the passage on the Greek temple.

The work of art's excess lies in its being "the taking place of truth" (*das Geschehnis der Wahrheit*). What is *uncanny* is the *relation* of the work of art *and* truth. What kind of relation is this? What does the work of art have to do with truth? Heidegger posits the relation of the work of art and truth in terms different than Nietzsche, as if in Heidegger *not* to have art would entail losing truth and perishing from oblivion. The danger here is not, as with Nietzsche, truth but the modalities of oblivion, of which the essence of technology is the most pernicious. By redressing the relation between truth and work of art, Heidegger weaves an *intrigue* between creating (*Shaffen*) and preserving (*Bewahrin*). The work of art is position (*Setzung: Ins-Werk-Setzen*) and taking place (*Geschehnis*). It is through this articulation that Heidegger's essay accomplishes a transformation of *figuration*. What is at stake in "The Origin of the Work of Art" is the retrieval of the saying *of truth's uncanniness*, a saying more original than those shaped by illustration, representation, or reproduction (*mimesis*).

But why is it that truth becomes *uncanny* (immense, measureless)? "Truth is the unveiling of being (*Unverborgenheit*) as such. *Truth is the truth of being*"(PLT 63). Truth is without comparison and no thing is similar or equal to it because it "overflows" the logic of identity (confrontation, opposition, equivalence), and therefore it cannot be measured in ontic terms—neither the predicative utterance nor the judgment are the original sites of truth. Truth is the taking place of what is incomparable, the "coming forth" as such (*phainesthai, scheinen*), the appearing of what appears. Truth is therefore understood as *alêtheia* or un-concealment. Heidegger conceives the "logic" of this un-concealment as "bringing into the open" (*ins Offene bringen*), opening (*eröffnen*) and uncovering (*entbergen*). By breaking with the logic of identity Heidegger's essay restores and installs a more originary saying—the saying of the open, of unconcealment as the initial (*Anfang*) moment of truth. Truth's enormity, its uncanny essence, lies in the *initial* moment of what is incomparable. Heidegger sounds the depths of the work of art to hear/listen to the saying of the open (*das Offene*) or of the opening (*die Offenheit*).

It should be clear by now that Heidegger's essay is not a contribution to the regional discipline called aesthetics, which has not prevented this essay from being treated as such by some scholars. Even if his point of departure is Hegel's aesthetics and he repeats Hegel in view of reopening the historical emplacement of art, Heidegger does not aim to stipulate a theory concerning the work's point of origin. The work of art *is* the saying of un-concealment as the initial moment of truth, a saying of its incomparable immensity. The saying is the *Ursprung*, the leap—of the origin and the work of art, its *schematism*.

In the work of art understood as the "setting up to work of truth" (*das ins-Werk-Setzen der Wahrheit*), a saying of the immensity unfolds. How does this *uncanny* coming of truth that breaches all identity, all familiarity, occur in the work of art? The work of art is *not* a thing *like* any other thing. To reach the "immediate and full reality of the work of art"(PLT 20/4), Heidegger must first eliminate the traditional (metaphysical) determinations of the thing, the thing as bearer of traits, as the unity of the manifold of sensations and as formed matter. That the work of art is not a thing *like* any other thing means that it can only be thought in terms of its self-identity. The originality of the work of art—its origin—

announces itself in its inaugural (classic) determination as allegory and symbol. But these terms do not remain untouched throughout the essay. Heidegger's text accomplishes a reversal and a reinscription of their classical determinations that in turn transforms the text of "The Origin of the Work of Art" into an *uncanny* text, an incomparable text, the text *of* the leap (*Ursprung*).

Allegory is the *uncanny*, the *uncanny* as the other than the ordinary or familiar, as the saying of the other than beings. "The artwork is, to be sure, a thing that is made, but it *says something other than the mere thing itself is*, *allo agoreúei*. The work makes public something other than itself; it manifests something other (*etwas anderes*); it is an *allegory*" (PLT 19–20/4). At stake in the work of art is a difference, an *allegorical difference* that is the *figuration of*—truth, a *figuration* of what is *without figure*. The allegory is the *uncanny* because the "something other" (*etwas anderes*) that it makes manifest in its bringing together (*Zusammenbringen*) is not a thing: "das Kunstwerk eröffnet auf seine Weise das Sein des Seienden" (PLT 19/24). The bringing together thus names the cobelonging of being and entities. The work of art does not make manifest another entity that it would represent in its absence. The classical determination of the sign or symbol is therefore not pertinent here, nor the schema of *Verweisung*, reference, or assignment, elaborated in *Being and Time*, but what is pertinent is the difference as *ontological* difference.

The work of art is this *allegorical difference* as ontological difference. In this mutation of the allegory, the *allo* refers to the unfolding of the double fold (*Zwiefalt*), rather than to what in a more classical register would have been the mere "is" of an "other *thing*" as "present-at-hand"(*Zuhandenheit*), according to the modalities of being made explicit in *Being and Time*. The allegory the work of art *is* (allegory of nothing—else but itself) means the taking place and unfolding of the double fold. The bringing together of the work consequently should not be equated with an enumeration or inventory of entities, since what it gathers is unnamable. The work of art speaks; its saying says the unnamable before it can be put into words. The saying of the work of art is a *Zeigen*, a determination of language that was absent from *Being and Time* and that appears for the first time in Heidegger's commentaries on Hölderlin. Only as a *Zeigen* can the saying of the work say the unnamable: "the unconcealment of being" (*das An-wesen des Anwesenden*).

So if allegory is traditionally the operation of a thing *like* another thing, the allegorical fold of the work of art becomes the operation of the "wholly other"—of the other that is the same for all things. The work of art allows Heidegger to elaborate one of the guises of the double fold; the *Sprache* as *Sage* will be the other, whose duplicity exceeds any duplication or duplicate since it is reversible. Heidegger reinscribes this reversed allegory in what he calls the *nonadverse* (*ad-versus, die Gegenwendigen,* and not *opposition,* as the English translation reads) of being and beings that becomes implicit through the nonadversity of world and earth and the play of *Lichtung* (clearing) and *Verbergung* (concealment), of their reciprocal belonging.

Towards the end of the essay, this reversed and reinscribed allegory receives another name, *Dichtung.* Heidegger defines the essence of the work of art as *Dichtung* understood, in an almost Kantian formulation, as the condition of possibility of any art. Heidegger *restitutes* the essential belonging of language to the work of art that was lost in national aestheticism. Poetry (*Dichtung*) is art's essence in the sense of *poíesis* or setting forth of truth, insofar as the installing of truth is a bestowing (*Schenken*), a founding (*Gründen*), an inauguration (*Anfangen*), an *Ursprung*—the originary exposition and safeguarding of the being of entities.

In the interval that opens between the transformation of allegory and its renaming as *Dichtung,* Heidegger elaborates the work's essential determination as "the setting-into-work of truth" (*das Ins-Werk-Setzen der Wahrheit*). A work of art is such only insofar as its *Setzen* is neither a transmission nor a transposition, which means that the work of art is not a replica, a reproduction (*Wiedergabe*) of a thing or product.

What are the main determinations of the work of art as the "disclosing of being in its truth"? Heidegger speaks in terms of *Setzen* and *Stellen.* Through Van Gogh's painting Heidegger makes the transformation of figuration explicit. Heidegger voids all the terms that ground the understanding of figuration as a process of replication or reproduction (*Wiedergabe*), illustration (*Veranschaulichung*), imitation (*Nachahmung*), or copy (*Abschilderung*). There is excess in the working of the artwork that allows Heidegger to remark the economy of figuration. The example of Van

Gogh's painting brings about the mutation of figuration as the mutation of reproduction (*Wiedergabe*):

The equipmentality of equipment (*das Zeugsein*) first genuinely (*eigens*) arrives at its appearance (*Verschein*) through the work and only the work. What happens here? What is at work in the work? Van Gogh's painting is the disclosure of what the equipment, the pair of peasant shoes, is in truth (*was das Zeug, das Paar Bauernschuhe, in Wahrheit ist*). This entity emerges into the unconcealedness (*Unverborgenheit*) of its being. (PLT 36)

"*Dieses hat gesprochen*," the painting spoke in such a way that the oblivion that ordinarily comes to the being of a piece of equipment does not occur.

However, the question is how it spoke. Heidegger wants to show that the painting does not represent anything ontic, but rather the essence of a particular set of entities, equipment. A familiar, common (*Gewöhnlich*) product functions as the point of departure of the demonstration, and to better facilitate its intuition (*Veranschaulichung*), Heidegger employs a "pictorial representation" ("*bildiche Darstellung*"). A reversal occurs; the "And yet" ("*Und dennoch*") functions as a rhetorical signal that introduces Heidegger's breaching of the logic of illustration and the economy of representation. An image that should supposedly help us with the intuitive apprehension of such an ordinary thing as a pair of shoes, veers into an allegory of one of the modes of being's dispensation. Nevertheless, this does not occur without a series of argumentative slippages that are dependent on what seems to be an arbitrary choice—Heidegger's decision to treat the painted shoes as a peasant woman's shoes. This series of slippages compromises the critical force of the "overcoming of aesthetics," of its rhetorical remarking:

A pair of peasant shoes and nothing more. And yet (*Und dennoch*)—
From the dark opening of the worn insides of the shoes the toilsome tread of the worker stares forth. In the stiffly rugged heaviness of the shoes there is the accumulated tenacity of her slow trudge through the far-spreading and even uniform furrows of the field swept away by a raw wind. Under the soles slides the loneliness of the field

path as evening falls. In the shoes vibrates the silent call of the
earth. . . . This equipment is pervaded by uncomplaining anxiety. . . .
this equipment belongs to the *earth* and it is protected in the *world* of
the peasant woman. From out of this protected belonging the equipment itself rises to its resting within-itself. (PLT 34)

Heidgger's description keeps a rather tenuous connection with the pictorial traits of Van Gogh's canvas. "From the dark opening of the worn
insides of the shoes" refers to an observable material pictorial feature.
What follows from it can easily be put under the heading of a vision and
even a hallucination, since the shoes are invested with a series of fantas-
matic or ideological features, as if through the painting and Professor
Heidegger himself a *Lebenswelt* were making itself present.[24] It appears that
in spite of Heidegger's efforts to preserve the unfamiliar he gets caught
up in the familiar. Against all the protocols of the phenomenological
presentation of the thing in sight, he states an implicit valorization of the
autochthonous.[25] The earth, a nonmetaphysical figure of being's modalities of manifestation, is soiled by its attachment to a metaphysical soil.
This soil refers to more than the nothing that enables the being of equipment to appear; it refers to a worldview with which Heidegger cannot
fully break. Even if the analysis is questionable, Heidegger concludes that
it is thanks to the work of art that equipmentality (the being of the
shoes) does not "waste away," does not "sink into mere stuff" (PLT 35).
By speaking, the work takes us "somewhere else than we usually tend
to be."

What is at work in the work, what figuration figures, is the coming
into appearance, the appearing. *Setzen* therefore means *"zum Stehen bringen,"*
to institute. Figuration figures the being of the entity: *"Das Sein des Seienden
kommt in das Ständige seines Scheinens"* (PLT 21/37). But this *Scheinen* as working of the artwork is not the production of a simulacrum, but rather the
figuration of the appearance of what appears; what appears in the stele or
figure (*Gestalt*) is the *figureless* appearing as such: "The work, therefore, is
not the reproduction (*Wiedergabe*) of some particular entity that happens
to be present at any given time; it is on the contrary, the reproduction /
restitution (*Wiedergabe*) in it of a common presence of thing" (PLT 37/22).
Wiedergabe appears twice in the space of two lines, between copy (*Abbild*)

and opening (*Eröffnung*); this repetition, this remarking signals the double play of the work of art, the transformation of the same into the other—*allegory*.

Outside any determination of the work of art as reproduction or imitation, the example of the Greek temple allows Heidegger to elaborate a different status for *Wiedergabe*. We now come across the *Stellung*, the second essential determination of the work of art. If traditionally figuration was conceived as substitutive, it is now transformed into a constitutive or institutive operation. The Greek temple is the bringing forth of a *Feststellung*, a constituting that establishes and convokes a world. This constituting sets forth a world that is neither an assemblage nor an inventory of entities. World here is the being-world of what is "in-the-world," whose essential determination is "the world worlds" ("*die Welt weltet*"). When dealing with the type of relations that the work of art entertains, Heidegger posits once again, as in the case of the Van Gogh painting, the question of truth, but this time "with view to the work" and not to the being-thing of the thing (equipmentality), as with the shoes. At issue here is the belonging of the work, that is, "the realm that is opened by the [work] itself. . . . For the work-being of the work only unfolds its being in, and only in, such opening" (PLT 41). So as to better highlight the unfamiliar or uncanny (*un-geheure*) "happening of truth in the work," Heidegger introduces a nonfigurative form, a Greek temple, a pure façade that represents nothing, that portrays nothing and that is made "in the image of nothing" (*ein griechischer Tempel, bildet nichts ab*) (PLT 27):

Standing there, the building rests upon rocky ground. This resting of the work draws up out of the mystery (*das Dunkel*) of that rock's clumsy yet spontaneous support. Standing there, the building holds its ground against the storm raging above it and first makes the storm itself manifest in its violence. The luster and gleam of the stone, though itself apparently glowing only by the grace of the sun, yet first brings to light the light of the day, the breadth of the sky, the darkness of the night. *The temple's first towering makes visible the visible space of air.* The steadfastness of the work of art contrasts with the surge of the surf, and its own repose brings out the raging of the sea. Tree and grass, the eagle and bull, snake and cricket *first enter into their distinctive steles or figures (Gestalt) and thus come to appear as what they are. The Greeks early called this emerging and rising in itself and in all things phusis.* It clears and illuminates, also, that on which and in which man bases his dwelling. We call this ground the earth. What this word says is not to be associated with the idea of a mass of matter deposited somewhere, or with the mere astronomical idea of a planet. Earth is that whence the arising brings back and shelters everything that arises without violation. In the things that arise, earth is present as the sheltering agent. (PLT 42/ HW 31)

The temple gathers being as a whole (*phusis*), what in the conferences and courses on Hölderlin Heidegger calls the sacred, the open (*das Offene*) that offers itself as the clearing (*Lichtung*). The temple thus delineates the clearing into which entities can appear, and as operation of the *Wiedergabe* it institutes a world and brings forth the earth. Heidegger is quick to distinguish the meaning of earth from the way in which it is unveiled in technology, that is, as reserve (*Bestand*); here earth and world have a pre-metaphysical meaning. In the language of metaphysics it would be possible to say that being (*Sein*) as ground (*Grund*) issues from the abyss (*Abgrund*), or that it originates from the nothing understood as the negation of all entities. However, in the language of the "other thinking," the world opens up in the opening of the sacred, which in turn is the source of history.

As operation of the *Wiedergabe*, the temple is the instantiation of unconcealment and withdrawal, "the temple-work, standing there, opens up a world and at the same time sets this world back again on earth, which itself only thus emerges as native ground" (PLT 42/HW 32), which explains why all the series of *des Stellung* are inscribed in the *Wiedergabe*, *Stellen* being the working itself of figuration.[26] *Stellen* is "ins werk Setzen," *thesis* in the Greek sense, figuring. The series of *Stellungeng*, figurations, articulates an older and more originary logic than that of a logical and grammatical predicative statement conceived in terms of *homôiosis* or *adæquatio*, that is, the derivative metaphysical determination of truth that forgets its inaugural essence. Here it is instead a question of the installation (*Aufstellung*) of a world in the splendor of its appearing; the temple is *Herstellung* (production) of the earth's withdrawal; it brings forth (*her-*

stellt) the withdrawal into the open. *Herstellung* is a "placing in front" of what has no intra-wordly antecedent; it is the absolute giving place of being. In the reversibility of the *Festellung* and of the *Zurückstellung*, figuration figures a vacant place, a non-place: the *offene Stele*. Exposing the site of the open is the essence of figuration as it occurs in the work of art, which indeed is a strange way of defining the working of the artwork. Nothing could be more *uncanny* with respect to an aesthetic conception of artistic figuration.

The *Wiedergabe*'s operation thus unfolds between world and earth, between the "coming into presence" (*zum Leuchten kommen*) and the "withdrawing into itself" (*sich verschliessen*), which entails that one cannot equate *Wieder-* with the *re-* of "*re*production"; the working of the artwork, *Wieder-gabe*, is the figuration-repetition in which the giving that gives itself "makes itself a figure," the incessant repetition of the *Geben* as aspect or splendor (*Glanz, Abglanz*). Within the economy of Heidegger's argument, the temple adds another turn to the movement away from the paradigm of the model and the copy (*mimesis*) initiated in the reading of Van Gogh's painting. It also allows Heidegger to displace and reinscribe the placing of both *Schinnen* and *eidolon* in figuration. It is the statue of the god that appears as pure exposition or figuration; the statue "is not representation of the god" but a work that "lets the god himself come into presence, and . . . is therefore god himself." The temple does not bring the face of the god into representation; it makes visible its aspect or splendor (*Glanz*). We are dealing here neither with an *eidolon* nor with an *idol*. The work of art does not make visible what is visible, but rather the invisible. *Wiedegabe* is the restitution of a "common presence (*Wesen*) of things" (*phusis*), a lightning that *at the same time* keeps in reserve; restitution/repetition of being and of the entity: a duplication that is traditionally called "beauty" (PLT 57/8–38–9). This duplication, however, does not reproduce the aspect of what appears from a different preexisting entity; *Wieder-* indicates the endless "origination" of the "vacant place" (*offene Stelle, offene Mitte*). *Glanz* is the strangeness (*Un-geheure*) of the *Wieder-gabe*. *Wiedergabe* (bestowing, gift, repetition) is the work's "originality," *figuration* in all its modes and under all its aspects. All arts are the putting into play of the "efficiency of the work" (*Wirkung das Werkes*).

If *Wiedergabe* does not substitute the entity, what is the status of this *restitution* then? What does this constitution institute? Truth happens in the work of art as the *rift* of world and earth, "the intimacy with which the non-adverse (*die Gegenwendigen*) belong to each other" (PLT 44/ HW 55):

The opposition of earth and world is a striving (*Streit*). But we would surely all too easily falsify its essence if we were to confound striving and discord and dispute, and thus see it only as disorder and destruction. In essential striving, rather, the *non-adverse* (*die Gegenwendigen*) raise each other into the self-assertion (*Selbstbehauptung*) of their essences. . . . In the struggle each *non-adverse* carries the other beyond itself. Thus the striving becomes ever more intense as striving, and more authentically what it is. The more the struggle overdoes itself on its own part, the more inflexibly do the *non-adverse* let themselves go into the intimacy of simple belonging to one another (*umso unnachgiebiger lassen sich die Streitenden in die Innigkeit des einfachen Sichgehörens los*). The earth cannot dispense with the Open of the world if it is itself to appear as earth in the liberated surge of its self-seclusion (*Sichverschliessens*). The world, again, cannot soar out of the earth's sight if, as the governing breadth and path of all essential destiny, it is to ground itself on a resolute foundation. (PLT 49/HW 37–38, translation modified)

Strife is the unfolding of the single fold of being into the double fold of the difference between world and earth. Strife cannot be envisioned as the fight between two opposing heavyweight champions coming from different places, but rather as the encounter in the reverse (*reversus*) of the fold of what is, essentially speaking, nonadversary (*non-adversus*). Earth and world are the two sides (*versus*) of the difference's fold; they weave the *intrigue* of being as withdrawal and unveiling, as truth.

What the working of the artwork institutes is a place, a *topos*: the locality (*Ort*), the constitution of the space (*Raum*). Locality and space are the inscriptions of the difference that the allegory and work of art are in their putting into play (PLT 48/30). The temple is the pure enclosure of the sacred: "It is the temple work that first fits together (disposes) and at the same time gathers around itself the unity of those paths and relations . . . that grant the human being the stele (figure) of its destiny"

(PLT 58/35, translation modified). What is at work in the temple is spacing, a dispensation of sites. "In its standing there (*Darstehen*) the temple gives to things their *look* and to men their *outlook* on themselves. This *view* remains open as long as the work is a work" (PLT 44/28).

Spacing, emplacing, disposing, erecting (*Einrichten/Errichten*), the production of the *Richtungen*, the directions (sense), even before the structure of *Verweisung* (assignment or reference) could be established. It is the *Stellung*, the articulation of installing, bringing forth, establishing and withdrawing, that secures spacing and direction. How does spacing relate to figuration (*Wiedergabe*)? Spacing and figuration are operations of the "rift-design" (*Riss*), operation of the *reissen* and *aufreissen*: tracing. However, this tracing is not something that comes to be added to a preexisting flat space. *Riss* is the tearing, rift, that establishes a space; it is its constitution. Spacing does not mean the effectuation of a uniform and homogeneous extension; the *Riss* folds and this folding supposes a logic of the fold. World, earth, spacing, and tracing are the fourfold of figuration. This operation of the trace presents different modalities, but in all of them the trace is *Gezüge*, *Gefüge*, joining: the joint of the appearing and truth (PLT 71/50). Inasmuch as *Gezüge*, *Gefüge*, the trace constitutes the *Gestalt* (stele, figure) and as the taking place of the tracing (*aufreissen*), the stele is rhythm, since it is the form of the joining: rhythm is the event of spacing. If tracing and spacing (*einräumen* and *aufreissen*) are the working of the artwork as bringing forth of truth, *Wiedergabe* (figuration) is a re-marking: at the same time positing (*Setzung*) and instituting (*Stiftung*). The work of art is an anarchic, uncanny, origin (*Ursprung*).[27]

Plot and Intrigue: From Being's Other to the "Otherwise than Being" (Language, Ethics, Poetic Language in Levinas)

Is it possible to write the other without assimilating or reducing it to the same, to an object or a thing, to concepts, categories or descriptions? What is this O/*other* that at times is my neighbor and at times wholly other (*tout autre*), whose alterity issues from infinity or even God? Levinas's works suggest that the interruption of the subject's power, "I have no power over the other" (*je ne peux pas pouvoir*) (TI 39), is a precondition for welcoming the other, but of course this does not happen as a resolution willfully taken by a free and autonomous subject. Writing the other is impossible if the focus or point of departure is an ego or consciousness, but even if the power of consciousness were to be relinquished or interrupted, there is still something that resists comprehension.

Psyche (*psychisme*), the trope that defines the preoriginary *intrigue* of the other in the self in *Otherwise than Being*, is the "form of a peculiar dephasing (*déphasage*) of identity" (AE 86/OB 68). The other is an event that exceeds the grasp of consciousness and of its present-oriented temporality, thus overflowing the frames of narration. The approach of the other comes to haunt sensibility, a "subjectivity without subject," according to Blanchot;

it is the traumatism of "the other than being" (Levinas) constitutive of a subjectivity, unable to give itself to itself in the present, and unable to bring this preoriginary affection into the present. The other is a ghostly event, or the other's temporality is the ghostly temporality of the event.

A subjectivity unable to catch up with the other's affection and to reduce the past of this affection to the present of recollection becomes the knot of *substitution* (the one-for-the-other), the emphatic trope of the other's welcoming. This trope organizes the "arrhythmia" of an *intrigue* overflowing the spatio-temporal frames of narration that Derrida renders with the French future anterior, "he will have obliged" (*il aura obligé*) (P 38–39). This tense escapes the time of the present because it simultaneously points towards a future and a past. The subject of the phrase, he-it (*il*), is not copresent to himself; the subject contracts an obligation that comes from a past and whose response does not assimilate the past to the present of consciousness. The response unfolds in a future that bypasses presence while its spatiality is that of a nonsequential writing that attests the other's affection of the same in an "après-coup." This affection produces a reversal of the middle, beginning and end of narratives. In fact, no plot can do justice to this intrigue, to its inextricable and dispossessing force; *intrigue* names what Blanchot calls "the unstory" (*le non-récit*), "that which escapes quotation and which memory does not recall" (ED 49/ WD 28).

It is therefore important not to overlook the distinction between plot and *intrigue*.[1] Following Levinas, *plot* refers to the correlation of consciousness with a represented content: "a present represented, a theme 'placed' before it [as] a perception of a presence in 'flesh and bone,' a figuration of an image, symbolization of a symbolized, a transparency and a veiling of the fugitive and the unstable in an allusion" (AE²46/OB 25).

Totality and Infinity narrates the plot of a return to a "*profond jadis*" by which memory seizes time, while *Otherwise than Being* takes a step back from this ontological plot and conceives time in terms of proximity's "immemorial past." Subjectivity thus becomes a "preoriginary *intrigue*" with the other. However, in both cases it is a question of an opening, a breaching, that takes the form of a relation with a surplus always *exterior* to totality (being).

I reserve the term *intrigue* for the inextricable diachronic structuring of subjectivity as "the other in the same." For Levinas *proximity* is a difference, a non-coinciding, an arrhythmia in time, a diachrony refractory to thematization and to the reminiscence that synchronizes the phases of a past, where "the unnarratable (*l'inenarrable*) other loses his face as a neighbor in narration. The relationship with him is *indescribable* in the literal sense of the term, unconvertible into a history, irreducible to the simultaneousness of writing (*simultaneité de l'écrit, à l'éternel présent*), the eternal present of a writing that records or presents results" (AE 258/OB 166). If the other is both unnarratable and indescribable, how to write the other and to conceive of this writing as its welcoming? What has to occur to writing in order to be up to this unheard-of exigency?

To answer, I must first provide the main articulations organizing Levinas's thinking. I will deploy the basic concepts and make explicit the main shifts between *Totality and Infinity* and *Otherwise than Being* in relation not only to Levinas's conception of language, but also to the place reserved for poetic writing in the determination of ethics as "first philosophy." This chapter thus has a preparatory function for an understanding of the strategies that Levinas employs to write the other. Although the point of departure is Levinas's first conception of language in *Totality and Infinity*, my reading proceeds from the perspective of what Levinas accomplishes in *Otherwise than Being*, where as the result of a profound revision in his conceptions of language and his practice of writing, he manages to bear witness to the *intrigue's* "peculiar dephasing (*déphasage*)." He does so by neither reducing it to a narrative plot nor to a hermeneutic adventure that could assimilate the *intrigue* to a form of knowledge or comprehension.

I must stress the philosophical protocols that Levinas deploys in order to secure an ethics as "first philosophy" against the privilege that Husserl grants to transcendental consciousness and Heidegger to the "question of Being," as well as rhetorical ones. While distinguishing his own method from those of transcendental philosophy, Levinas claims that in the latter an idea is always justified when one reaches its foundation. However, if the point of departure is the approaching of the human being, "there is another sort of justification of one idea by the other: to pass from one idea to its superlative, to the point of its emphasis. You see that a new idea—in no way implicated in the first—flows or emanates from the overbid (*surenchère*)" (DQV³ 141–42/GCM 89). As an example of this way of proceeding, Levinas refers to the concept of the world's *positing* (*thesis, position*) and of its emphatic transformation into *ex-position*. This "to be posited in a superlative manner" illustrates the passage from an ontological structure to an ethical subjectivity. Although this seems to be a discrete example, it illustrates the constructive principle of *Otherwise than Being* or what Levinas calls "exasperation" as a "philosophical method."⁴

Emphasis and hyperbole, the figures that accomplish the concept's mutation, are decisive for understanding Levinas's writing of the other: first, because they bring about a displacement and reinscription of phenomenology, Levinas's philosophical horizon, within a space that is no longer determined by the correlation between consciousness and phenomena; second, because they transform the plot of being into the quasi-narrative dimension of the approach of the other, the *intrigue*. Although narration is an unavoidable dimension, it is not the stratum that determines where the writing of the other understood as its welcoming occurs. This becomes more evident in *Otherwise than Being*, where Levinas conceives of subjectivity as the trace of a traumatism, as a heteronomy whose temporal and spatial location escapes the parameters of presence and consciousness, and that cannot be plotted as narrative. Both emphasis and hyperbole produce a transmutation of the dominant ontological plot line of *Totality and Infinity* into an *ethical intrigue* in *Otherwise than Being*.

While I am not suggesting that the philosophical analyses are of secondary importance, the rhetorical and textual dimension of Levinas's thinking and the place he accords to art and poetic language are crucial for my reading.⁵ Although aesthetics is not a decisive dimension for Levinas, its relation to ethics is the site of conflicting operations that reveal the tensions in his conception of language. Also, since Levinas's thinking authorizes a certain "ethical turn" in contemporary literary studies, an assessment of his reflections on art and poetic language is in order, especially because of Levinas's own ambiguity on these issues.⁶ In what follows, I analyze in detail two configurations where Levinas articulates ethics as the question of language, as well as the place that poetic language occupies within them. By making explicit the function of language and art in Levinas's philosophy, my goal is to isolate the different threads that weave the preoriginary *intrigue* of the other.

Ethics as the Question of the Other

Up to a certain point, Levinas agrees with Heidegger on the need to question the derivative nature of "ethics." According to Heidegger:

> along with "logic" and "physics," "ethics" appeared for the first time in the school of Plato. These disciplines arose at a time when thinking was becoming "philosophy," philosophy, *episteme* (science) and science itself a matter for schools and academic pursuits. In the course of a philosophy so understood, science waxed and thinking waned. Thinkers prior to this period knew neither a "logic" nor an "ethics" nor "physics." Yet their thinking was neither illogical nor immoral. . . . The tragedies of Sophocles—provided such a comparison is at all permissible—preserve the *ethos* in their sagas more primordially that Aristotle's lectures on "ethics." (LH 232–33)[7]

For Heidegger ethics, as a region of philosophical questioning, comes after metaphysics (knowledge and theory) and is determined by the effect of oblivion that Plato's philosophy institutes. Here we find Heidegger's typical gesture for signaling his departure from an intellectualist tradition for which theoretical comprehension is the starting point of thinking. According to Heidegger ontology is primarily determined in a noncognitive way, by modes of existence that are more basic than the intellectual grasp of the concept. As we saw in chapter 3, it is through its dialogue with poetry that thinking fundamentally becomes a letting be (*sein lassen*), a bringing of being to language, understood as the dwelling or sojourn, since in being-there men "let the world and truth *spring forth*" (*Ursprung as entspringen lassen*) (KPM 136/148). Thinking as act becomes a "compliance with being" (TK 47), an "ethics" in the sense of guarding or keeping watch of the open site.

However, for Levinas Heidegger does not sufficiently think the exposition to the other, and thus the provenance of ethics becomes even more primordial than the determination that grounds being and its history, since it comes *before* the basic tenets of an existential analytic. This pri-

macy is neither temporal nor logical but rather anarchic since it constitutes the opening of time. Levinas subtracts the term "ethics" from the
systematic building erected by Aristotle and conceives it as an abyssal
and infinite anteriority. This re-traction from the space of theoretical
thinking and from fundamental ontology into that of sensibility (ethics
entails a redefinition of subjectivity) undermines metaphysic's basic conceptual opposition between reason and sensibility.[8]

There is therefore something excessive in Levinas's handling of the
term *ethics* since it does not yield a set of norms or an art of living, not
even an art of the self. Under the heading of ethics, a profound redefinition of reason takes place, as well as a rethinking of subjectivity that
leaves any philosophy of identity in disarray. If, as we saw in the previous
chapter, for Heidegger the work of art can preserve the *ethos* in a "more
primordial" way than a philosophical treaty, and the poem can be the
royal path to dwelling, for Levinas the suture of fundamental ontology
to art does not allow for a "more primordial" way of thinking ethics. Art
has a *tragic* matrix for Levinas, but this is due more to art's inhumanity
than to the human dimension of ethics.

Levinas defines the ethical relation in terms of the question of language, which here means two things. On the one hand, continuing Heidegger's dismantling of the logical and grammatical metaphysical
determinations of language, Levinas questions the primacy of language at
play in structuralism and analytic philosophy. He even mobilizes some
of the concepts and recourses of the linguistic turn in order to expose
what for him is the derivative determination of language that these modalities of thinking presuppose. Yet, on the other hand, Levinas makes
us read and think the question of language as a given word (*parole donnée*),
as if he were welcoming the underside of language or responding to its
call even before comprehending its content. In this sense, Levinas radically changes the form of the question of the other.[9]

It is necessary to understand ethics as the *question of the other* and not as
the questioning proper to an autonomous consciousness. This is because
Levinas disputes the primacy of the metaphysical subject, which constructs itself in isolation from its relation to the other. The subject of
metaphysics is not his point of departure because, since Descartes, it is *in*
the subject that questions and answers originate. This self-sufficiency of

thinking undergoes a profound revision in Levinas. He also contests the sufficiency of the Kantian autonomous subject that precedes and conditions not only its thinking of the other but also its relation to the other.[10] The question of the other, therefore, makes itself heard neither in the form of questioning nor as a dialogue between two copresent alter egos.[11] These two modalities entail an exposition of the other and its assimilation to the same. The question of the other is a matter of *proximity* for Levinas or, in the language of *Otherwise than Being*, an "allegiance to the other by the same" before any questioning or dialogue. The other concerns the self as "otherwise than" an ego.[12]

Levinas's rethinking of ethics, for which the current label "ethical turn"[13] is inappropriate, dependent as it is on an autonomous conception of the subject, revolves around language. It is even possible to claim that the ethical relation is language, if the form of this traditional statement were able to resist Levinas's transgression of formal logic. That the ethical relation is language means that the latter is primarily neither a system of signs whose goal is to represent—thus reducing the other to the same—nor a play of differences, but rather *expression* and *communication*.[14]

Levinas maintains the basic premises of his philosophy throughout his work. For him the ethical relationship comes before knowledge; language is the possibility of the ethical relation before being a system of signs, and the saying of responsibility is a giving to the other. There are two versions of the relationship between the ethical saying and language in general. In each of these versions Levinas stresses a series of elements, an understanding of which is decisive for his conception of poetic language, as well as for his writing of the *intrigue* of the other.[15]

In *Totality and Infinity* (1961) Levinas emphasizes an ethical language which is pure immediacy: the face (*visage*) of the other faces me, concerns me (*me regarde*) without mediation. The face, "the nonmetaphorical unity of body, glance, speech and thinking" (WAD 128), exceeds the grasp of representation and overflows form, but in so doing it shapes my answer; the face is discourse. Levinas conceives the sincerity or straightforwardness of discourse in opposition to rhetoric and other forms of representation, including those of artistic works. In the face as the source of signification, "prose" comes to interrupt the "charm of poetic rhythm" (TeI 222/TI 203).

We will see below that this conceptual opposition between prose and poetic rhythm is underwritten by a privileging of presence, and that this conceptual articulation undergoes a radical revision and reformulation in *Otherwise than Being*. In this later work Levinas replaces a logic of binary oppositions—being/entity, totality/infinity—with that of the "amphibology of being," according to which language is conceived as a dual structure. Within this "amphibology" being is said, but the "otherwise than being" is a saying that substracts itself from the grasp of being and its categories. The interplay between these two dimensions of language makes up the "clandestine *intrigue* of the other" that *Otherwise than Being* exposes and to which it responds.

In *Totality and Infinity* the transcendental founding experience is beyond form and representation, although there is a residue of representation, the face, that poses a series of difficulties. Levinas describes the face in opposition to the phenomenon and foregrounds its lack of horizon and nonmanifestation. Yet the face *reveals* and *expresses* itself and *beyond itself*. The *face-to-face*, the form of the ethical relation, is neither a mystical fusion nor a cognitive relationship; it is speech, a "relation in which the terms absolve themselves from the relation, remain absolute within the relation" (TI 59/64).

While in *Totality and Infinity* the face bypasses language as representation, in *Otherwise than Being* (1974) the ethical saying occurs in language. Language is "an original relation with an external being" that is "produced only in the face to face" (AE 100/OB 61).[16] In *Otherwise than Being* Levinas deploys the concept of trace as a way of thinking an ethical language that is no longer primarily determined by the plenitude of speech. In the distinction between the said *"le dit"* (writing as representation, synchrony, essence, discourse, history) and saying *"le dire"* (writing as testimony, face, passivity, diachrony), he elucidates the ethical saying as an original presemiotic dimension inhabiting each historical language.

An immemorial trace haunts language and bears witness to "the glory of the infinite" or the proximity of the other to the same. In order to manifest itself, this preoriginal saying is destined to fix itself in a said or predicative proposition. It thus becomes a theme, the object of a narrative and is subordinated to a linguistic system woven by ontological categories. However, for Levinas the said's enunciative peripeteia is derivative and secondary and presupposes the gravity of a responsibility incommensurate to being and to the language in which it is said:

A methodological problem arises here, whether the preoriginal element of saying (the anarchical, the nonoriginal, as we designate it) can be led to betray itself by showing itself in a theme (if an an-archeology is possible), and whether this betrayal can be reduced; whether one can at the same time know and free the known from the marks which thematization leaves on it by subordinating it to ontology. Everything shows itself at the price of this betrayal, even the unsayable. In this betrayal the indiscretion with regard to the unsayable, which is probably the very task of philosophy, becomes possible. (AE 18/OB 7)

The necessity of this betrayal constitutes the *clandestine intrigue* that *Otherwise than Being* deploys in opposition to philosophical narrative. The "otherwise than being" must be said, but at the same time it must subtract itself from the structures that characterize the said (propositions and narratives).

In an attempt to elucidate the ethical relation, Levinas utilizes all the recourses proper to phenomenology. However, when it no longer approaches what exceeds the grasp of the phenomenon, he employs a series of "poetic recourses"—a wide range of practices that make evident the textual dimension of philosophical writing: semantic, pragmatic, rhetorical and intertextual. This is what in 1977 Levinas calls "exasperation as a philosophical method" (DQV 142).[17] It is through this textual dimension that he inscribes what can only be said in terms of the order of discourse, but which discourse cannot assimilate: the trace of the other, the "otherwise than being."

The Face and the Contact of Speech

Totality and Infinity tells a story whose pivotal point is the concept of *separation* in which a being, a creature, is given to itself by what is neither an entity nor being: the infinite. The relation between the infinite and the creature involves neither origination (it is anarchic), nor causation (it is not shaped in terms of a creationist theology); it is *signification*. The infinite orients the creature and its world (it gives sense), enabling the former to escape the grasp of pure being (*il y a*). The main sequences of this separation are corporeity, nourishment, habitation, possession, labor, economy, knowledge, and technique. Separation is plotted in terms of the story of a joyous ego that, after a harmonious fusion with the feminine other (a familiar alterity), must confront an even more rigid other towards whom no appeal of responsibility is possible.

The subject is the egotistic singular concretization of the totality, the truth of the real or being in general, that from which one cannot escape and which admits no exteriority. *Totality and Infinity* is a treatise on exteriority, which suggests that a way out of the subject's power is at stake: an evasion from being, a breaching of totality that the infinite's generosity and fecundity accomplishes: "we call this calling into question (*mise en question*) of my spontaneity *ethics*" (TeI 13/TI 43).

Levinas's critique of Heidegger's fundamental ontology revolves around the specific status of the other's exteriority (*autrui*). The encounter with the other shakes the horizon of the world in which *Dasein* finds the other; the intensity of this shock becomes more hyperbolic in *Otherwise than Being*. Levinas takes issue with Heidegger's idea according to which "the others are encountered from out of the world in which concernfully circumspective *Dasein* essentially dwells" (BT 155/119). For Levinas the validity of Heidegger's phenomenology, whose novelty lies in the broadening of the concept of understanding beyond its classical determination as theoretical attitude, finds its limit precisely in the question of whether the other can be exclusively understood "from out of the world."

By determining the encounter with the other from the horizon of the world as being-with (*mit-Dasein*), Heidegger's break with classical intellectualism reveals itself as more apparent than real. The Heideggerian notion of understanding still preserves the traces of a tradition from which he strives to break away—the pretension to limit any exteriority within the horizon of a comprehension issuing from the subject: "comprendre c'est ce rapporter au particulier qui seul existe, par la connaissance qui est toujours connaissance de l'universel" (EN 17).[18]

For Levinas, the face is signification, but signification without context; the face's signification does not derive from a network of relations (income, profession, social standing, gender, age, race), but from itself. It signifies *kath'autó*, and because it overflows visibility and representation, the face cannot become a correlate to knowledge (EeI 90–1). The face that regards me has the singular "power" of neutralizing the context in question, which means that the relation to the other, ethics, exceeds understanding or is more fundamental than the alleged nonintellectual determination of a fundamental ontology. By opposing the face's signify-ingness (*signifiance*) to the signification derived from the horizon of the world, Levinas thus contests the primacy of Heideggerian ontology (EN 23).

But there is more. Behind Heidegger's elucidation of the being-with structure is the concern of the self (*soi*) for preserving the proper distance or difference from the other(s) that is at stake. Thus the structure of distancing (*Abständigkeit*) in which the hold the others have on the self is revealed—subjection (*Botmässigkeit*) and the dictatorship of the "they" (*das Man*) (BT 163–68/126–30), which are the existential modalities of being-with proper to everyday life.[19] We can say, in Levinasian terms, that in Heidegger the self is also "hostage to the other" (OB 125–66), but when encountering the other, the existential analytic can only see a threat and a danger without ever envisioning the possibility that this subjection could be interpreted in terms of obligation or commandment. Levinas reverses and reinscribes the structure of subjection into the ethical rela-tion as a way of reopening what he perceives to be an insufficient account of the exposition to the other in Heidegger.

The other of *Totality and Infinity* is an external alterity that dispossesses the ego only to give it sense; the book's narrative describes the ego's process of identification along with the identification of the world's oth-erness. The ego's enjoyment endows sensibility with a concrete character and, at the same time, is the condition of possibility for a metaphysical desire that opens it to the other, transforming subjectivity into hospital-ity. The book's argument follows an ascendant path, from the ego or same to the transcendence of the other, the turning point being the face-à-face with the other.

It is the encounter with the concrete character of the other's face that breaches totality and that disarms an ego whose law is war, the law of being (TeI 3/TI 21). Alterity occurs in the encounter with the face (*visage*), which institutes "a relation with being beyond the totality" (TeI 6/TI 22). Levinas conceives the breaching of totality as a concrete event—the face-à-face with the other (*autrui*) in which infinity (*l'infini*) indicates itself without appearing or rather without exhausting itself in the appearing. The breaching of totality can only occur in terms of a self (*moi*) and as the questioning of the self's powers—will, freedom, egoism, enjoyment. "Ethics" is the name of this rather bizarre and extraordinary relation with infinity, even if it unfolds in the most everyday manner, and that consists entirely in the putting into question of my egoism by the face of the other.

The experience of the face is a concrete event, an empirical occurrence, except that Levinas endows the empirical with an unheard-of status; it is the other (*autrui*), an entity who is promoted to the dignity of being the source of signification. There is a *crossing out* (*biffure*) of the empirical and the transcendental that is at the same time scandalous and innovative. This crossing out leaves neither the empirical nor the transcendent untouched; it is precisely what touches, at times by the severe and disconcerting face of the other, at others by the more traumatic, anarchic engagement of the-other-in-the-same or substitution.[20]

The title, *Totality and Infinity*, is indicative of a certain trajectory. If it is true that the exposition begins with the structure of being (totality), infinity has always already produced a *separation*.[21] If totality is a warrior, an arid dimension of self-perpetuation in isolation, infinity is fecund and generous. Infinity names the anarchic noncausal intrigue of the other to which the plot of *Totality and Infinity* fails to do justice completely, as the radically different protocols of *Otherwise than Being* make evident.

The experience of the other is concrete because the face of the other calls me, questions me (*m'interpelle*), thus producing my most concrete ipseity. It is signification and as such is fundamentally justification of my freedom; the self finds his meaning in the very questioning of his power. Approaching the face in discourse presents a series of challenges; for once, the face can only be what it is by deranging, dephasing the genre under which one would pretend to place it so as to better apprehend it. The face overflows form, even the form called face, manifesting itself before being said and in calling me. It produces itself as an address before any articulated word is ever pronounced. And although Levinas is exposing a "concept" of the face, it is useful to keep in mind that the experience of the face is always the encounter with a singular other.

How is it that we began talking about infinity, the other, and con-cluded with the singular other? The passage from the other, from infinity to the other (*autrui*), does not go without saying. Is Levinas describing the absolute singularity of the human being, or the absolute originality of the infinite? Levinas states: "The other person is not the incarnation of God, but precisely by his face, where it is disincarnated, the other person is the manifestation of the height where God reveals himself" (TeI 4/TI 34). The face is the relation between two terms, but how? What is this infinity (*infini*)? Is it different from what metaphysics calls God?[22] In Levinas one goes from the other to infinity and from infinity to God by a concatenation that may very well give the impression of a confusing ambiguity. There is ambiguity—this is certainly the case—although it would be wise to refrain from attaching negative connotations to it, since ambiguity is a positive operator of Levinas's discourse. What is at stake is an *intrigue*, an inextricable relation that is ambiguous through and through and that defies formal logic and the principle of identity.[23]

Infinity exceeds the category of being; it is nothing at all, neither exis-tence nor essence. It only makes itself felt in the force of its calling to whatever is, in the upheaval it inflicts to the immanence of being, in the trace with which it signifies the coming of a face. The infinite gives itself in the experience that endures it: the experience of the encounter with the other, a giving (*donation*) that does not belong to the regime of pres-ence. To do justice to the unheard-of character of this giving, in *Otherwise than Being* Levinas will have to introduce the notions of trace, echo, and even rhythm, which will enable him to write its indirectness and its inter-ruptive force, establishing a new alliance between poetic and prophetic language.

The other shatters the conception of consciousness understood as a correlation with the world. In spite of all the subtleties in Husserl and Heidegger, the phenomenon, the world, is still complicit with the stasis of being. To expose the originary shattering of being one has to turn away from the world and its appearing, that which gives meaning to any appearing. It is not enough to say that the other, infinity, cannot be enclosed in a given form appearing here in the world. One must also state that this overflowing of the world's horizon does not entail a beyond-the-world, but rather an exigency to engage with this world here. By instantiating separation, infinity becomes the animation, the inspiration of whatever is. Although the infinite refuses to "fixate" itself into a form, it would be a mistake to conclude that it is as formless as the Platonic One; the infinite is a deformation which, in its overflowing, is in solidarity with any form.

It is necessary to wrest the world as the ultimate structure of manifestation, which entails an original detour through infinity in its radical invisibility. This detour leads to the heart of the phenomenon, the face, which is also the border of phenomenality, as it shows itself in refusing to appear as a form. In marking a limit between inside and outside, the face announces itself in its withdrawal. This explains why Levinas refuses any "transcendental reduction" (Husserl) in which consciousness appears as the absolute power of envisioning, consciousness's power to identify itself as a self-presence to which nothing escapes—being as self-appearing. As with Heidegger, in Husserl the world is an instance for manifestation, which explains why for the former it becomes the fundamental structure of being. For Levinas, what Heidegger calls the ontological difference between being, a pure dynamism, and beings, what is substantial and individualized in the light of being, remains inherently a part of being. Due to the reciprocal belonging of being and appearing, Heidegger's nothing *(das Nicht)* loses its radical force. Heidegger's nothing is what fuels the appearing of being and cannot envision any "otherwise" than being. There is no possible overflowing to the monotonous duet of being and appearing.[24]

Everything revolves around the interruption of being because manifestation owes everything to the other. The face, the knot between the singular concrete other and infinity, therefore bears the trace of this interruption and as such is expression—the coinciding of manifestation and what is manifested. The face thus appears in language as an interlocutor. Levinas distinguishes between two types of communication, an impersonal one that goes from the same to the other without crossing the barrier of cognitive reason, and an apologetic communication in which the self justifies its freedom before the other. The original phenomenon of reason consists in this self-justification when faced with the other; but this justification of the self comes from the other. Interlocutors speak as singular faces in an asymmetrical relationship instead of being symmetrical and abstract senders and receptors of messages. The essence of language is found in this asymmetrical relationship.

Although the face is the empirical singular encounter with the other, it is not an ordinary phenomenon, since its ethical character endows it with a surplus exceeding the grasp of the phenomenon. The face cannot be seen; it overflows its own form and its encounter cannot be organized around the dynamic of vision; the face gives itself without appearing to my gaze. Further, the face's excessive way of giving itself produces an inversion of the cognitive relationship organized around the subject/object polarity. I cannot fix the face in a form, but the face looks at me and concerns me (*me regarde*). The face presents itself as a nonformal concretization, as a de-formalizing operator. The face escapes its own form that formally "assigns" the self:

> The way in which the other presents himself, exceeding *the idea of the other in me*, we here name face. This *mode* does not consist in figuring as a theme under my gaze, in spreading itself forth as a set of qualities forming an image. The face of the Other at each moment destroys and overflows the plastic image it leaves me, the idea existing to my own measure and to the measure of its *ideatum*—the adequate idea. It does not manifest itself by these qualities, but καθ'αυτό. It expresses itself. (AE 42/TI 50–1)

The face's overflowing of the idea, its undermining of the regime of *adæquatio*, "means concretely [that] the face speaks to me and thereby invites me to a relation incommensurate with a power exercised" (TeI 216/TI 198). *Teaching* is an example of this relation in which what comes from the outside puts into question the identity of the self. However, Levinas breaks with Socratic *maïeutics*, since in this method he sees the primacy of the same at work. In Socratic teaching one "receives nothing of the other but what is in me, as though from all eternity I was in possession of what comes to me from the outside" (TeI 43–44/TI 50–51). Moreover, *maïeutics* is a relearning of what has always already been in me, a form of repossession, so that there is a correlation between what is to be thought and thinking. The ideal of Socratic truth thus rests on the self-sufficiency of the same, philosophy as "egology."[25] Whether the other speaks to me from above (height) or whether his voice comes from the "other shore" (proximity), the teacher's word exceeds the grasp or cognition I can have over him. There is something traumatic in the relation of teaching, as the putting into question of the student's self that instantiates separation; it is the presence of the infinite making a break-in to the closed circle of totality.[26]

Teaching does not entail the communication of contents but rather the indication of transcendence. "Teaching signifies all the infinity of exteriority. And all of the infinity of exteriority is not first produced and afterward taught. Teaching is its very production" (TeI 173/TI 199). Teaching is an instantiation of infinity that does not depend upon the correlation of the contents of a statement and its form, said or *dit*. In Heideggerian terms it would be possible to say "teaching teaches," as it does in an eminent way in the face of the other, who faces me not to impose his domination upon me or mastery upon things but to open me to the strangeness of exteriority. The teacher speaks from a height; teaching means a fundamental and structural asymmetry, since no exchange of positions occurs.[27] However, "height" here does not denote a social hierarchical relationship but the nonviolent questioning of the autonomous subject by the other. Teaching is a figure for the primary dimension of ethics, a "one-way transcendence . . . bound up with metaphysics and with God."[28]

The speaking of the face is the "primordial essence of language" or signification, whose being consists in "putting into question in an ethical relation constitutive freedom itself" (TeI 225/TI 206). This is why meaning is the face of the *Other* (*autrui*) and also why any linguistic exchange takes place "already within this face-to-face of language" (TeI 225/TI 206). Language unfolds in the effect of this "personal signifier," expression, upon the anonymous signifier of speech. Only in this way can the face be epiphany, discourse, or originary word in the medium that is the impersonality of language. This effect is also an affirmation, a rupture with any preceding sign:

Every language as an exchange of verbal signs refers already to this primordial word of honor. The verbal sign is placed where someone signifies something to someone else. It therefore already presupposes an *authentication of the signifier*. (TeI 220/TI 202, my emphasis)

This "authentication" is problematic, however, because it means that expression precedes the act. In other words language precedes the activity of its product or *érgon*. Ultimately, signification supposes an overflowing of its content by the signifier.

The other (*autrui*) reveals itself at a distance that one must safeguard; it must remain a proximity, while at the same time the face is encountered in the face-to-face or the immediacy of presence. In *Totality and Infinity* Levinas endows discourse with a capacity to assist itself; as in Plato's *Phaedrus*, it is "a living presence" unlike the simulacrum of writing. The face signifies in itself and by itself, without reference to an external sign; it gives meaning (*sens*) its general orientation. However, for this to take place, the face must assist its own speech (TeI 60/TI 65). The face, speech coming to its own assistance, is the plenitude of discourse:

Manifestation *kath'autó* consists in a being telling itself to us independently of every position we would have taken in its regard, *expressing itself*. . . . The face is a living presence; it is expression. . . . The face speaks. The manifestation of the face is already discourse. He who manifests himself comes, according to Plato's expression, to his own assistance. (TeI 61–2/TI 65–6)

As could not be otherwise, the reactivation of the scene of full speech goes hand in hand with a denunciation of rhetoric as nondiscourse, as an oblique way of approaching the other. It is only by renouncing rhetoric that one can face the other and be "in a veritable conversation" (TeI 95/TI 209) and, therefore, institute justice. In this sense, "language lays the foundations for a possession in common. The world in discourse is no longer what it is in separation; it is what I give: the communicable, the thought, the universal" (TeI 96/TI 209). Furthermore, the presence of the other in language arrests the terrifying precession of simulacra, given that speech "surmounts the dissimulation inevitable in every apparition" (TI 97–98/TI 209–10). This surmounting of rhetoric and the simulacrum also entails the surpassing of poetic activity, since the straightforwardness of discourse or prose "dispels the charm of rhythm . . . which enraptures and transports the interlocutors" (TeI 203/TI 222). In *Totality and Infinity* there is a return to Plato, a thinking of the "beyond being" or *epekeina tés ousias* that would later become the "otherwise than being." This explains why Levinas's determination of rhetoric is classic; its nature is to be "propaganda, flattery, diplomacy" (TI 70). He understands rhetoric in its Platonic-Aristotelian determination as an act of persuasion, a technique for achieving eloquence.[29] Most importantly this classical determination is still too dependent on truth (*le dit*), on its synchronic manifestation, and cannot fully accommodate the double temporality of the teaching of the other (infinity) or saying. That this is too limiting a view becomes evident in "Langage quotidian et rhétorique sans eloquence" (1981),[30] in which the opposition between nakedness and eloquence no longer holds.[31]

It is now time to assess the implications of Levinas's conception of language for his understanding of art. There is an ambiguity in how Levinas evaluates the place of the poetic or literary within the ethical breaching of totality, or the saying (*le dire*) expressing *psychisme*. One finds a hiatus or caesura between what Levinas does with poetic language and what he says about what poetic or literary language does or does not do. It is as if Levinas's said (*le dit*) about poetic language had not undergone the ethical reduction necessary to liberate its saying (*le dire*).[32] So massive is the evidence that it is possible to affirm that a philosopher for whom the question of the other is both an obsession and a passion ends up subscribing to an eminently traditional treatment of poetic language. Although in Levinas poetic language is not the site from which to derive a heterology, one cannot interpret the traditional approach to art found in his texts as humanistic. It is necessary then to carefully weigh the reasons that compel a philosophy that defines itself as a "humanism of the other man" to deprive itself of a traditional humanistic use of art while at the same time eschewing its post-humanistic uses.[33] This double refusal explains only *in part* the oscillation at play in Levinas's assessment of art. There is also an ambiguity in the rhetorical modalities that Levinas employs in order to expose without exposing or to bear witness to the trace of the other. Why is it that for Levinas *only* the language of philosophy can recount and, for this reason, betray this *intrigue*?[34] Why is it that the ethical interruption of ontology (knowledge, representation, manifestation, and narration) can *only* take place by a saying, *unsaying* the conceptual statement?

For Levinas poetic language is neither the other (*alter, alius*) of philosophy nor a type of other (*heteron*) able to interrupt the working of totality and thus give access to the "otherwise than being." At times it is a fake, an other that totality can easily assimilate and reduce to propositional utterance or, at best, "the preeminent exhibition in which the said is reduced to a pure theme, to absolute exposition. . . . The said is reduced to the beautiful, which supports Western ontology" (AE 70/OB 40). At other times the poetic saying lays bare language's possibility to exceed the order of discourse (AE 263–4/OB 169–70).

What are the reasons and protocols that sustain this ambiguity in Levinas's thought? Whatever they may be, it indicates that his indictment of art cannot settle once and for all the conflictive proximity of aesthetics to ethics that Levinas establishes early on in his work.[35] This traditional philosophical protocol unfolds in the essay "Reality and Its Shadow,"[36] and, despite some of its shortcomings, its argument becomes an integral part of *Totality and Infinity* and other crucial texts. For example, in "Détermination philosophique de l'idée de culture" (1983), written more than a decade after the publication of *Otherwise than Being*, and in which Levinas's understanding of language leads him to reassess the ethical "potentialities" of poetic language.[37]

It is true that in "La Transcendance des mots: À propos de *biffures*" (1949) Levinas focuses on the potentialities (*virtue*) of a poetic language (the crossing out or bifurcation) that subtracts itself from the classical categories of representation and identity, a potentiality that reveals the fundamental ambiguity (*equivoque*) of thinking. However, he is too quick to dismiss it as still operating under the unifying grasp of discourse (*dit*). It will take him several more years to implement "toutes les possibilités de l'approfondissement de la pensée pensante au contact même de la matière sensible des mots" (HS 203) in his own ethical writing.[38]

Levinas's ambiguity concerning poetic language is not only visible at the level of evaluation or judgment (*critique*), but also at the level of the most basic determination of the ethical relation. If, as we saw above, the ethical relation is language, it remains to be seen whether it is "poetry" or "prose," saying or said; said betraying the saying or saying unsaying the said. Also ambiguous is whether in "Reality and Its Shadow" Levinas is *simply* deploying a conceptuality inherited from Sartre (even if the essay is an explicit condemnation of the theory of committed literature) or trying to accommodate an idiom that is neither Sartrean nor falls prey to Heidegger's sacralization of the work of art.

The hypothesis guiding my reading is that, although the explicit target of "Reality and Its Shadow" is the function that a philosophy of freedom reserves for art, the conceptual matrix that Levinas deploys is that of "Some Reflections on the Philosophy of Hitlerism" (1934).[39] It is the shadowy presence of this matrix that explains the virulent condemnation of art through which Levinas stages an ethico-political summons of Heidegger's thinking. This devaluation of art goes hand in hand with a valorization of technology and a commitment to rational philosophy. According to Levinas, Heidegger's denigration of technology is the other face of a dangerous rootedness in a place that produces "the very splitting of humanity into natives and strangers."[40] While the work of art "makes this prehuman splendor glow," allowing "the sacred [to filter] into the world" (HGN 301/HGU 232), technology suppresses the privilege of this rootedness. Levinas's condemnation of art passes sentence on the *paganism* of Heidegger's philosophy, as well as being an affirmation of Judaism, which like technology has "demystified the universe. It has freed nature from a spell" (HGN 303/HGU 234). And while this is a Judaism that has relinquished imagination, it "has discovered man in the nudity of his face" (HGU 234/HGN 303). It is necessary to assess whether this biblical humanism manages to articulate a condemnation of art that does not fall prey to the same shortcomings as Greek humanism. In *Existence and Existents* the realm of aesthetics is severed from the sobriety and seriousness of ethics.[41] The *il y a* or pure being, the restricted economy to which Levinas confines art, ought to be surmounted, because of its "barren, haunting and horrible nature and [of] its inhumanity" (EE 12).[42] The space of the *il y a* corresponds to that of the "elementary feelings" or "primitive powers" that characterize the primal and even primitive nature of "the philosophy of Hitlerism," but also to that of the "prehuman splendor" by which "the sacred filters into the world" (HGN). The question of art is the hinge that organizes Levinas's critique of Heidegger's political ontology.[43]

At this stage in Levinas's thinking, an ethical and political condemnation of art, which cannot be distinguished from Heidegger's "ontological use," is combined with two other crucial features. On the one hand, Levinas fails to positively locate a place for pure being in the general economy of the "otherwise than being." On the other hand, there is no satisfactory conception of language, which explains why Levinas fails to describe what subtracts itself from ontology and the modalities of this subtraction. It is because of the former that art is severed from ethics and it is because of the latter that Levinas's ambiguity towards the work of art remains a negative one well into the mid-sixties.[44] The signifying complex that Levinas analyzes in "Reality and Its Shadow" (rhythm, icon, image, and the statuesque dimension of art's temporality) is devoid of the expressive force of verbal utterances and belongs to the neutral and impersonal dimension of pure being.[45]

The task ahead is to deploy the conceptual system that allows Levinas to situate the work of art within a pre-ethical realm, a move that enables him to put in question Heidegger's ontological use of art. I undertake this analysis through a reading of "Reality and Its Shadow," as well as by situating this essay within the context of a series of texts predating *Totality and Infinity*. As we will see in the following chapter, in these texts Levinas articulates his first conception of language, as well as the notion of *il y a* or pure being, both of which play a crucial role in his definition of the work of art.

Art's Inhumanity: "Reality and Its Shadow"

Exoticism and the Work of Art

The face-à-face describes a non-intersubjective and nonviolent relation between the other and the self guaranteed by the straightforwardness of discourse that takes place on this side of pure being, the impersonal and anonymous *il y a*. The subject liberates itself from the *il y a*, without totally breaking away from it, except when the other faces him.[1] Given that the *il y a* plays a central role both in Levinas's thinking as well as in his determination of the nonethical nature of the work of art, I now turn to its role within the context of the works predating *Totality and Infinity*. This enables me to assess the full extent of Levinas's condemnation of art in "Reality and Its Shadow."

Levinas places transitional layers between the anonymous rumbling of the *il y a* and the order of the world or totality. Logically prior to all propositions, including negative ones, but unable to be itself negated, the *il y a* serves as a moment of being's foundation. However, if the *il y a* necessarily precedes the constitution of any world, it posits an implicit, irreducible challenge to the world's autonomy and stability. Levinas therefore defines the *il y a* as "the impossibility of death, the universality of existence even in its annihilation"(EE 61/100).

The *il y a* is an "experience" whose elaboration is common to both Levinas and Blanchot. Consequently, it shares many of the same characteristics: the presence of the absence of beings, its nocturnal provenance, its dissolution of the subject in the night, its horror, the return of being at the heart of every negative movement, and the reality of irreality.[2] For Blanchot, the presence of absence is felt as an expulsion outside of the world, in which the distinction between inside and outside collapses and with it, the subject of that experience. Levinas describes this collapse in analogous terms:

There is not determined being, anything can count for anything else. In this ambiguity the menace of pure and simple presence, of the *there is* (*il y a*), takes form. Before this obscure invasion it is impossible to take shelter in oneself, to withdraw into one's shell. One is exposed. The whole is open upon us. Instead of serving as our means of access to being, nocturnal space delivers us over to being. (EE 96/56)

Levinas conceives the exposure of consciousness to the *il y a* as a horror that throws subjectivity into an "impersonal vigilance, a participation" (EE 98/60) from which no escape is possible. This is precisely what distinguishes Levinas's analysis of the *il y a* from Heidegger's description of the pure nothingness (*das Nichts*) that the experience of anxiety exposes, in which the negation of the totality of entities reveals *Dasein*'s authentic being.[3] But while for Levinas horror must be left behind, for Blanchot the nocturnal "impersonal vigilance" gives way to fascination. In this relation the other preserves its alterity and gives itself neither as manifestation nor as presence to an instance that is no longer a subject.[4] For Levinas horror refers to the return of being after the negation of all entities has taken place, a return that takes the form of a "haunting specter" (*revenant*) (EE 100/61). Blanchot retains the modality of this return but reserves it for the nonphenomenal core of the phenomenon, the outside, from which fascination has expelled the subject. Unlike Sartre's, Blanchot's fascination does not empower the subject to assimilate the other, nor prevent, as in Levinas's concept of participation, subjectivity from encountering the other.

In *De l'évasion* and *Existence and Existents* Levinas analyzes the dimension underlying the constitution of the world. A different order with its corresponding array of forms exists on the hither side of cognition, and the work of art gives access to this order that Levinas calls "existence without a world." The first analysis that Levinas devotes to the work of art takes place under the heading of "Exotism," the first chapter of the section titled "Existence without a World." It is the work of art and the realm of aesthetics that makes it possible to specify the contents of one of his crucial concepts, the *il y a*. However, as we will see, the work of art not only provides contents for a determination of the *il y a*, even if this concept is by definition what is deprived of any content, but allows for a shift in the nature of the analysis. Levinas's position regarding the realm of aesthetics attenuates the implications of this shift.

The central operation of *Existence and Existents* is to perform a reversal of Heidegger's ontological difference through detailed phenomenological analyses of experiences such as fatigue, insomnia and the instant.[5] However, there is a shift in method in the presentation of the main insight of the book: the discovery of a paradoxical *intrigue* transcending being from the obverse of its forms and in the direction of an exoticism that does not coincide with manifestation. At this juncture of the argument, Levinas asks the reader to "imagine": "let us imagine all beings, things and persons, reverting to nothingness"(EE 57/93).

What kind of imagination is at play here? Is this the "disengaged," "evasive," "irresponsible," or "possessed" imagination that, according to Levinas, characterizes the poet? Or the more classical philosophical imagination that reconciles reality and unreality and thus accomplishes a mastery of what is unreal? Does this imagination belong to the level of "passivity" that Levinas discovers in the aesthetic realm or rather to the activity of a sovereign consciousness? In the answer to these questions lies the key to assessing whether Levinas's analysis of the work of art is ethical, in the Levinasian sense of the word, and whether his claims may be valid for an ethically informed literary critique. It is important to remember at this point that the work of art is part of a series of "experiences," such as fatigue and insomnia. This means that it is one of the figures of desubjectivization and possesses negative connotations, since it still refers to the impossibility of fully breaking away from the impersonal and anonymous being.

Imagination thus comes to supplement and to alter the scene of phenomenology, and the element where the power of imagination unfolds is that of the materiality of aesthetic sensation:

The movement of art consists in leaving the level of perception so as to reinstate sensation, in detaching the quality from the object of reference. Instead of arriving at the object, the intention gets lost in the sensation itself, and it is this wandering about in sensation, in *aisthesis,* that produces the aesthetic effect. Sensation is not the way that leads to an object but the obstacle that keeps one from it, but it is not of the subjective order either: it is not the material of perception. In art, sensation figures as a new element. Or better, it returns to the impersonality of *elements.* (EE 85–86/53)

Two points are worth stressing here. First, Levinas isolates an aesthetic materiality, the "in itself" of sensation that he locates at the margins of the world—neither inside nor outside—and uses the term *alterity* in order to refer to what happens in this "in-between" (*entre-deux*).[6] The exoticism of the work of art has to do with its disengagement from the world; it points to an outside without reference to an inside, and this lack of correlation receives the name of alterity.

However, for Levinas not all artwork preserves this alterity. Classical and romantic art conceive the subjectivity of the artist as an alter ego that assimilates this alterity. By undoing the subject/object binary opposition as inside and outside poles of the perceptive realm, Levinas questions a first form of the exotic outside in which a correlation with an inner constitution still exists.[7] This is not the case with the exoticism at play in modern art, since it functions independently of objective perception and cognitive inwardness: "[in contemporary painting] . . . the discovery of the materiality of being is not a discovery of a new quality, but of its formless proliferation. Behind the luminosity of forms, by which beings already relate to our 'inside,' matter is the very fact of the there is (*il y a*)" (EE 90/57). Like the face, the work of art offers the "in itself" of represented objects, their naked materiality, as if a principle of deformalization were at play in the work of art.[8] However, although the plasticity of the artwork occurs at a different level than the face's overflowing of form, Levinas adds an aside that authorizes bringing the work of art to the face: "the real nakedness which is not absence of clothing, but we might say the absence of forms, that is, the nontransmutation of our exteriority into inwardness, which forms realize" (EE 84–85/53).

In the modern work of art objects undergo a deformalization that makes the reduction of the other to the same impossible. This is because the material elements of the artwork (colors, shapes, words) preserve the exteriority of things and "uncover the things in themselves" (EE 85/53). This evacuation of form does not signify *kath'auto*; the in-itself of the thing is neither the luminous plenitude of a presence nor the severe nakedness of the other's proximity in the face, but an obscure dimension of the material world.

The second point that needs to be stressed regarding the materiality of aesthetic sensation concerns the obscure dimension of the *il y a* or neutrality that Levinas ties to the fate of the work of art and that allows him to claim that *the fate of the work of art is Fate*. It is possible to cipher the crux of Levinas's argument in this apparently tautological statement since it captures the ineluctable destiny of art, its pagan spatio-temporal schema which, unlike Heidegger's, is not the condition of possibility of truth, of the strife of the world and earth and the foundation of *Dasein*'s dwelling.[9] In spite of the alterity that the aesthetic realm offers, as well as the structural similarities between the presentation of the "in itself" in the face and in the work of art, the realm of aesthetics is severed from the sobriety and seriousness of ethics.

It is necessary to surmount the *il y a* given its "barren, insistent and dreadful character and its inhumanity"(EE 11). But due to its inhuman neutrality, the surmounting cannot be "aesthetic," even if the work of art makes a rehabilitation of sensation understood as an originary quality independent of any object possible. The work of art cannot accomplish a surmounting of the *il y a* in spite of Levinas's claim that exoticism is a modality of the "in itself" divested not only of its form, but also of its relationship with a subject of knowledge or perception, a subject divested of power, two of the preconditions for welcoming the other.

The exoticism of the work of art consists mainly in a cancellation of *interesse*, the mediation of being among objects oriented towards their possession or dominion. This is the same type of *interesse* that, for example, one finds at play in the reconciliation between what is real and unreal and which, as we will see, imagination and certain versions of the imaginary accomplish. In other words, Levinas does not acknowledge the aesthetic interruption of *interesse* even though it bears striking similarities to what he calls passivity, the most naked form of subjectivity or *psyche* (*psychisme*) (AE 116–20/OB 68–72), in which the self is already preoccupied and obsessed by the other. In order for this to happen, Levinas must accomplish a reversal of the *il y a*, and this occurs in *Otherwise than Being*, after he elucidates the modality of openness proper to the other— substitution.

Image and Resemblance

In "Reality and Its Shadow" Levinas proposes a distinction between rational forms of cognition and the aesthetic realm, where knowledge is not at stake.[10] In order to ground this distinction, Levinas criticizes Sartre's doctrine of committed art (*art engagé*) but also Heidegger's conception of the work of art as the unconcealment of truth.[11] Sartre's philosophy plays a central role at that time in France, and Levinas's essay appeared in Sartre's journal *Les Temps Modernes* alongside a curious note stating, "Sartre's ideas about literature's engagement are only partially examined."[12]

Be that as it may, it is evident that Levinas endorses several Sartrean theses in order to argue just the opposite, that art is in fact disengaged and evasive. For example, Levinas subscribes to Sartre's analysis of the image and the imaginary, as well as to the thesis regarding the contiguity of art and dreams. However, while for Sartre a recuperation of the imaginary's negative dimension is possible, the realm of the image is not at the service of consciousness's freedom for Levinas. Art is mute, it is not a language, and if left to itself cannot affect reality in a positive way. Criticism must come to its rescue; it has to speak in its name and reintegrate it to the human order, given that art's temporality and spatiality are inhuman.

In "Reality and Its Shadow" Levinas questions some of the most cherished ideas on modern aesthetics. He also develops two other theses: the originary character of sensation, which he calls "resemblance," and the exoticism of the work of art. Before evaluating the nature of Levinas's indictment of art, an analysis of the concepts of image and resemblance is in order. "Reality" refers to the natural presupposition of critical philosophy, whose fundament and purpose revolve around the notion of cognitive truth, while "shadow" refers to an image already exiled from the real: the sensible or sensation. Based on Husserl's thetic neutralization, Eugen Fink first introduced the concept of shadow by showing that in the image there is an element of "unreality" which depends upon and is given simultaneously with positional reality (the latter becoming the medium of "unreality"). The distance existing between both regions belongs to the same constitutive intentional act whose objectivity is appearance and not truth.[13]

Although coinciding with Fink's schema, Levinas disputes phenomenology's conception of the image's transparency. He is more interested in the opacity or shadow than in the luminosity of the image. For this reason, he endows the image with an allegorical function and with the capacity to alter the being of the absent object. It is precisely this function that distinguishes the "manifestation" proper to the face from that of the work of art, even if caricature is a structural possibility of the former:

A being is that which is, that which reveals itself in its truth, and, at the same time, it resembles itself, is its own image. The original gives itself as though it were at a distance from itself, as though it were withdrawing itself, as though something in a being delayed behind being. The consciousness of the absence of the object which characterizes an image is not equivalent to a simple neutralization of the thesis, as Husserl would have it, but is equivalent to an alteration of the very being of the object, where its essential form appears as a garb that it abandons in withdrawing. (RS 779/CPP[14] 7)

At issue is a movement between the two realms that, nevertheless, differs from the Platonic thesis of representation according to the hierarchy and temporality of the original and the copy. Reality does not present itself in a univocal and linear fashion—first its essence and then its reflection, as in Plato—but as ambiguous and dual: its light or obverse, truth, and its shadow or reverse, its nontruth. This shadow precedes the luminous concept and neutralizes its reference to the apprehended object. The image or shadow subtracts itself from idealization; it is a nonconceptual sensation. In the image, the object becomes a nonobject; it remains at a distance, withdrawn or altered, without, however, being neutralized as in the phenomenological reduction that favors the image's resemblance: "a represented object, by the simple fact of becoming an image, is converted into a nonobject. . . . The disincarnation of reality by an image is not equivalent to a simple diminution of degree. It belongs to an ontological dimension where commerce with reality is a rhythm" (RS 776/CPP 5).

When descending to the bottom of life and once the zone bathed by the light of the concept is left behind, it is possible to discover an obscure and ungraspable essence different from the "essence revealed in truth" (RS 780/CPP 7). In chapter 3 I showed that in Heidegger the work of art is an allegory of truth, of its uncanny "origination" (*Sprung*), the schematism of what gives beings their "outlook" by bringing their being into unconcealment. The truth of the work of art also unfolds as the strife between world and earth through which a ground for human beings may be secured.[15] For Levinas, however, the work of art is world-less, exotic, and thus does not secure any autochthony; it leads to a dispossession of the self (*soi*), since the *il y a* is its unique and final destination.

As we saw in the previous chapter, for Levinas the fundamental determination of existence is not the relation with being (neither an "in itself," nor a "for itself") but rather the "for-the-other" (*pour-l'autre*), of which the face is its basic instantiation. It is a question of preserving the trace of transcendence of which the human face bears witness, a trace that does not belong to the economy of the same, to being or truth (*alêtheia*). Therefore, what is at issue for Levinas is revelation and whether the work of art is up to the task of preserving the trace of the infinite.

Unlike the unconcealment of truth, revelation announces the manifestation of a hidden reality, which is as such inapprehensible by sensation. The face enables the invisible to be seen, not as a full visible phenomenon, but as what withdraws into its non-phenomenality. To assess whether the work of art can preserve the infinite, it is necessary to focus on sensation's nontruth and to make its difference from the essence of truth explicit. Levinas calls this obscure and ungraspable essence *shadow* or *resemblance* and distinguishes it from Heidegger's "letting be" (*Seinlassen*), since sensation does not reveal our being-in-the-world where "objectivity is transmuted into power" (RS 774/CPP 3). Instead, the originary contact with sensibility opens in its "blind nakedness, to the other." To this obscure essence, which is a methodological specter of Husserlian intersubjectivity, Levinas adds the mark of an inaugural, passive root (*passivité foncière*), different from the passive and affective force that Husserl locates at the foreground of consciousness.

The sensible impression retains what is felt and this retention engenders a resemblance that, according to Levinas, has a "function of rhythm" (RS 776/CPP 5).[16] For this reason, there is a mutual summoning of elements in the image that affects us without having to appeal to a receptive will. When our will awakens, rhythm has already invaded us; we already participate in it. This rhythm is neither conscious—it invades and paralyzes our freedom—nor unconscious, since all the situational articulations are present in an "obscure clarity":

Rhythm represents a unique situation where we cannot speak of consent, assumption, initiative or freedom, because the subject is caught up and carried away by it. The subject is part of its own representation. It is so not even despite itself, for in rhythm there is no longer a oneself, but rather a sort of passage from oneself to anonymity. (RS 775/CPP 4)

Levinas compares this rhythm to the automatism of marching or dancing (RS 775/CPP 4). However, there is something negative in the spell the plastic and rhythmic hold of the image exercises. This negative dimension of art competes with ethics because, although affecting subjectivity's autonomy, it does not allow the self to open itself to the call of the other.

To the exoticism and anonymous immersion of poetic rhythm, Levinas opposes the uninterrupted contact of *prose*, to which he attributes the immediate expression of the face. Rhythmic repetition's rhetorical effect is alienating; it produces an encompassing same in which a departure from the face occurs. The poem's discontinuous expression substitutes the immediate expression of the face in speech; it is a constant rupture and beginning. The artwork's expression (an expression of itself) puts a mask or façade before the opening of presence, the "in itself" of the author or of his circumstance before the expressive urgency of the other. Further, it delays and leads the other's presence astray, as if writing itself were unable to respond to the other in a face-to-face.[17]

It is true that Levinas's opposition, as well as his negative evaluation of rhythm, make sense in light of his definition of sensibility's opaque image and of the *il y a*'s rumbling. These two determinations characterize the delay of the classical (pagan) artwork.[18] The poetic rhythm Levinas has in mind is that of rhetorical, formulaic poetry. However, he does not consider the possibility that beyond its uniform resonance, rhythm may be both intermittent and discontinuous. In this essay at least, Levinas refers to a concept of rhythm that belongs to a tradition for which perception and the restricted phenomenon of poetic rhythm are the starting points of a much broader investigation. This is a tradition in which the association of rhythm and movement is *de rigueur* and thus repeats Plato's inaugural assimilation in *Laws*.

By correcting this Platonic assimilation, Emile Benveniste showed that rhythm should not be confused with periodicity, regularity and repetition, but that it is rather a form in time, which makes the separation of order and movement impossible.[19] Benveniste's reassessment paved the way for a series of approaches that go beyond the framework of a restricted poetic understanding of rhythm and beyond the empiricist attachments at play in more semiotic theories of the sign.

For Meschonic, for example, rhythm becomes force and energy, a principle of disruption of the linguistic sign, *signifyingness*, the organization of signification in discourse.[20] While for Court, rhythm refers to the cobelonging of corporeality and temporalization: "l'élan, c'est le bond en avant, la dimension de l'avenir, le projet."[21] The *ictus*, the moment when the *thesis* becomes the starting point of a new *arsis*, of a new leap forward, becomes something other than a dead time (*temps mort*); it is a contact, a relation (*liaison*), or "le principe ordinateur du temps [qui] engendre l'ordre du temps, [qui] produit le temps."[22] In the interval of the *ictus* both a caesura and an articulation occur, and the experience of time itself unfolds. Not unlike the drives that, according to psychoanalysis, animate psychic life, this experience of time is founded on the fundamental rhythmic kernel of tension and relaxation, awaiting and remembrance.

Although the more rigid opposition between speech and writing that underwrites Levinas's conception of rhythm suggests solidarity with a metaphysics of presence, it does not sufficiently explain why Levinas brackets some of the elements that would suggest a more dynamic conception of rhythm and implements them at a different register. The opposition between speech and writing, however, becomes harder to sustain in light of the ethical performative writing that Levinas claims to have produced in *Otherwise than Being.*[23]

Is this ethical writing "prose" or "poetry"? As we will see in chapter 6, the rhythmic scansion of this book, its "quasi-hagiographic style," is a type of writing that by unfolding thematically and stylistically in a "spiraling movement" (*en vrille*) (AE 76/OB 44), prevents both the *said* from being uttered all at once and the ethical saying's synchronization. The reduction's "two times" (*contre-temps*) enables the *intrigue* of the other to resound as an irreducible diachrony, and allows Levinas to displace rhythm from an aesthetic context and to reinscribe it as an ethical trope.

One has to wait until *Otherwise than Being* to see this schema of rhythm at play not only at the level of its own textual mechanism (exasperation, style "en vrille"), but also at the level of the ethical tropes par excellence: substitution, psychosis, breathing. In other words, rhythm is no longer an ontological trope, but becomes an ethical one. In "La Transcendance des mots" (1949), however, there are some indications that will help us think through a different relation between the voice of the other and the space of writing. But before engaging in a reading of this essay, we will focus on the image.[24]

Versions of the Imaginary

SARTRE'S WAY OUT OF FASCINATION.   It is time to fully assess Levinas's approach to the image by situating his analysis within the context of contemporary phenomenological analyses of the imaginary, the most influential of which, in the French context, is Jean-Paul Sartre's *L'Imaginaire* (1940).[25] Basing his analysis on Husserl's formulations of the quasi-reality of the imaginary, Sartre emphasizes the negative character of imagination when compared to perception. The image refers back to consciousness's "fonction irréalisante":

The characteristic of the intentional object of the imaginative consciousness is that the object is not present and is posited as such, or that it does not exist and is posited as not existing, or that it is not posited at all. . . . However lively, appealing or strong the image is, it presents its object as not being. (I 25–26/PI 12–13)

In his analysis of "hypnagogic images" (I 55–74/PI 41–56) Sartre introduces a dimension of fascination in the imaginary space and speaks of consciousness's captivity when encountering images. However, for Sartre it is always the case of a consenting captivity. Consciousness ought to be able to choose whether to let itself be fascinated by images: "it is necessary (*il faut*) that the reflexive consciousness give way to fascination" (I 65/PI 50). Throughout the book, Sartre's goal is to safeguard the activity and spontaneity of consciousness when faced with experiences that could potentially put it in question.

The image's proximity to the concept is a constant danger, given the possibility of falling under the spell of a "nonreflexive thinking" that hides the ideal structure of its object behind its material structure: "the image carries within itself a suspicious persuasive power that comes from its *ambiguous nature*" (I 231/PI 251, my emphasis). For Sartre an imagined object is unreal inasmuch as it calls for a split self that has to become unreal in its turn. If there is incantation, magic and spell at play in the image, its pernicious effects are only felt at the cognitive level.

The imaginary object is the shadow of an object that is also endowed with a shadow of space and of time, and consciousness can only enter this world by becoming unreal itself. As the shadow of reality, the imaginary seems to imply a correlative shadow of consciousness. However, Sartre does not grant a positive value to this modality of consciousness. This situation becomes clear when, after analyzing a series of disquieting features of the imaginary world, Sartre dismisses them by appealing to the fundamental spontaneity of consciousness in general and of the imagining consciousness in particular. The integrity of consciousness is systematically opposed to the void evoked by the image.

Sartre's main concern is what features to confer on a consciousness endowed with imagination and the ability to produce images. This ability that goes beyond reality is the condition of possibility of a free consciousness. And, since this unreal outside-the-world is the product of a free consciousness that remains in the world, the negative dimension of the imagination quickly reverses into a positive one. The apparent passivity of consciousness when facing the image yields to the freedom and activity of the imagining consciousness, whose goal is to master both the represented object and the imaginary world to which it accedes through images.

In the end, this proves to be a more powerful mastery than that of perception. It is in this context that the work of art is also defined as unreal (*irréel*) (I 239), since in aesthetic contemplation "there is in fact no passing from one world into the other, but only a passing from the imaginative attitude to that of reality. Aesthetic contemplation is an *induced dream* " (I 245/PI 225, my emphasis). The work of art thus participates in the economy of activity and mastery. If at first it seemed that the imaginary could withdraw the world, it turns out that its true nature is to put the world at the disposal of a sovereign subject's freedom. The unreal (*l'irréel*) is nothing but a necessary detour for the affirmation of the only possible type of real, that of a subject master of self and world.[26]

LEVINAS: IMAGE AND IDOLATRY.   Levinas's image shares many of Sartre's characteristics: its negative character, its dimension of absence, its closed familiarity with shadow and resemblance, its fundamental ambiguity, and captivating force. However, while Sartre bridges the gap between the imaginary and the real and preserves the unity of consciousness, Levinas stresses a hiatus in the very structure of being. Unlike Sartre, in Levinas the image excludes the concept and its effective grasp of the object. Contesting many of the received ideas of modern aesthetics (art as revelation, creation, disinterest and freedom), Levinas claims that the proper dimension of art is obscurity or non-truth and that the production of images entails a form of magic. The artist is a possessed individual whose irresponsibility, disengagement, and evasion are dangerously contagious.

Levinas's way of understanding the relationship between image and resemblance is not Platonic *in principle* since no degree of essence is involved in the distinction between image and copy (resemblance). However, since Levinas's interpretation of the image issues from the biblical condemnation of representation, it enters into a resilient and lasting alliance with the Platonic critique of the degraded nature of the image as copy and simulacrum. His view of the image as erasure of the infinite thus preserves some Platonic features. Levinas's indictment of art, even if its language is that of a "philosophy of art," is situated in the space of revelation: "la proscription des images est véritablement le suprême commandement du monothéisme, d'une doctrine qui surmonte le destin—cette creation et cette révélation à rebours" (RO 776), that is, from the perspective of the biblical prohibition concerning the representation of images (Ex 20:4; Dt 5:7) and whose most important antecedents in the Jewish anti-iconic tradition are Maimonides and Rosenzweig.[27]

The Bible denounces sculptures and images as instigators of idolatrous practices: "their idols are silver and gold, made by human hands. They have mouths, but cannot speak, eyes, but cannot see; they have ears, but cannot hear, nostrils, but cannot smell," the psalmist sings (Ps 115:4–6). However, what seems to be the target of the biblical text is a certain type of image: one whose configuration takes the form of a self-subsistent, closed presence in itself; a complete image in itself open to nothing, unreceptive, unresponsive, deaf and mute: "dumb." The prophets (Ez 7:22; Mi 1:7; Na 1:14) teach that when coming across an idol one must turn the face (*panim*) the other way, since the God who speaks to the Hebrew people at Sinai should not be confused with an image or sculpture of human proportions. This confusion entails the risk of losing the meaning of their true vocation: to stand fast in facing the invisible, to listen and respond to it. What is at stake in this condemnation is not the image in itself, so much as the look that one brings to it.

The idol (*pésel*) is a man-made God and not the representation of a God; its inauthenticity consists in its being fashioned by men. Moreover, the idol is an image (*témouna*) that posits its value as issuing from itself and not from the object that it represents; it is an image that is itself a divine presence (which explains why it is usually made of lasting and precious materials). In the Bible the idol is, for the most part, a carved form (a pillar, a stele, a burning bush), a category of man-made objects whose names cover a very broad semantic field; all of which have been translated into Greek as *eidolon*, without necessarily belonging exclusively to the field of vision or visibility.[28] Although Levinas takes as strict an attitude against images as the biblical prophets, the interpretations of the Jewish law (*Halakha*) and the discussions among the sages tend to indicate that the meaning of the prohibition falls upon the sculpting or carving of the human face, since there is a risk of forgetting the invisible source animating the human face. The idol's danger consists in misleading men to believe that they can approach the invisible through the sensible.[29]

Issuing from an anti-iconic tradition best represented by Maimonides and Rosenzweig, Levinas's interpretation of the image as idol stresses its pernicious effects: its saturation of the visible, its hiding and suppressing of the visible and, most importantly, of what withdraws from it: that whose occurrence belongs neither to the realm of entities nor being. The idol's opacity is pernicious because it arrests the light's descent.[30] The god of paganism can be conceived as adequate to the idea because it bestows full visibility without shadow.

The idol thus refers to a mute immanence that leads to an irreversible ontological solitude. The proximity of the idol and the image and the degrading of the image into an idol bear witness to the mute immanence that the beautiful is, to the danger it entails. When the rhythmic incantation of the beautiful image or icon isolates us in lonely satisfaction, its opacity or shadow can pass for the light of revelation. At issue is the mute, dispossessing satisfaction that blocks our disposition for the coming of an "idea of God" beyond the visible, a God that from an unrepresentable, invisible, and immemorial past, fills our desire without ever satisfying it. We are compelled to envisage responsibility in the face (*visage*) of the other, to renounce the mute satisfaction of the beautiful and finally to speak. Speaking here entails saying "me voici" to the concrete and singular human being, while the idol-image erases the withdrawal from which responsibility proceeds.

For Levinas, faithful as he is to this tradition, the image is an "allegory of being" that produces an "erosion of the absolute." He consequently disqualifies the image by putting it under the heading of idol, a concept that brings together the opacity of aesthetic materiality and the fixed temporality of the work of art: "to say that an image is an idol is to affirm that every image is in the last analysis plastic, and that every artwork is in the end a statue—a stoppage of time, or rather its delay behind itself" (RS 701/CPP 8). The concepts of image, idol, and statue make up the coordinates of art's indictment and are related to the way in which time temporalizes itself in the work of art. Moreover, idol is a superlative and perfect image, the image par excellence. The idol-like or statuesque character of the work of art refers to an instant that does not pass and that "endures without a future" (*dure sans avenir*) (RS 782/CPP 9): "the artist has given the statue a lifeless life, a derisory life that is not master of itself, a caricature of life. . . . *Every image is already a caricature*. However, this caricature turns into something *tragic*" (RS 782/CPP 9, my emphasis). If the "disincarnation of reality by an image is not equivalent to a simple diminution of degree" (CPP 5), as in the Platonic schema of model and copy, how should one think the term "caricature"? Does the image's caricatural nature not suggest a degrading or a perversion, an inversion of the classic hierarchical opposition of essence and accident?

Levinas claims that "in the instant of the statue, in its eternally suspended future, the tragic, simultaneity of necessity and liberty, can come to pass: the power of freedom congeals into impotence" (RS 783/CPP 9). Here too, as in Sartre, we must compare art with the oneiric realm: "the instant of a statue is a nightmare" (RS 783/CPP 9). Against the modern humanistic aesthetic credo, art fails to accomplish loftiness and instead produces a relapse into destiny, an entry into the hither side of time, monstrous and inhuman.

The plasticity of the image, the statuesque perfection of its rhythm in the idol leads to a pernicious time: a time of dispossession of the self— "the meanwhile" (*entre-temps*). Image, idol and "the meanwhile" are systematically tied to the pagan destiny of art:

The fact that humanity could have provided itself with art reveals in time the uncertainty of time's continuation and something like a death doubling the impulse of life. The petrification of the instant in the heart of duration—Niobe's punishment—the insecurity of a being which has a presentiment of fate, is the great obsession of the artist's world, the pagan world. . . . *Here we leave the limited problem of art. This presentiment of fate in death subsists, as paganism subsists.* (RS 786/CPP 11, my emphasis)

In the artwork, we face the fate of paganism, as well as its pernicious survival. Levinas's indictment of art is fundamentally shaped in terms of Rosenzweig's critique of paganism.[31] This may also explain why he subsumes the concepts of image and rhythm under Lévy-Bruhl's evolutionist category of participation, a type of belief-structure proper to primitive societies.[32] Levinas's is a religious indictment of art even if he claims that with this type of condemnation "we leave the limited problem of art." Indeed we do leave it, because what is really at play here is a condemnation of the "ontological use" of art and, therefore, the essay is much more than a religious argument. The "meanwhile" of the work of art is the "irreversible time" of a present in which "there lies the tragedy of the irremovability of a past that cannot be erased and that condemns any initiative to being just a continuation" (RS 65). This is the conception of "reality and destiny" that underlies the "philosophy of Hitlerism," as well as Heidegger's ontology.

Paganism subsists; it is the danger of a sacred that is rooted in an ontology and in a conception of the artwork as cultic restoration of the sacred. For Levinas, atheism is just one moment in the breaching of totality and cannot be confused with ecstasies or enjoyment. It is the moment when the self finds its identity again through what happens to him, the encounter with the face of the other, which can only prevent any fusion with being as in the work of art or the soil. The work of art is an inverted revelation, an occultation of revelation, an aborted separation: "l'être séparé doit courir le risque du paganisme qui atteste sa separation et où cette separation s' accomplit, jusqu'au moment où la mort des ces dieux le ramènera à l'athéisme et à la vraie transcendance" (TeI 115–6).

In chapter 3 we saw that for Heidegger the sense of the everyday, the meaning of a pair of shoes, issues from the work of art; the essence of the thing is made visible by the work of art in an eminent way as a common presence with the earth. The call of the earth, of which the painting is a silent echo, restores the shoes to the earth's belonging and shelters them in the peasant woman's world.[33] The essence of the thing thus comes from further away, and it is the Greek temple that gives sense to the earth as soil on which the peasant woman's world rests. Heidegger defines the temple as the setting forth of a human world in its strife with the earth. The temple is envisioned as human installation which, in letting the thing come into the world, also brings the earth to its own; with the temple Heidegger introduces the reciprocal play of the earth and world. The aspect of the thing that the work of art brings into play originates beyond its usage, in a signification that subtracts itself from the essence of technology understood as the dominant mode of unconcealment: the appropriation of the earth, dwelling or *poîesis*.

The poem sings the strife of world and earth as the site of the god's proximity and distance. In Levinas's eyes this way of conceiving dwelling amounts to a resacralization of the earth; the peasant shoes and the temple hear the silent appeal of the earth and answer to this call through a cultic configuration. Heidegger approaches the thing, quotidian existence, through the sacred; it is in the temple that the god can be present, but it is by the call that issues from the temple that the light can fall upon things. The world of references or assignments does not end with the piece of equipment, as in *Being and Time*, but with a cultic consecration: "in its standing there (*Darstehen*) the temple gives to things their *look* and to men their *outlook* on themselves. This *view* remains open as long as the work is a work" (PLT 59). The temple is both the starting point and end of the unconcealment of the meaning of being, a meaning that primarily shines "as in a holiday."

The call of the earth, whose hearing makes up the adventure of being, becomes the source of an enjoyment of an elementary materiality that convenes me and that comes from nothing (*das Nicht*). From this initial call the earth's sacred nature emerges along with its historial signification. The earth is the gift of being that the poet must guard; the language of the poet (*Ur-sprache*) is an ontological production (the unveiling of truth) destined to a historical people. It is the work of art that restitutes the historical signification to a cultic site. According to Levinas, "Heidegger aura méconnu le caractère laïc dans le monde et la sincérité de l'intention" (EE 65); this is so because the sacred in the end endows things with meaning. The call of the earth that the poet hears and guards acquires the sense of native soil only by reference to the bringing forth of the temple, a linkage that has a sinister ring, the premonition of a disaster.

In "Reality and Its Shadow" Levinas frames his analysis of the image and art with two sections on criticism: "Art and Criticism" and "For Philosophical Criticism." The work of art appears surrounded by discourse, as if it were necessary to mark its borders in order to prevent the reader from falling under its spell. In the first section, Levinas contests critical approaches that see art as a form of knowledge and that "still [have] something to say when everything has been said" (RS 772/CPP 2). This way of understanding criticism has to do with a failure to assess the disengagement of the work of art at play in its completion; a completion by which the work of art "does not give itself out as the beginning of a dialogue" (RS 773/CPP 2). The work of art disengages itself from dialogue and communication, and this detachment takes place on the hither side of time, the dimension of evasion that precludes the aesthetic from opening itself to becoming.

The work of art is mute and cannot enter into a dialogue with this type of criticism, which is deficient because "it does not attack the artistic event as such, that obscuring of being in images, that stopping of being in the meanwhile" (RS 788/CPP 12–13). However, in the second and final movement of the essay, to this "still preliminary criticism" Levinas opposes a "philosophical criticism" whose logic "we cannot here broach," but for which "the value of images lies in their position between two times and their ambiguity" (RS 788/CPP 13). Levinas does not undertake the "logic" of a philosophical approach to art because of the need and the impossibility of introducing "the perspective of the relation with the other" (RS 788/CPP 13). A philosophical exegesis of art supposes a previous ethical determination of being and time. And although this "logic" is lacking here, Levinas pronounces a critical philosophical proposition concerning the essence of the work of art—"an event that eludes cognition" (RS 789/CPP 13). The work of art is myth (*muthos*) and as such calls for an interpretation (*lógos*).

If in the case of criticism the work cannot enter into a dialogue (the idol turns its face against language, it is a radical indifference to language, a pure opacity), it can nevertheless be reintegrated to the human order by the language of "philosophical criticism." This type of criticism gives life to the work of art. Does this rendering of *mythos* into *lógos* not entail a form of theoretical and cognitive violence? Can the simple reference to "the perspective of the relation with the other" be enough to justify a distinction between mere criticism and a philosophical (ethical?) exegesis of the work of art?

The nonimplementation of a philosophical approach to art in "Reality and Its Shadow" does *not* lie in the impossibility of introducing "the perspective of the relation with the other." Indeed, all the major elements of this "perspective" could have been *explicitly* introduced in the argument, since they were either outlined or developed in *Existence and Existents* and in *Time and the Other*, before their more systematic elaboration in *Totality and Infinity*. However, what is truly missing in the argument is an understanding of language that would have allowed some potentialities of the work of art to be conceived in their own right. It is not by chance that in *Otherwise than Being* Levinas nuances his position when he claims that:

> To fail to recognize the said *properly so-called* (le Dit *proprement dit*) (relative as it may be) in the predicative propositions which every artwork—plastic, sonorous or poetic—awakens and makes resound in the form of *exegesis* is to show oneself to be as profoundly deaf as in the deafness of hearing only nouns in language. (AE 71/OB 41)

In the realm of art the distinction between the said and saying becomes relevant, on the one hand, only when Levinas manages to find a place for being in the general economy of the "otherwise than being," and on the other, when his critique of Heidegger is attenuated and the work of art ceases to be the privileged terrain on which to wage war against "fundamental ontology."[34] Only at that moment does the work of art become not only a pure said, able to speak of and against the violence of the order of discourse, but perhaps something else. We know by now that the statuesque (plastic) temporality of "the meanwhile" ought to be transformed into discourse. It needs to be put at the service of the order of time in the same way that in Sartre the anomalies of imagination serve the autonomous self. At this stage, it may be risky to assimilate this transformation with what Levinas calls the *unsaying* of the said in *Otherwise than Being*.

Levinas must still bridge the distance between a religious indictment of the work of art in "Reality and Its Shadow" and the ethical exegesis of the given-word (*parole donnée*) he develops in *Otherwise than Being*. "Reality and Its Shadow" is a remarkable multilayered essay. If read alongside "Reflections on the Philosophy of Hitlerism," one finds at one level a dismantling of the myth of art and of the cobelonging of myth and art.

The latter phenomenon is no longer seen as the fulfillment of communication and signification or as the myth of a communal and authentic signification, but as a shadow or a nontruth whose fascination is mortally dangerous and that one must escape. However, this *evasion, hypostasis,* or process of deneutralization is *not* the work of an isolated subject. In the subject's adventure to secure a world and to live among entities, there is always a risk of relapsing into the *il y a.* The process of deneutralization has a new meaning only in "the proximity of the other structured as an asymmetry."[35] Levinas deploys the term *deneutralization,* which ciphers a movement "that finally let us catch a glimpse of the ethical meaning of the word *good*" (EE 12), not only against Heidegger's ontology, but also against Blanchot.

At another level of "Reality and Its Shadow" Levinas attempts to reintegrate the work of art into the human realm and thus preserve traces of a classic moral conception of art. The work of art continues to be, if not a major obstacle, at least something that keeps disrupting the space of ethics. One can find a different approach to writing and, more implicitly, to rhythm in "La Transcendance des mots," an essay Levinas wrote in 1949 on Michel Leiris's *Biffures.* In this essay it is possible to detect some indications of how an ethical writing might look, of how the "otherwise than being," in which transcendence indicates itself and, at the same time, hides and shelters itself from manifestation, can signify without congealing into an image or idol. This writing of the other must unfold as a clandestine *intrigue,* able to render the manner in which the "otherwise" than being leaves its traces.

By bifurcation and/or erasure (*biffure*), Levinas understands an implausible and unheard-of process of accretion of meaning that unfolds by means of a proliferation of associations beyond contiguity, since what matters is "la présence d'une idée *dans* l'autre" (HS 199).[36] In the procedure called "biffures" Levinas locates "une pensée par-delà les catégories classiques de la représentation et de l'idéntité" (HS 199), as its originality lies precisely in positing the multiple as simultaneity and the state of consciousness as something irreducibly ambiguous. These are important features that Levinas's writing will make his own: the principle of hetero-affection, of the other-in-the-same that produces a coimplication of all the major concepts; the simultaneous proliferation of the multiple, which will become writing as "exasperation." The appositive bifurcation of concepts and ambiguity or the amphibology of the said are all constitutive features of *Otherwise than Being*, a treatise on the ethical *biffure* of ontology: the unsaying of the said, the ethical subtraction of the saying from the space of identity or said.

But in this essay all these features are still subsumed under the primacy of the spoken word, which is the defining feature of *Totality and Infinity*. It explains why Levinas is quick to delimit the potentiality (*vertu*) of this literary writing by reducing the ambiguity of the *biffures* to the shaping or configuration of a space (HS 199). By bringing together Leiris's writing and Charles Lapicque's paintings without any explicit reason, except perhaps the implicit axiom that "all art is plastic" (TI 140/149), Levinas links the spatial and the visual. He exposes the immanent economy of being within which these artistic forms operate, thus leading the philosopher to declare that "tous les arts, même les sonores, font du silence" (HS 201).

Faithful to his determination of the essence of art, Levinas speaks of a transformation of language and of its engulfing of images in which the nontruth of being emerges. We are back in familiar territory; the muteness of the work of art was why in "Reality and Its Shadow" Levinas surrounded it with a double ring of criticism. But in "La Transcendance de la parole" Levinas does what he refrained from doing in "Reality and Its Shadow." He introduces the "perspective of the other" within the frame of an "ethical criticism" of art. If all arts "font du silence," it is the very impossibility of speaking that, at the same time, elicits a "besoin d'entrer en relation avec quelqu'un malgré et par-dessus l'achévement et la paix du beau" (HS 201), a critical need (*besoin critique*). Criticism is now placed under the heading of need.

The critical need is thus a response to the completeness of the work of art, to its immobilization of time, to the violent immanent holding of its plastic rhythmic schema and erasure of the absolute, even if Levinas claims that Leiris's text belongs to a regime of incompleteness (a postmodern and even a post-beautiful regime). By "peace of the beautiful" we by now know that Levinas means a violent indifference to the other. The aesthetic delectation of the work of art leads us to an "en deça" without hope of redemption, a world already closed and finished in itself.

So a breaching of this always-complete world of vision (totality or being) and the work of art must occur: a resounding, a roar, a scandal—a sound. If the image entails a stoppage of time, a delay with respect to itself, the sound produces an overflowing of the sensible by itself, of the form by the content, a tearing of the world by something that cannot be reduced to a vision and that, therefore, exceeds the sensible: "entendre véritablement un son c'est entendre un mot. Le son pur est verbe"(HS 201).

As in *Totality and Infinity*, the spoken word (*parole proferée*) plays the role of a transcendent origination of meaning; it is the real presence of the other that matters, a situation

dont le privilège se révèle à Robinson quand, dans le splendeur du paysage tropical, n'ayant rompu ni par ses utensils, ni par sa morale, ni par son calendrier, aucun lien avec la civilization, il connaît dans la rencontre avec Vendredi le plus grand événement de sa vie insulaire; où enfin un homme qui parle remplace la tristesse inexprimable de l'echo. (HS 201–2)

The insular life of aesthetic enjoyment supposes a form of violence to the self; a self-positing that gives itself as a spectacle that only the other who speaks can counter. Robinson here embodies the figure of the *chez soi*, the self-sufficient self (*soi*) that in *Totality and Infinity* is the precondition for encountering the other, a figure of totality; while Friday belongs to the biblical series of the other, "the widow, the orphan, and the stranger." It is Friday who speaks and in speaking he exposes the constitutive insufficiency in the position of the subject (Robinson): "le sujet qui parle ne situe pas le monde par rapport à lui-même, ne se situe pas purement et simplement au sein de son propre spectacle, comme l'artiste—mais par rapport à l'Autre" (HS 203). As we established it in the previous chapter, here we come across the questioning of the self's spontaneity or ethics in terms of a set of premises Levinas had introduced in *Totality and Infinity* through the concrete event of the encounter with the other.

The artist, the poet loses the privilege he had in Heidegger; he is neither the guardian of being's truth nor the semigod whose signs are "prophetic" and who thus announces the primordial word of the sacred (EH 136–39). In Levinas it is only the face of the other in its nakedness that can teach. By teaching, Levinas refers in this context to a "wrench-ing" of experience from its aesthetic self-sufficiency—the very operation that, not without violence, Levinas performs upon Leiris's text—the "critical saying" to the other by which art is completed. As in Sartre, "le langage de la critique nous fait sortir des rêves—dont le langage artistique fait intégralment partie" (HS 202). While the artist situates himself in relation to himself, inside his own spectacle, the speaking subject situates himself in relation to the other: "par la parole proferée, le sujet qui se pose s'expose et, en quelque manière, prie" (HS 203). He speaks in the anarchic language that dissolves the "mythical format of the element" (TeI 140/TI 149).

The work does not speak, it is mute, its beauty guards this silence; no address, no message stems from it. One cannot retrieve a fable of the origins, a "poem before the poem," as in Heidegger, nor hear the ground-ing attunement as mourning that issues from the departure of the ancient gods and the awaiting the coming of the new gods. By being restricted to the *il y a*, the absence of a world, the work plunges us into horror, trapping us in an existence without a world.

Nevertheless, the critical need arising from this deadly silence seems to indicate that there is a language that must be delivered from this inhuman hold. The critic is the one who resurrects the infinite that inhab-its the finitude of the said. He must elevate a saying that is in excess with respect to the immanence of what is said: "Closer to us than any present, the Unpresentable will not be represented in the poem. It will be *the poetry of the poem*. Poetry signifies poetically the resurrection that sustains it: not in the fable it sings, but in its very singing" (NP 13).[37] This is a strikingly Heideggerian formulation, except that once conceived in its relation to infinity, "the poetry of the poem" implies an ethical potentiality. We will see how this potentiality (*vertu*) of poetic saying unfolds in *Otherwise than Being*. However, for this to occur Levinas must also implement a different understanding of rhetoric, which he begins to elaborate in the 1980s, as the essay "Langage quotidien et rhétorique sans éloquence" (1981) con-firms. By questioning the classical determination of rhetoric as a tech-nique for mastering language, Levinas aims to ground the ethical saying in the empirical order of the everyday life, beyond its determination as the unveiling of being and of *Gerede* or chatter, the improper or inauthentic everyday existential determination of language, according to Heidegger.

Heidegger approaches the everyday on the basis of structures of existence (care, being-in-the-world) and posits it as an inner possibility of a proper, authentic existence that can only be secured through more essential modes of being—poetry, thinking, political foundation—than the everyday. The everyday, which is "a fundamental mode of being-in-the world" (BT ¶ 37), is improper, inauthentic, and is thus conceived in terms of a set of relations and as impersonal existence (*das Man*) in which a technological leveling down of experience may occur. In chapter 2 we saw that the essence of technology brings into play an obfuscation of the manifestation of being. Only poetic language can reestablish the initial unveiling of being (*phusis*), the sacred, and grant us the possibility of a dwelling. Levinas's everyday is grounded in enjoyment (*vivre de*); the ego's happiness is the way in which the infinite posits itself and opens the self (*soi*) from within. Moreover, Levinas understands everyday language in light of the distinction between said (*dit*) and saying (*dire*), a distinction that, as we will see in chapter 6, plays a decisive role in the ethical writing of *Otherwise than Being*. It enables him to reverse the traditional understanding of language as proposition (*dit*) to the exclusion or subordination of the saying (*dire*).

It is in the saying that one must expose "an *intrigue* that does not reduce itself to the thematization or exposition of a said, to the correlation in which a saying would make the being of an entity appear" (HS 192). Levinas subtracts *apophansis*, the Heideggerian inaugural determination of language as the showing of truth, from the economy of being and transforms it into a modality of the approach of the other (*autrui*). Before being the manifestation of the being of an entity, the proposition is what I propose to another human being. The saying (*dire*) is "an approche du prochain" (HS 193) beyond any signification; everyday language is that language in which the saying as approach of the other is not absorbed in the said or proposition.

This is a radical way of defining everyday language, since as we saw in the previous chapter, it presupposes that the empirical is already invested by a trace of infinity. For this reason everyday language understood as saying is "a nonindifference to the other, susceptible of an ethical signification to which the utterance of the said subordinates" (HS 193). This already means that the "this as that" (the basic hermeneutic structure of signification) is derivative with respect to this noneloquent quotidian language. In the proximity of the other human being, a proximity in which he is *at the same time* wholly other (*tout autre*), the signifyingness (*signifiance*) of a transcendence is born, with its archi-original metaphors "capable of signifying the infinite" (HS 193). *Otherwise than Being* weaves an *intrigue* of the other with the threads of quotidian language and the potentiality of poetic language to communicate these archi-original metaphors.[38] A process of desacralization of the work has began, a separation from the truth of the appearance that is essentially mixed to the true (DSS 90), and which the work of art cannot accomplish due to its inextricable participation in being's nontruth.

"THE RESEMBLANCE OF CADAVERS": BLANCHOT. It is tempting to read Sartre and Levinas as representing the "two versions of the imaginary" that Blanchot refers to in *The Space of Literature*. The more conventional version would reserve for the image and the imaginary the dialectical function of bridging the gap between intelligibility and the negative dimension of art. The less conventional would stress its inassimilable negative dimension, its "shadow." Nevertheless, such a neat division does not hold, since a version (*versant*) supposes a movement of reversal and, therefore, a certain unavoidable contamination. This ambiguity is not accidental but something that "comes from the initial double meaning produced by the power of the negative and the fact that death is sometimes the work of truth in the world, sometimes the perpetuity of something that does not tolerate either a beginning or an end" (EL 351/SH 424). Therefore, one cannot simply choose one version over the other because "an art which purports to follow one version (*versant*) is already on the other" (PF 321/SH 388). We could replace the word "art" with "philosophy" here so as to locate this reversal in Levinas's argument.

As I have shown, the Levinasian critique of the image's hold points to a ghostly temporality, a mute and inhuman dimension, "the meanwhile," which strictly speaking belongs neither to presence nor to absence. Nevertheless, Levinas conceives this negative dimension in terms of the idol, a figure which suggests a form of full-fledged presence, albeit a mute one.

The ghostly temporality of the "meanwhile," the fact that the "meanwhile" is, becomes the statuesque glow of the idol in which no ambiguity survives. The "meanwhile" belongs to *il y a*'s "elementary materiality" that must be surpassed by the approach of the other human being whose face bears the trace of transcendence.

Blanchot's version of the imaginary shares many of the features found in Sartre and Levinas and takes its point of departure precisely from what Levinas's analysis leaves out: "the position an image occupies between two times and their ambiguity" (RS 788/CPP 13). Although Blanchot does not reject the possibility of reintroducing this negative dimension in the order of the day, he is interested in the particular and irreducible negative character of the image. In Blanchot there is neither a call for an evasion of the *il y a* nor a process of deneutralization. Writing faces this "elementary materiality" and thinking implies keeping watch (*veiller*) on this movement of dispossession. Literary language is the site where Blanchot comes face-to-face with a dimension of the negative that dialectics cannot sublate, and which he elucidates under four different headings: the experience of the night or outside, the neuter, the disaster and the return (ED 95/WD 57).

One of the names of this experience of the night is, of course, the *il y a*. While Levinas assimilates the *il y a* to the category of being, Blanchot approaches its negative dimension as what is on the hither side of being and ontology: neither being nor nonbeing. If for Levinas the ethical reduction of being's neutrality and anonymity energizes itself from a writing that bears witness to the trace of the other, writing in Blanchot marks a "step *not* beyond" (*pas au-delà*). It is a perpetual errancy faced with an inhospitable other that one must welcome in the absence of any dwelling place and independently of its inhuman character. Levinas's other (*autrui*) is a human other whose face bears witness to the trace of transcendence; it is the immanent site of transcendence. But Blanchot's other is prehuman and conceived in terms of the structure of difference, although the human dimension does appear years later in *The Infinite Conversation*.[39]

Given that for Blanchot the image is the oscillation of the two versions, or the very deployment of ambiguity, it gives access to the "elementary materiality" of the neuter. It pacifies and humanizes "the unformed nothingness pushed towards us by the residue of being that cannot be eliminated" (EL 341/SH 417). This humanizing aspect that the image accomplishes in the work of art brings the promise of "a pure happiness" and of the "transparent eternity of the unreal." In this version, the image affirms presence, even if this is the presence of an absence that it manages to dissimulate; it is the representation of a preexistent object that belongs to a preexistent world.

We are not far here from the imagination's "fonction irréalisante" (Sartre) and from the halting of the instant that Levinas isolates in classical art, but that he interprets as the plasticity of art in general. However, in Sartre the image's "fonction irréalisante" is relative; the image accomplishes the object's negation but preserves the world as its background. Against Sartre and more in line with Levinas, Blanchot relates the space of the image's negation with an "elementary materiality" that he calls the neuter (*neutre*). It is important here to emphasize the commonality between Levinas's *il y a* and Blanchot's neuter, as well as to stress that it is a commonality on which they also part ways. One should not forget that in Levinas the *il y a*'s "elementary materiality" must be surmounted, and that this can only occur by the approach of the other. This is not the case with Blanchot, who aims to preserve the neuter. However, since the terms *neuter* and *neutrality* are the site of friendly although contentious exchanges between them, we must pay some heed to how Blanchot determines this crucial "concept."

"The neuter emerges" (EL 477/IC 325) in the imaginary's second version. The image is no longer related to meaning and signification but rather "tends to withdraw [the object] from its meaning by maintaining it in the immobility of a *resemblance that has nothing to resemble*" (EL 350/SH 423, my emphasis). The image is a doubling of the object, but a neutral one, since the former appears neither as absence/presence nor as being/nothingness. The image is the hither side of objects that resists its own objective constitution and that the "elemental claims."[40] Further, this being claimed by the elemental is the very opposite of the process of idealization that the image's first version accomplishes. For this reason Blanchot chooses the corpse as the trope that will allow him not only to approach this dimension, but also to elaborate the notion of resemblance. Resemblance expresses neither the relationship between the image and its object (I 47–55), as in Sartre, nor the movement that for Levinas engenders the image. Blanchot equates the strangeness or the enigma of the image (EL 476/SH 331) to the corpse that resembles itself; it is a resemblance without antecedent and, as with the image, exceeds the dialectics of presence and absence, identity and difference. Although Blanchot reads the becoming-idol of the corpse as a movement of idealization (EL 346–47/SH 420–21), he quickly reverses the halting of time it brings about by focusing on the "haunting [of the] inaccessible which one cannot rid oneself of" (EL 348/SH 422). Resemblance names the anarchic nature of the image, its constitutive ambiguity without reference to a previous original model.

If for Levinas the work of art bears witness to the inhuman dimension of the *il y a* and must be either left behind or reintegrated to the order of discourse, this is not the case with Blanchot, for whom the question is "how to experience (*vivre*) an event as image" (EL 353/SH 425). As we saw in chapter 1, Blanchot takes as his point of departure the "space of literature" understood as the site where "the most profound question" (EI 12–35/IC 11–17) comes to thinking. The "space of literature" is also the site where the fascinating hold of the image liberates the irreducible ambiguity of the neuter, whose elucidation organizes Blanchot's writing in its different modalities, ranging from the novel genre and the *récits* to fragmentary writing.

"The Writing of the Outside," Blanchot with Levinas, or the "Potentiality" of Poetic Language in *Otherwise than Being*

Language would exceed the limits of what is thought, by suggesting, letting be understood without ever making understandable (*en laissant sous-entendre, sans jamais faire entendre*) an implication of meaning distinct from that which comes to signs from the simultaneity of systems or the logical definition of concepts. This possibility (*vertu*) is laid bare in the *poetic said*. . . . It is shown in the *prophetic said*.

—*Levinas,* Otherwise than Being

Tell us *"just* exactly" what happened? A story (*histoire*)?. . . . No. No stories, never again.

—*Blanchot,* The Madness of the Day

Wittgenstein's "mysticism," aside from his faith in unity, must come from his believing that one can *show* when one cannot *speak*. But without language, nothing can be shown. And to be silent is still to speak. Silence is impossible. That is why we desire it. *Writing or Saying* (Dire), *that precedes every phenomenon, every manifestation or disclosure: all appearing.*

—*Blanchot,* The Writing of the Disaster (translation modified)

One can imagine a voice that "comes from the other shore" and by saying "at this very moment here I am," "interrupts the saying of the already said." It is a voice that refuses to tell stories, much like the one in Maurice Blanchot's *La Folie du jour* (*The Madness of the Day*), a mad voice, "obsessed, persecuted," whose echoes disrupt the transparency of daylight, manifestation, and discourse. Yet even while refusing to tell stories this voice bears witness to an *intrigue* with the other in a "quasi-hagiographic style that wishes to be neither a sermon nor the confession of a 'beautiful soul'" (AE 81/OB 47). This is the voice of someone "out of breath" who underwent a fission exceeding any figure of support (*subjectum*) and inwardness and, therefore, exposes himself to "the outside where nothing covers anything" (AE 275/OB 179).

If in "Reality and Its Shadow" and in *Totality and Infinity* the aesthetic category of rhythm was characterized by its alienating force, in *Otherwise than Being*'s "emphatic mutation" it becomes ethical. The voice that welcomes the other can only be a matter of writing that, not unlike Blanchot's, precedes all phenomenon and form of manifestation. However, the mutation of rhythm is not an isolated phenomenon. It is as if the language of *Otherwise than Being* showed a different understanding of its own operations than that found in *Totality and Infinity* and were making peace with certain potentialities of poetic language.

I began this chapter by quoting a passage from Blanchot's *The Madness of the Day* and equated the "voice" of his *récits* to that of Levinas's *Otherwise than Being*. Even though the latter energetically refuses any form of mysticism and remains committed to a rational philosophy, there is something outrageous in this book. The "clandestine *intrigue*" of *Otherwise than Being* is "unnarratable and indescribable," two features that would certainly compel a philosopher like Wittgenstein to remain silent. It is the sort of preinvolvement that, strictly speaking, does not fully abide by the rules of discursive exposition and can perhaps be more easily tolerated in fictional writing. Nevertheless, Levinas's daring attempt to write what by his own account exceeds the order of discourse may justify my referring to it as the "writing of the outside."[1] I know that by employing this expression I may be going against Levinas's explicit intention, since for him writing can neither "effect the [ethical] reduction" by itself (AE 75/OB 44) nor allow access to the "otherwise than being."

Although Levinas does not develop a positive concept of writing, one can read his reduction of phenomenological discourse as a displacement and reinscription of a classical understanding of writing. It will therefore be necessary to explore how Levinas deploys the "question of writing" (Blanchot) and how he understands the "outside," as well as the apparently sudden *rapprochement* between Levinas and Blanchot. The justification for this connection is that *The Madness of the Day* is lurking somewhere in a corner of *Otherwise than Being*, much like the silhouette of the "different law" that appears behind the backs of the masters of discourse, in Blanchot's *récit*.[2] It is a question then of interrogating this textual witness according to the double logic that Levinas derives from it. First, in terms of the order of discourse, and second, in terms of a certain outside of discourse.

In *Otherwise than Being: or, Beyond Essence* language as expression and communication bears witness to an immemorial trace in which echoes of the primary scene of ethics resound, that of substitution (the-one-for-the-other). Substitution refers to an *intrigue* older than consciousness and presence that can be told neither in the time of narration nor in that of knowledge. The word *intrigue* refers to a knotting of subjectivity and the other that is no longer conceived as a clear-cut opposition between totality and infinity; the other of *Otherwise than Being* is not an entity; its mode of coming is that of the "otherwise than" being. In addition, *intrigue* refers to another way of conceiving the temporalizing of time, the "beyond essence." If in *Totality and Infinity* it was a matter of going back to a *"profond jadis,"* what is at issue here is an operation "produced in two times" (*à contre-temps*) (AE 76/OB 44). Levinas's quasi-narrative in *Otherwise than Being* aims not only to inscribe this *intrigue*, but also to welcome it; the book reads as the testimony of this *intrigue*.

So far I have focused mostly on Levinas's condemnation of the work of art in "Reality and Its Shadow," whose conceptual system is still present in *Totality and Infinity*. I also made reference to the fact that, in spite of maintaining this position, the essay on Leiris's *Biffures* already points to a different understanding of writing and poetic language. This means that Levinas reluctantly acknowledges "poetic" language's ability to suggest significations that exceed the order of discourse, and at times even endows it with a quasi-ethical force. The acknowledgment goes without saying, however, or is merely implied (*sous-entendu*), since in *Otherwise than Being* it appears only by way of an *allusion* to Blanchot's *The Madness of the Day*. As I will show in this chapter, this indirect reference marks the site of a complex intertextual grafting. What the poetic said simply suggests, that "language would exceed the limits of what is thought," becomes operative in Levinas's own text. It enables it to welcome the "otherwise than being" and to put into place a writing whose double temporality (diachrony) lets the other "come to thought, as approach and response" (Blanchot).

The purpose of this chapter is to make explicit how Levinas writes the *"intrigue* of the other." Although the main focus of my reading is the structure of *Otherwise than Being*, the book's main tropes compel me to ask what Levinas *does* with poetic language beyond what he explicitly claims. Since the key operation that *Otherwise than Being* performs, the ethical reduction of the said, is a textual operation that Levinas deploys in the proximity of a poetic text, the chapter aims not only to explain the writing of ethics, but also to elucidate the features of an ethics of writing. Writing of ethics, ethics of writing, is not a mere play on words. As we will see in the next chapter, this reversal will allow me to read the "unerasable difference" between Levinas and Blanchot.

Substitution—Writing the Other

Discourse, expression, communication, face, sincerity, witnessing, and *prophecy* are some of the terms that Levinas deploys in order to elucidate the ethical dimension of language, the *ethicity* of philosophical discourse. This constellation revolves around the crucial term *signification* and the two operative concepts of *the said (le dit)* and *saying (le dire)*. At the end of *Otherwise than Being,* Levinas sums up his analysis: "signification, the-one-for-the-other, the relationship with alterity, has been analyzed as proximity, proximity as responsibility for the other, and responsibility for the other as substitution. . . ." (AE 282/OB 184). What is striking about Levinas's style—and one can read the whole book as an expanded version of this type of sentence, an expansion that is also a permanent displacement and reinscription—is his refusal to abide by a conventional philosophical exposition.

Strictly speaking, Levinas defines none of the terms in the passage I quoted above. His refusal to comply with the procedures of a traditional exposition lies in the fact that "the alterity of the other is not a particular case, a species of alterity, but its original *exception*" (AE 279/OB 182). Definition, therefore, would entail a thematization, a synchronization of the saying in the said. By refusing the economy of definition, Levinas lets each of the terms resound "in other words" or as the *autrement dit.*[3] It is as if the archi-principle of substitution were already at play at the deepest level of the text, or as if the textuality of *Otherwise than Being* had already undergone a substitution that "dit [l'*Argument*] comme l'autrement qu'être au fond de la proximité" (AE 37/OB 19).

Otherwise than Being also lacks a progressive sequential narrative organization. Instead Levinas follows a different protocol and assembles the chapters, not according to the logic of conceptual exposition, but rather as if they were appositions:

The different concepts that come up in the attempt to state transcendence echo one another. The necessities of thematization in which they are said ordain a division into chapters, although the themes in which these concepts present themselves do not lend themselves to linear exposition, and cannot be really isolated from one another without projecting their shadows and their reflections on one another. Perhaps the clarity of exposition does not suffer here only from the clumsiness of the expounder. (AE 37/OB19)

The basic concepts unfold in the section "The Argument," which announces the *otherwise* than being and promises something "other than a said" (manifestation, representation, narration, and disclosure). It is in the central section, "Exposition," that a "clandestine *intrigue*" unfolds under the trope of substitution and that the "reduction of the said to the saying" (AE 77/OB 44) takes place. In this section the said undergoes a reduction and becomes "the saying of the otherwise than being." The text announces and, at the same time, performs an interruption of synchrony, of the correlation between the saying and the said. It is as if the whole text had gone through the "methodical operation" that Levinas calls "exasperation" (DQV 142). *Otherwise than Being* does not consist of a progressive narrative but rather of an emphatic or hyperbolic rewriting of the "argument" transformed into an *intrigue* or *ex-position*. Therefore, all the terms (signification, the-one-for-the-other, the relationship with alterity, proximity, responsibility for the other and substitution) can neither "be really isolated from one another without projecting their shadows and their reflections on one another" (AE 258/OB 166) nor put into correlation by either thematization or narration. Levinas finally implements some of the ideas on writing he pointed to in "La Transcendence des mots," making *Otherwise than Being* a "crossed out, 'bifurcating'" text: a treatise on the ethical erasure, remarking, writing over (*biffure*) *of ontology*.

Language for Levinas is the "structure" of both the retraction and the inscription of infinity (*l'infini*); this same "structure" is what Levinas calls *ethics*. It is thus possible to affirm that in Levinas there is no ethical turn without a certain linguistic turn, one in which the a priori of language is interrupted by an anteriority whose a priori character is enigmatic. This is due to the fact that language is elevated to a metaphysical category (not an ontological one, according to the distinction that *Totality and Infinity* establishes) that exceeds the simple "giving out of signs" (*délivrance de signes*) (AE 81/OB 48) or communication: "saying is communication, to be sure, but as a condition for all communication, as exposure (*exposition*)" (AE 82/OB 48). Signification precedes and gives fundament to language as proximity and contact with the other and not as the "vicissitude (*peripetia*) of the thematizing intentionality" (AE 216/OB 137). It also names an enigmatic pre-diction that challenges the primacy that language, understood as a system of signs, enjoys in other philosophies, structuralism and analytic philosophy, for example.

How can Levinas locate an enigmatic inscription in language that bears "an allegiance to the other"? What does he understand by signification? As happens with most of his terms, signification is ambiguous. Its scope extends to manifestation or disclosure and to proximity, a form of "allegiance to the other" that he situates on the hither side of manifestation. Levinas locates this dimension in the discontinuity of manifestation, a temporality that goes "beyond essence" and is unsynchronizable in a linear narrative: "the intrigue of proximity is not a *plot*, a modality of cognition" (AE 52/OB 48, translation modified).

On the side of manifestation, beings and entities show themselves in the said to a consciousness able to synchronize their manifestation in the present. However, beneath manifestation and exceeding the grasp of ontology, Levinas locates proximity, a different modality of openness in which the same is involved with the other before the other appears in any possible way to consciousness. This "exposure precedes the initiative a voluntary subject would take to expose it" (AE 276/OB 180). Levinas refers to this modality of openness as subjectivity, the other in the same, an allegiance of the other before any manifestation and representation. In turn, he characterizes subjectivity as the restlessness of the same disturbed by the other. The same is disturbed to such an extent that subjectivity is "without rest" and undergoes a substitution. If on the side of manifestation it is possible to assemble a signification according to the play of differences, on the side of proximity there are echoes of a saying whose signification consciousness is unable to assemble.

The crux of *Otherwise than Being* is both to allow the vibrations of this echo to reach the reader and for the inscription of its trace to interrupt the all-encompassing assimilation of the saying by the said. This echo is not the resonance of essence or of the saying assimilated by the said: "the said, contesting the abdication of the saying that everywhere occurs in this said, thus maintains the diachrony in which, holding its breath, the spirit hears the echo of the *otherwise*" (AE 76/OB 44).

If subjectivity is my substitution for the other and this substitution is the *signifyingness* of signification, for the text to make sense it is necessary that the "I" *who* writes be himself a substitution, be *assigned*. This does not mean that the "I" sends signs that the reader must decipher. In this *intrigue* with the other, *denouement* does not play a role. This *intrigue* suggests an inextricable relation in which the "I" "se fait signe, s'en va en allégeance." Therefore, it is possible to pose to *Otherwise than Being* the question that Blanchot poses to Beckett's texts: "Who speaks?"[4]

The philosophical book called *Otherwise than Being* has a meaning that at first seems to be nonsense (*contre-sens*). Its aim is to refer what, by definition, cannot be narrated, indeed what escapes the order of narration—the interruption of the logic of essence, or substitution. However, for the text to be able to bear witness to this interruption, a textual substitution must take place *as* writing and *in* writing. This writing is that of "a voice that comes from the other shore," that is no longer the voice of full speech, but of a trace:

The "who?" of saying is not simply a grammatical necessity . . . nor a withdrawal before the paradox of a language that could not be the saying of anyone, that would be the language that speaks and that would hang in the air. It is not the I of the I think, subject of cognition, nor Husserl's pure ego, transcendence in the immanence of intentionality, radiating from this ego (a subject that presupposes the subject-object correlation and refers to the correlation of the saying and the said). The who of saying is inseparable from the *intrigue* proper to speaking (*l'intrigue propre du parler*), and yet it is not the for-itself of idealism, which designates the movement of consciousness returning to itself, where the self consequently is understood as identical to the return movement, a knowing of knowing. Nor is it the pure form in which the Kantian I think appears. Nor the identity of the Hegelian concept, in which, under the apparent naturalness of expressions such as "for oneself," and "by oneself" all the singularity of the recurrence to oneself disappears, a recurrence without rest (*sans repos*)—the genuine problem of the subject. (AE 80, n. 2/OB 190, n. 33, translation modified)

In this passage that reads like a discursive translation of Beckett's *The Unnamable*, Levinas discards all the philosophical figures of the speaking subject in order to affirm that one cannot detach the genuine problem of subjectivity from the *intrigue* of the other that speaking presupposes. The who of saying suggests a recurrence without rest (*sans repos*) and therefore calls for a determination of space other than the one that prevails in ontology. The theme of inwardness must be turned inside out, since this voice comes from the other shore, the outside, and is that of passivity.

A Forgetting Older than the "Forgetting of Being"

If signification extends to both sides of manifestation, language also presents an ambiguous structure. On this side of manifestation, one can conceive language either as a system of nouns, according to the inaugural distinction that Plato's *Cratylus* establishes, or as an excrescence of the verb. According to Levinas, ontology has widely understood language as a system of nouns, and this becomes evident when analyzing the structure of the apophantic utterance in terms of amphibology or ambiguity.

The correlation saying/said is proper to manifestation or apophansis, whose privileged vector is nomination, the reduction of all significations to nouns. This correlation annuls alterity since it rests on the correspondence between verb and noun. Levinas analyzes predication in terms of a partial identification between predicate and subject and shows how designation can be derived from predication to the advantage of the assimilating power of identification—the "this as that." Moreover, even if in identification there is an enigmatic reference to an already said,[5] ontology forgets it and also forgets that "the signification of the saying goes beyond the said." For that reason Levinas is able to claim that ontological difference is not the last: "behind being and its monstration, there is now already heard the resonance of other significations forgotten in ontology" (AE 66/OB 38). For Levinas the difference of ontological difference is a redoubling, since the verbalness of the verb ("the red reddens," or "A is A") does not fully break with the substantiality of the noun: "the said, as a verb, is the essence of essence" (AE 67/OB 39).

It is within this context that art becomes the "preeminent exhibition in which the said is reduced to a pure theme," and that poetry is "productive of song, of resonance and sonority, which are the verbalness of verbs of essence" (AE 68/OB 40). Art is still *exotic*, "isolated, without a world, essence in dissemination," but the schema of rhythm I isolated in "Reality and Its Shadow" becomes a more positive element here, since art exposes the ambiguity of the verb *to be*. Yet in art "the said is reduced to the beautiful, which supports Western ontology" (AE 68/OE 40).

Although Levinas's description of rhythm is purged of the hypnotic overtones we encountered in "Reality and Its Shadow," this is still an eminently classical and partial determination of art whose main goal is to secure the sublime character of the ethical. Art exhibits a reduction of the said to a pure theme since in artistic exhibition the *kérygma* of the said and the signifyingness (*signifiance*) of the saying vanish. If in "Reality and Its Shadow" and in *Totality and Infinity* art failed to reveal being (it "let go the prey for its shadow"), here Levinas seems to endorse a view of art not very different from Heidegger's: the essences of things resound in the work of art. What the poem says is "absorbed in the said," even if this said is "prior to communication." That is, even if being could "manifest itself as already invoked in silent and nonhuman language by the voices of silence, in the *Geläut der Stille*" (AE 211/OB 135), this language would amount to nothing more than a resounding of the said because "any radical nonassemblable diachrony would be excluded" from it (AE 211/ OB 135). Everything seems to indicate that the amphibology that characterizes language, that language is and that the work of art exposes in a superlative way, voids any possibility of thinking the diachronic temporality of the *intrigue* in the poem.

However, there are some indications that the poem's poeticity may allow a hetero-affection as anarchic as that of the ethical saying. Inspiration, witnessing, and prophecy are tropes that refer to the ethical saying. Is poeticity a case of the saying or is the saying a case of poeticity? Levinas does not posit things in these terms, nor does he settle the issue here. He states that the ethical saying "is already a sign made to another, a sign of this giving of signs, that is of this nonindifference, a sign of this impossibility of slipping away and being replaced, of this identity, this uniqueness: here I am" (AE 227/OB 145). In a footnote that immediately follows this passage, he adds: "as a sign given of this signification of signs, proximity also delineates the trope of lyricism: to love by telling one's love to the beloved, the possibility of poetry or art" (AE 227/OB 199). The anarchic ethical saying is the possibility for the origin of poetry. The question remains whether proximity delineates the trope of lyricism or whether *poïesis* delineates the trope of proximity beyond the metaphysical determination of aesthetics.

"*Loosening the Grip of Being*": Ethical Reduction As Writing

Levinas locates the possibility of a saying that exceeds the grasp of the said (although not without being betrayed by it) in the amphibology of language. This betrayal and the irreducible echo of the saying encompass the infrastructure of language or ethicity. In order to expose this infrastructure, Levinas must accomplish a reduction:

It is clear that the verb to be, or the verb to consist, is used in the formulas from these first pages that name the hither side of being. It is also clear that being makes its apparition and shows itself in the said. As soon as saying, on the hither side of being, becomes dictation, it expires or abdicates, in fables and in writing. If being and manifestation go together in the said, it is in fact natural that if the saying on the hither side can show itself, it be said already in terms of being. However, is it necessary, and is it possible that the saying on the hither side be thematized, that is, manifest itself, that it enter into a proposition and a book? The responsibility for another is precisely a saying prior to anything said. The surprising saying which is responsibility for another is against the "winds and tides of being," is an *interruption of essence.* . . . Philosophy makes this astonishing adventure—showing and recounting as an essence—intelligible, by loosening *the grip of being.* A philosopher's effort, and his unnatural position, consists, while showing the hither side, in immediately reducing the eon which triumphs in the said and in the monstration, and, despite the reduction,

retaining an echo of the reduced said in the form of ambiguity, of diachronic expression.
For the saying is both an affirmation and a retraction of the said. . . . It is the
ethical interruption of essence that energizes the reduction. (AE 75/
OB 43–44, my emphasis)

The "for the other" at the heart of the one names the dynamism of
the signifier and the preceding proximity constitutes *le Dire*, saying or
preoriginal language. Language, the structure encompassing both *langue*
and *parole*, bears the trace of this preoriginary language. By referring to
saying (*le dire*) as "la signifiance même de la signification," or "le propos
de l'avant-propos" (AE 6), Levinas stresses the total immersion of the
trace in every part of discourse. Saying, however, cannot be totally contained in the proposition, and while each of its parts accomplishes the
saying's negation, it manages to affirm itself at the same time.

Since the correlation saying/said is the price that any form of manifestation must pay, the distinction between being and entity is already included in the said. And although the said lies and betrays, it does not
contain within itself the whole process of signification; it nonetheless
makes its reduction possible. Language's façade can give access to what
subtracts itself from a system of differences, "the otherwise than being."
Levinas calls this process *ex-ception*, as if it were an obverse of being or its
otherwise. Saying is the *ex-ception* to the said inasmuch as it overflows its
themes while pronouncing them to the other. It is for this reason that
one cannot simply conceive the saying as a non-said, as a part of the said
that remains silent or unspoken. The said is an echo of the saying or
saying is an echo of the reduced said.

Because being is delayed with respect to its own manifestation, its
delay signals a diachrony (*contre-temps*) hidden behind the synchrony that,
in turn, negates a content by affirming its presence. The affirmative utterance accomplishes a negative act in an illocutionary way. Nevertheless,
negation negates the saying without fully capturing it because it is contained within the limits of the proposition, while the saying takes place
even beyond non-being, in a subjectivity that Levinas equates with the
soi-même, understood as nonindifference and restlessness.

This *soi-même* expresses a passivity without agent (as in the French
reflexive pronoun *se*), although it goes beyond this passive/active verbal

reference that is still tied to the understanding of being. This *se* refers to an inner occurrence acting within us and above the reduction that has taken place in the said, or as hidden and implicit language: a pure accusative or pronominal mark that does not depend on a nominative case. With this *se* Levinas refers to the nonspatial site corresponding to subjectivity as the "pure receptivity" of a past never present—the outside (*dehors*). This saying prior to anything said "bears witness to the glory" of infinity (AE 220/OB 145) since it is a "dedication to the other" and therefore "sincerity." This is a saying that does not narrate any manifestation and is thus irreducible to the truth of disclosure. As a nonthematic saying, it is a witnessing or prophecy.

The reduction of "the said to the saying beyond *lógos*" (AE 77/OB 45) is a philosophical operation that Levinas characterizes as the "return of skepticism." Skepticism is a hyperbolic figure of philosophy through which Levinas renders a "return of the diachrony refusing the present" (AE 258/OB 169). The "return of skepticism" after it is refuted allows Levinas to anticipate the objection that would accord discourse the total power to capture and mend any form of interruption (AE 198/OB 155). The philosophical speaking that "betrays in its said the proximity it conveys before us *still remains*, as a saying, a proximity and a responsibility" (AE 257/OB 168, my emphasis). This does not mean that Levinas assumes a skeptical posture, but rather that in the history of philosophy the very movement of the return of an irreducible diachrony is best testified by skepticism's refusal. This is a refusal to synchronize in a single stroke both the implicit affirmation that the saying contains *and* the negation that this affirmation states in a proposition. The force of skepticism's refusal lies in that it "makes a difference and puts an *interval* between saying and the said" (AE 261/OB 168). Ultimately for Levinas "language is *already* skepticism" (AE 263/OB 170) because in it the "two times" of diachrony unfold within it without achieving a final synthesis.

Nevertheless, when Levinas claims that the "impossible simultaneousness of meaning, the nonassemblable but also inseparable one-for-the-other, is an excluded middle signifying as equivocation or an enigma" (AE 258/OB 169), he supplements the hyperbolic figure of skepticism with the *poetic said*. He needs to show that language can exceed the limits of what is thought and that it allows "a possibility of meaning distinct from that which comes to signs from the simultaneity of systems or the logical definition of concepts" (AE 259/OB 170). For Levinas, this possibility is "laid bare in the *poetic said* and the interpretation it calls *for ad infinitum*" (AE 259/OB 170).

The *poetic said* exposes the possibility of a subversion of essence and accomplishes a dismantling of the normative and violent dimension of coherence. The re-traction in the direction of the saying (*le dire*) towards what is prior to the "amphibology of being and entities in the said" (AE 74/OB 4) is thus made possible. Without forcing the argument, it is possible to claim that for Levinas, poetic language is already skepticism in a superlative manner, even if he does not explicitly phrase it in these terms. This can be shown in two ways.

First, because a double temporality exceeding the grasp of discourse can be located in the *poetic said*. This is the dimension of poetic language that Levinas explicitly recognizes and valorizes, but he does so in terms of potentiality. Indeed, the refutation of skepticism, the oppressive dimension of the order of discourse and its refusal of anything that could escape its grasp, is curiously described in terms of a text Levinas only alludes to, Blanchot's *The Madness of the Day*.[6]

Levinas does not explicitly refer to the *poetic said* that lays bare the possibility of an ethical saying. In fact, there is no explicit reference, mention, or quotation of Blanchot's *récit*, but only an *allusion*. It is as if the poetic text were still a silent witness to the glory of the infinite and not the testimony to a different possibility of interrupting the order of discourse. This allusion comes at a very strategic moment; it takes place before Levinas's performative inscription of the ethical saying, an operation *of* writing that marks the ethical interruption of essence (AE 262–63/OB 169). Further, it is placed before the last chapter titled "Outside" ("*Au Dehors*"), in which Levinas elucidates the form of openness that pertains to substitution. Substitution, the master trope of ethics, supposes a "writing of the outside" in which space ceases to be simply the condition for the openness of entities in the light of the day. The outside names an absolute exteriority that Levinas characterizes with the hyperbolic feature of being "out of the world." Can one claim that a *substitution*, a one-for-the-other of literary and philosophical writing, takes place here, even if two pages later Levinas, once again with Heidegger in mind, questions poetry's ability to "reduce rhetoric (the said)"?[7]

Second, from *The Madness of the Day* Levinas *implicitly* takes a set of figures and uses them to describe the order of discourse, as well as to account for the textual principle of his own book. Because the first use of these literary figures responds to a classical philosophical use of tropes, Levinas does not hesitate in qualifying it as a said. This said belongs to ontology and offers a satisfactory description of totality's topology. The second use, however, does not belong to this configuration. It is the poetic saying that, while going unacknowledged, silently provides Levinas with a formal structure to describe and inscribe the ethical saying as what exceeds ontology and totality.

Given the complexity of Levinas's gesture, it is necessary to pay attention to this double use of literary figures. The *poetic said* allows Levinas to describe how discourse accomplishes the mending of the saying's "latent diachrony," what we can call the "first version of interruption":

Coherence thus dissimulates a transcendence, a movement from the one to the other, a latent diachrony, uncertainty and a fine risk.

Are the rendings of the logical text mended by logic alone? It is in the association of philosophy with the State and with medicine that the breakup of discourse is surmounted. The interlocutor that does not yield to logic is threatened with prison or the asylum or undergoes the prestige of the master and the medication of the doctor. . . . The discourse then recuperates its meaning by repression or by mediation. . . . It is through the State that knowledge and force are efficacity. But the State does not irrevocably discount folly, not even the intervals of folly. It does not *untie the knots*, but cuts them. The said thematizes the interrupted dialogue or the dialogue delayed by silences, failure or delirium, but the intervals are not recuperated. Does not the discourse that suppresses the interruptions of discourse by relating them maintain the discontinuity *under the knots with which the thread is tied again?* (AE 263–64/OB 170)

Levinas conveys the violence of coherence, its dissimulation of the *intrigue* in terms of a literary scene that presents the "association of philosophy with the State and with medicine." Repression and mediation appear here under the guise of the ophthalmologist and the psychiatrist, the two figures who interrogate "the interlocutor that does not yield to logic" and, therefore, who resists the complete assimilation of the saying to the said, as well as the violent suppression of the saying. However, Levinas still refers to literary writing as a *said*, without mentioning the interruptive force of Blanchot's *récit* as the *saying* that subtracts itself from the order of discourse.[8] Nevertheless, it is this literary scene that makes it possible to ask whether there is another way of dealing with interruption. Is there "a second version of *interruption*" that does not depend on the violence of coherence, the forceful extraction of a testimony by interrogation, which is precisely how Blanchot figures the coercive nature of the order of discourse and the law of narration?

It is the poetic *saying* that provides Levinas with a formal structure to describe this other version of interruption and to inscribe the ethical saying, since what he is finally proposing is the possibility of understanding interruption as different from interruptions in discourse. Levinas focuses on what discourse represses, on what a conventional version of interruption evacuates, but nonetheless preserves on the underside of its fabric or tissue. Although the pattern or thread of a violent continuity comes to the forefront as the dissimulating effect that the first version of interruption accomplishes, it is the inscription of a no less forceful interruption that sparks Levinas's interest—the series of knots. How does Levinas seek to relate these two series? He must comply with two conditions. First, he must expose the discursive work of interruption, its thread, and show that this is a broken thread unable to fully reduce the knots of interruption. Second, he must interrupt the interruption of discourse and demonstrate that the continuous thread and the knots of interruption no longer relate to each other in terms of simultaneity or correlation.

As can be seen, Levinas's *allusion* to the potentialities of poetic language goes hand in hand with a deployment of a series of *textual* tropes (thread, knots, tissue, and weaving). This deployment makes the ethical reduction of the said possible since in the *poetic said* language suggests "an impossible simultaneousness of meaning" (AE 262/OB 169). It is precisely this simultaneity of meaning that philosophical discourse betrays and that Levinas attempts to write. I will now follow Levinas's deployment of these textual tropes and his performance of the ethical reduction:

Every contesting and interruption of this power of discourse is at once related and invested by discourse (*relatée et invertie*). It therefore recommences as soon as one interrupts it. . . . This discourse will affirm itself as coherent and one. In relating the interruption of discourse or my being ravished by it, *I retie the thread* (*j'en renoue le fil*) . . . and are we not *at this very moment* in the process of barring up the exit which our whole essay is attempting, and encircling our position from all sides? (AE 262/OB 169, my emphasis)

And a few lines further down, within the context of his allusion to *The Madness of the Day*, Levinas states:

The said thematizes the interrupted dialogue or the dialogue delayed by silences, failure or delirium, but the intervals are not recuperated. Does not the discourse that suppresses the interruptions of discourse by relating them maintain the discontinuity under the knots with which *the thread is tied again* (*sous les nœuds où le fil se renoue*)?

The interruptions of discourse found again and recounted in the immanence of the said are conserved like *knots in a thread tied again* (*dans les nœuds d'un fil renoué*), *the trace of a diachrony that does not enter into the present, that refuses simultaneity*.

And I still interrupt the ultimate discourse in which all discourses are stated, in saying it (*en le disant*) to the one that listens to it, and who is situated *outside* the said that the discourse says, outside all it includes. That is true of the discussion I am elaborating *at this very moment*. This reference to an interlocutor permanently breaks through (*perce*) the text that the discourse claims to weave (*tisser*) in thematizing and enveloping all things. (AE 264/OB 170, my emphasis)

The reduction of the said that brings about the *intrigue* of the other takes place in two times (*à contre-temps*) (AE 76/OB 44), which as I noted at the beginning of this chapter, is the double movement of Levinas's quasi-narrative: to inscribe an intrigue of the other and to welcome it. In the first moment, Levinas relates the interruptions according to the temporality of the said (*le dit*), that is, according to the order of discourse and ontology. The ethical interruption of ontology leaves its marks, but as soon as one attempts to fill them with some content they are tied back to the order of discourse and lose their ethical force. *At this very moment,* Levinas is describing what is taking place when he attempts to exceed the order of discourse, but he is also accomplishing ("*I retie the thread*" [*j'en renoue le fil*]) what he is describing. From the viewpoint of discourse's totality, interruption fails. However, in the second moment of the reduction it is possible to locate an alteration and displacement that produces an excessive remainder, "the trace of a diachrony that does not enter into the present, that refuses simultaneity."

The repetition of Levinas's gesture under the heading of the *at this very moment* interrupts the recounting of interruptions in the immanence of the said and makes it possible to preserve them "like knots in a thread tied again (*dans les nœuds d' un fil renoué*)." Levinas's repetition interrupts the expository line of his argument and this interruption is preserved at a different level than that of a philosophical exposition. The interruptions of the said (discourse, ontology, knowledge, narration) occur as the tearing of a continuous tissue or fabric now preserved in a discontinuous surface in which the series of interruptions can no longer be retied by the unifying thread of discourse. Further, the reduction interrupts these series of interruptions by *saying* it to the interlocutor, to the other. The final interruption takes place under the modality of the address (*parole donné*) that is prior to the language of ontology, the saying of the *intrigue* of the other: an adjacent supplement that keeps the two series out of sync.[9]

Levinas refers to this supplement with a different series of tropes (breath, breathing and inspiration), as if to stress its nontextual nature. It is the "restlessness of respiration" (AE 276/OB 180) that keeps the series of the mended thread, the recuperated interruptions in the said, and the series of knots (the saying as interruptions of the said) separated and in constant animation. This chain of tropes brings about an "emphatic mutation" of the aesthetic category of rhythm that now becomes ethical. The alienating force of aesthetic rhythm becomes the ethical trope of substitution. The interlocutor, the other who comes from the outside, is "a fission of the subject beyond lungs. It is a fission of the self, or the self as fissibility" (AE 277/OB 180).

Levinas reverses the classic values of breathing as the sign of a vital force and transforms it instead into the movement by which "I already open myself to my subjection to the whole of the invisible other (*à tout l' autre invisible*)" (AE 278/OB 181). The final reduction of the said, the one that keeps the "two versions of interruption" apart, is "the breathing opening to the other and signifying to the other in its very signifyingness" (AE 278/OB 181). The ethical reduction is not a punctual movement, but rather an "incessant unsaying of the said"(AE 278/OB 181).

Allusion

Levinas invokes the poetic said *at this very moment* in which he determines language as "skepticism" and energizes his ethical reduction of discourse through a textual matrix that bears striking similarities with *The Madness of the Day*. In *Otherwise than Being* the destiny of the "possibility (*vertu*) of the *poetic said*" unfolds on the hither side or beyond the region that in *Existence and Existents* Levinas called "existence without world." It is also no longer simply cast as a shadow, as in "Reality and Its Shadow," but envisioned as a "parole donnée." However, while in *Existence and Existents* Levinas acknowledges Blanchot's "description of the *il y a*" by explicitly referring to *Thomas the Obscure* (EE 103, n. 1), in *Otherwise than Being* he does not mention *The Madness of the Day*.

It is crucial to consider the reasons for Levinas's discretion. Inasmuch as the allusion functions under a double register, the possibility of poetic language falls on the side of the said (*le dit*) and thematization (order of discourse). However, a textual grafting takes place in *Otherwise than Being*; the matrix of a double law that unfolds in *The Madness of the Day* becomes the model of the ethical reduction of the said and the possibility of a word whose spacing subtracts itself from the law of discourse (totality, the same). In the *poetic said* Levinas localizes a double temporality that could potentially exceed discourse's power of assimilation. It is this dimension of poetic language that Levinas explicitly recognizes and values under the heading of "possibility" (*vertu*). Levinas describes the refutation of skepticism, the oppressive dimension of the order of discourse and its rejection of anything that could escape its grasp in terms of *The Madness of the Day*. He alludes to this text at a strategic moment, before the performative inscription of the ethical saying, an operation *of* writing that marks the ethical interruption of essence (AE 262–63/OB 169) and before the last chapter titled "Outside" (*Au Dehors*), in which Levinas elucidates the form of openness that pertains to substitution, an ethical form of openness different from Heidegger's "letting be."

As I described in detail above, because the first use of these literary figures responds to a classical philosophical treatment of tropes, Levinas does not hesitate to qualify it as a *said*; it belongs to ontology and offers a satisfactory description of totality's topology. The second use, however, does not belong to this configuration. We could call it a poetic *saying* that, while going, silently provides Levinas with a formal structure to describe and inscribe the ethical saying as what exceeds ontology and totality. The *poetic said* allows Levinas to describe how discourse accomplishes the mending of the saying's "latent diachrony," what we may call the "first version of interruption": "coherence thus dissimulates a transcendence, a movement from the one to the other, a latent diachrony, uncertainty and a fine risk"(AE 263–64/OB 170).

Levinas conveys the violence of coherence and its dissimulation of the *intrigue* in terms of a literary scene that presents the "association of philosophy with the State and with medicine." However, Levinas still circumscribes the *possibility* of poetic writing to a said, without mentioning or elucidating the interruptive force of Blanchot's *récit* as the saying that subtracts itself from the order of discourse. This literary scene, that strictly speaking is neither literary nor aesthetic, allows Levinas to question whether another way of dealing with interruption is possible. Is there a second version of interruption that does not depend on the violence of coherence, the forceful extraction of a testimony by interrogation, which is precisely how Blanchot figures the coercive nature of the order of discourse and the law of narration?

It is as if the language of *Otherwise than Being*, which shows a different understanding of its own operations than that of *Totality and Infinity*, were making peace with poetic writing. One can claim that a *substitution* of "poetic" and "philosophical" writing has taken place. Yet doubts still remain, given Levinas's discrete acknowledgment of the "possibility" (*vertu*) of literary language to unsay the said. The only way to dispel these doubts is by supplementing Levinas's allusion with a reading of his 1975 essay "Exercises on *The Madness of the Day*."[10] However, to do so entails shifting away from discretion and into the concept of *ingratitude*, a concept in which Levinas ciphers an ethics of reading.

SEVEN

The Unerasable Difference
(Levinas in Blanchot)

Thus there are not two discourses: there is discourse—and then there would be dis-course, were it not that of it we 'know' practically nothing. We 'know' that it escapes systems, order, possibility, including the possibility of language, and that writing, perhaps—writing, where totality has let itself be exceeded—puts it in play.

—*Maurice Blanchot*, The Writing of the Disaster

Thinking otherwise than he thinks, he thinks in such a way that the Other might come to thought, as approach and response.

—*Maurice Blanchot*, The Writing of the Disaster

Although the friendship between Levinas and Blanchot is known to have begun in the mid-1920s when they were both students in Strasbourg and spanned several decades,[1] for Blanchot their relationship cannot be simply reduced to a series of facts or episodes. "Friendship" names a relation to the other that exceeds the forms of "influence," "priority" and "misinterpretation":

We must give up trying to know those to whom we are linked by something essential; by this I mean we must greet them in *the relation with the unknown* in which they greet us as well, in our distance (*éloignement*). Friendship, this relation without dependence, without episode, yet in which all the simplicity of life enters, passes by way of the recognition of the common strangeness that does not allow us to speak of our friends but only to speak to them, not to make them a topic of conversations (or essays), but the movement of understanding in which, speaking to us, they reserve, even on the most familiar terms, an *infinite distance*, the *fundamental separation* on the basis of which *what separates becomes relation*. (A 328/F 29)[2]

"Friendship" is therefore one of the knots of the *intrigue of the other* because it supposes the nonreciprocal relation between Blanchot and Levinas. Deploying many of the same terms that in *The Infinite Conversation* describe the relation to the other, for Blanchot friendship is a "relation of the third kind" in which the encounter between two persons opens to a radical otherness, outside or neuter. Blanchot's elucidation of this relation takes place through a "conversation" with Levinas's *Totality and Infinity*.

The purpose of this chapter is to articulate how Levinas's and Blanchot's texts encounter each other and leave an indelible mark, *an unerasable difference*, on the intrigue of the other. Although they take a common experience (the *il y a* and its nocturnal determinations) and philosophical horizon as their point of departure, they also diverge in fundamental ways. "Friendship," the figure of their encounter, supposes that what one "gives" the other be reinscribed in another space. What follows is an assessment of how in speaking *to* the friend the movement of understanding preserves "the *infinite distance*, the *fundamental separation* on the basis of which *what separates becomes relation*" (A 328/F 29).

What Blanchot gives Levinas as a question for thinking is the other that (poetic) writing releases in a modality that is not manifestation but the night, the neuter, the outside, and the disaster. Although writing is a concept for which Levinas has no decisive place in his philosophy, the question of poetic writing, as we saw in the previous chapters, constantly surfaces in his thinking. How does Levinas finally respond to this question?

What Levinas gives Blanchot is the question of the other as ethics, which manifests itself in the face of the other human being, bearer of the trace of transcendence. Even though the question of the other as the approach of the other human being is not crucial for Blanchot, its ethical force imposes itself in *The Infinite Conversation*. This text marks an important turning point in how Blanchot conceives the alterity of writing and the task of thinking. How does Blanchot think the human dimension of Levinasian ethics?

The Question of Writing

Readers of Blanchot know that his texts present numerous difficulties. His questioning and disruption of the ontology of writing disarms criticism, inasmuch as one of Blanchot's most decisive effects is the dismantling of the Romantic myth of literature. By interrogating literature's essential concepts and figures (work, author as source of expression, the relation of writing to the world), Blanchot undermines all the certainties on which to ground a critical commentary.[3] Deprived of these critical certainties, the interpreter comes face to face with Blanchot's strange materiality of writing.

Blanchot's reflections on the question of writing belong neither to literary theory nor to philosophy proper but to a space difficult to categorize since it points to what resists categorization itself. However, this resistance is not due to the ineffable character of his writing. Blanchot is far from subscribing to a mystical conception of language. The resistance is due to the fact that one must think and write language's materiality as the underside of categories. Critical discourse struggles with Blanchot's constant transgression of conventional discursive genres or modes and it has responded to this situation in two distinct ways.

First, by positing the need to bracket Blanchot's own reflections on literature in order to dismantle the textual operations of his fictional writing (most commonly of the *récits*). This approach presupposes that one can separate his "reflexive" and "fictional" texts along clear lines and thus accommodate the heterogeneity of Blanchot's writing according to this binary distinction. The pitfall lies in that this approach cannot elaborate protocols for reading the specificity of both types of texts. It also has trouble when attempting to think their peculiar interdependence, whose modalities cover a wide range: motivation, remotivation, translation, retranslation, allusion, intertextual and intratextual reference, to mention just a few.

In spite of a cautious attempt to guarantee an autonomous experience of reading sensitive to the movements of Blanchot's prose, this approach has to transgress its own principle, since the need to refer to Blanchot's "literary thinking" is unavoidable. It can also only limit itself to one task: to provide the reader with a repertoire of the transgressions that Blanchot's writing commits against the hermeneutic code. Blanchot thus becomes unreadable inasmuch as "it is at the very first stage of reading—the constitution of a fictional universe in the reader's imagination or its 'concretization'—that the hermeneutic *challenge* takes place."[4] Underlying this claim is the fact that when a hermeneutic reading fails to grasp or to make sense, it begins to use only one ear, attuned to the difficulties and noises affecting comprehension and understanding.

In this sense Brian Fitch's conclusion is irreproachable: Blanchot's *récits* are unreadable, and the only task left is to mark those places where the text "does not work" (LR 14). If one conceives this "not working" in a traditional manner, as a deficiency or opacity that the critic fails to bring to light, then one risks missing the peculiar type of negativity at play in Blanchot, as well as the crucial interruption of working and the work (*désœuvrement*) that the text performs. In other words, if the text "does not work," the critic has to do more than simply resign himself; he must propose a positive elaboration of the regime of the "unworking" and of the type of reading that this "unworking" entails. This does not mean that one has to make the interruption of meaning signify, even if one determines it in a negative way (as nonsignification).

"Unworking" is not simply a negative movement; it does not fall under the jurisdiction of nihilism and does not lead into silence or paralysis.[5] My claim is that by subtracting the space of writing from the jurisdiction of classical and romantic aesthetics, a "literature of good taste" destined to "rule [the world] in view of strengthening your self,"[6] Blanchot opens up writing's ethical and political dimension. In Blanchot writing obliges us to come face to face with the unknown without reducing it to what is already familiar.[7] It also makes possible an exposure to the unknown that contests the totalizing claims of technical rationality and power. This interruption of power is decisive in order to assess how Blanchot's writing is relevant for a thinking of community and politics.

If Blanchot interrupts the myth of literature (a romantic invention) and his writing engages the very possibility of politics, why refer to him as the "last Romantic," as some critics do?[8] What is at stake in this expression, above all if "Romanticism" names the interruption of the Enlightenment? For these claims to be feasible, Blanchot would have to belong to something like "romanticism" as an "unfinished project." However, the incompleteness would also decompose the concepts of end and finality. This would indeed be a strange romanticism that exceeded historical and literary categories, unless "romanticism," now a preromantic "romanticism," neither logically nor chronologically prior to what it predates, became a way of rendering more familiar what Blanchot refers to as "effroyablement ancien." When applied to Blanchot, "romanticism" would therefore be a way of naming an anarchic principle "older" than the principles of sufficient reason and identity: what resists assimilation and is the strange par excellence, the neuter, the outside and the disaster. The term "romantic" is clearly misguided here and does not do justice (justice being also a matter of *ratio*) to the formidable alteration of temporality that Blanchot's writing puts into play.[9]

Another way of approaching Blanchot and of circumventing the shortcomings of a hermeneutically grounded reading is to posit the interdependence of his two different types of texts. An observation such as "the *récits* are riddled with theoretical reflections"[10] acknowledges the difficulties in any approach to Blanchot. It also alerts us to the impracticality of bracketing Blanchot's "literary thinking." Nevertheless, it also runs the risk of situating him within the space of theory, which his writing constantly questions and exceeds. What could be more alien to *theória*, the realm of optical intelligibility, than Blanchot's writing? No theoretical considerations are grafted into Blanchot's *récits* since theory does not illuminate what writing "is" about. The reason why Collin's claim is alien to Blanchot lies in the external, albeit intimate, center of writing. This is an unlocatable point that announces itself as the *question of writing* and that eludes direct apprehension.

This question is an "exigency" that does not take the form of "what is" nor treat language as an object of reflection. And because it eludes identity, writing is refractory to the theoretical question. In summary, for Blanchot writing is irreducible to theory because they belong to different economies:

To write as a question of writing (*écrire comme question d'écrire*), question that bears the writing that bears the question, no longer allows you this relation to being—understood in the first place as tradition, order, certainty, truth, any form of rootedness—that you received one day from the past of the world, domain you have been called upon to govern in order to strengthen your "Self," although this was as if fissured, since the day when the sky opened upon its void.

I will try in vain to represent him to myself, he who I was not and who, without wanting to, began to write, writing (and knowing it then) in such a way that the pure product of doing nothing was introduced into the world and into his world. That happened "at night." During the day there were the daytime acts, the day to day words, the day to day writing, affirmations, values, habits, nothing that counted and yet something that one had confusedly to call life. The certainty that in writing he was putting between parentheses precisely this certainty, including the certainty of himself as the subject of writing, led him slowly, though right away, into an empty space whose void (the barred zero, heraldic) in no way prevented the turns and detours of a very long process. (PAD[11] 9/SNB 2, translation modified)

Writing is in question because it is the question *of* writing, and this intertwining of the question and of writing will preclude any claim to an inner substance from which to render writing as an object of comprehension. Moreover, no self-reflection is at play in this reciprocal implication, since no identity preexists it. This coimplication is enacted in the syntactical turns of its formulation by the symmetrical scansion of "écrire/ écrire" and "question/question," a reversal that alters both terms. The syntactical turns of this formulation subordinate, in an appositive position, the elucidation or determination of the question to the passivity of writing.

   In its absolute economy, the fragment cited above ties together several essential motifs in Blanchot. Among them is writing's intransitivity, understood as violence to representation, as well as its subordination to the ideologies of commitment, expression and reproduction of that very same order.[12] Writing liberates a nonintentional dimension that introduces a certain type of negativity in the realm of possibility. It also accomplishes a double bracketing of its own certainty and of intentional consciousness.

   A movement of comings and goings in an empty space articulates Blanchot's *récits*. The fragment, a sort of primal scene of writing, combines a discursive reflection on writing with a seemingly autobiographical narrative; seemingly, because writing reduces or brackets what one normally calls "life." The "question of writing," therefore, is the form that the exigency of the "otherwise than being" takes in Blanchot and that compels him to put into question all the values of presence. Although Blanchot accedes to the "question of writing" by means of literature, his response unfolds in a space adjacent to philosophy.

Blanchot and Philosophical Discourse

To write in ignorance of the philosophical horizon . . . is necessarily to write with facile complacency.

—*Maurice Blanchot,* The Writing of the Disaster

The negativity inassimilable to the order of discourse in Blanchot's writing bears witness to the end of theory's hegemony and disturbs all critical assumptions. If his writing transgresses literary and discursive genres, would a philosophical reading of Blanchot be able to "preserve" the other as other? Is the philosopher better equipped than the literary critic to approach the "other space without direction" in which "knowledge" inscribes itself, without committing treason against the other, as Odysseus did when faced with the Sirens' song?[13]

In "Le 'Discours Philosophique'" Blanchot questions the very possibility of philosophy and asks "if what one still calls by this name, and that perhaps has already disappeared, can be written."[14] At issue here is the status of philosophical language and by extension philosophy's fate. Blanchot asks whether the use of an eloquent language can accomplish this task, or "if it would have to be used in such a way as to withdraw its powers of direct or immediate signification from it in order to equate it to what it nonetheless wishes to say" (DP 1).[15] Blanchot is quick to point out that what is said indirectly traditionally belongs to the domain of "literature." Could the saying of "literature," characterized by detours and tropes, become a model for a philosophical discourse in search of a nontraditional language? Blanchot categorically rejects this option. As soon as the propriety of philosophical language is in question, one cannot simply sustain the validity of literature, which is itself a philosophical concept. One can only gain insight about the nature of this language by changing the form of the question: "perhaps there is no philosophy and one can also doubt the validity of the word literature" (DP 2). After canceling out both concepts and after exposing how philosophy's language determines the concept of literature, Blanchot refers to a very peculiar type of speech (*parole*):

The philosopher is always the man of a double speech: there is what he says aimed to prolong the infinite discourse, but behind what he says, there is something that withdraws him from words. This *dis-course* precisely without right, without signs, illegitimate, of bad omen, obscene and always of deception and rupture is, at the same time, by passing beyond any proscription, what is closest to the intransgressible Outside. . . . The philosopher must respond to this other speech. Speech of the other, that he however cannot render. (DP 2)

The inscription of this "double speech" appears at the very heart of philosophical language and is presented by a marker, a hyphen or *trait d'union*. This marker affects the function of the prefix "dis-" as signifier of continuity and unification (*discourse*: running about) and transforms it into what interrupts the "normal course" of affairs, the order of discourse. The prefix "dis-" (opposition, privation, exclusion and absence) comes to affect language in an unaffected way, and the philosopher must respond to this discrete alteration. The force of this interruption is that of an anarchic law introducing an unsettling responsibility. The philosopher must respond, but he cannot communicate this response since this speech does not belong to the realm of power: "here is a feature (*trait*) one must retain: philosophical discourse is first without rights. It says everything or could say the totality (*ou pourrait tout dire*), but it does not have the power to say it: it is something possible without power" (DF 1, my emphasis). The feature (*trait*) that one should retain is precisely marked by the *trait d'union*, although for philosophy this is an impossibility since it is the trace (*trait*) that withdraws the right to retention, the right to speak about what exceeds power. In other words, the *trait d'union* marks what affects philosophy and transforms it into something "possible without power."

What would something "possible without power" look like? Perhaps it would look like writing, given that the inscription of the "double speech" through an interrupting *trait d'union* introduces us to the question of the neuter (*neutre*): "a principle of paucity and excess; suspension and alteration; effacement and proliferation; a 'concept' whose aim is to conceptualize that which precedes all concepts."[16] The *trait d'union* performs what is left unthought by the philosopher's speech. The *trait* effaces the very marks of its interruption and reinscribes the terms in a quasi-conceptual space: neither philosophical, nor properly speaking, literary. Blanchot links writing to the neuter by using a *trait d'union* that enact the "unworking" of the neuter, and thus indicates "by a detour, in its own resistance to naming, the unthinkable and impossible margin of thought itself, the alterity that is at the origin of all thought as such."[17]

What is the duplicitous nature of this "double speech"? Blanchot employs a spatial figure in order to explain this question. He states that it affects discourse "from behind," in an illegitimate way, outside of what the former states about things. In other words, it affects the propositional dimension, the logical articulations allowing thematization and comprehension and the correlation between consciousness and its object. Because of its duplicitous nature, this speech "withdraws speech," but even so this affection cannot be taken as the subtraction of a given content.[18] Behind the supposed master discourse emerges "something that surprises, frightens, disturbs" (DF 3); for this "speech of the Other" to emerge, the philosopher must withdraw himself from the position of mastery. In order to welcome the speech of the other one must become the "last man" (*dernier homme*), since it is a "speech that, in any case, does not make our life easy and with which one cannot live" (DP 4).

As in Blanchot's homonymous *récit*,[19] the "last man," the dying convalescent man at the end of a life that prolongs itself indefinitely, is the figure of unapproachable death in life, of the death than one cannot die or accomplish. The "last man" is also confronted by an impersonality opening the self to an unknown outside that is, at the same time, menacing and fascinating. This "last man," therefore, points to a dimension of nonpower, and the philosopher is, regarding language, exposed to the same "experience" as he who wanders in an "empty space" (WD 9). He is no longer a vigilant consciousness able to synthesize an absolute knowledge, the master of language, but a totally unknown other whose intrigue with the neuter affects language. "Double speech" thus interrupts discourse by opening it to a radical heterogeneity.

Levinas Reading Blanchot

As we saw in previous chapters, Levinas locates a dimension of speech that exceeds totality and interrupts the order of discourse. He even goes so far as to make explicit some of its features in the proximity of a literary text, Leiris's *Biffures*, highlighting a logics of the crossing out, erasing or bifurcation not unlike the obscene *dis-course* that Blanchot places under the heading of the neuter. Moreover, Levinas implemented this unheard of writing in defiance of the principle of identity and binary logic as the only possibility for writing the other, that is, for an ethical writing. He did so by a complex intertextual grafting of Blanchot's *récit*, *The Madness of the Day*, to which he alluded in rather discrete ways. However, he also continues to express reservations regarding poetic language's access to the ethical relation. Is Levinas's thinking, oriented as it is toward an ethicity breaching totality, in a better position to approach Blanchot's writing? Are his texts up to the task of hearing this "double speech" that points to the hither side of being?

In the previous chapter I claimed that although Levinas was skeptical of poetic language's ethical dimension, Blanchot's texts proved to be an exception. The exemplary status of Blanchot in Levinas's texts, which span a twenty-year period, is also fraught with ambiguity. Levinas at first situates Blanchot within a philosophical context (the end of philosophy, the end of art, the closure of the System—a Hegelo-Kojèvian context) and then gradually places him within a space that is neither philosophical nor aesthetic. Levinas must first come to terms with writing's excessive dimension and redefine the scope of "poetry." Although he approaches Blanchot's writing in terms of ethics as "first philosophy," there are important differences in the way in which the former conceptualizes language; these differences unfold in three essays Levinas publishes between 1956 and 1975, later collected in *Sur Maurice Blanchot*.[20]

Levinas gives credence to a critical account according to which Blanchot would be the signpost of a "way out of Heidegger," a path that his own thinking sets as a goal in the early *De l'évasion*. The effects of this approach are still visible today in intellectual histories, as well as in more analytical works.[21] And although this account finds its justification in Blanchot's own critique of Heidegger, it hides as much as it reveals. It is within the context of this critical account that a certain term marks a point of total divergence between Levinas and Blanchot: the neuter.

For Levinas it names the impersonality of pure being (*il y a*) and the violent realm of ontology (including Heidegger's fundamental ontology) from which the other becomes the only way out and the only true process of *de-neutralization*. For Blanchot it indicates a space of subtraction from being that thinking must preserve in its radical alterity, without recourse to any form of presence. To be unable to endure the emptiness of the neuter entails a failure for thinking: the inability to respond to the injunction to keep watch on the other.

In his seminal "The Poet's Vision" Levinas attempts to situate the peculiarity of Blanchot's writing: "Blanchot's reflection on art and literature has the highest ambitions. . . . The book [*The Space of Literature*] is, in fact, situated beyond all critique and all exegesis" (SMB 9/PN[22] 127). Levinas is careful to point to the peculiar nature of Blanchot's writing and to stress its distance from traditional criticism or commentary. This approach to Blanchot and the concepts Levinas deploys to situate his writing recall Heidegger's attempts to displace traditional categories grounding classical exegesis or interpretations of artworks, as we saw throughout chapters 2 and 3. This displacement takes place when Heidegger tries to demarcate *Dichtung* from the traditional metaphysics of art.[23] Between the Heideggerian strategy of displacement and Levinas's reenactment there are major differences, however. While Heidegger elaborates a "space" adjacent to the metaphysics of art, Levinas seems to get caught midway.

Levinas begins by establishing a hierarchy according to which Blanchot's treatment of the literary work would belong to the proximity of philosophy. This dimension does not fully coincide with philosophy's traditional placement since, according to Levinas, Blanchot's writing does not belong to philosophy. Does this differentiation amount to recognizing the irreducibility of Blanchot's writing to philosophical discourse? Does it point to what takes place *for* philosophy in this writing?[24] Before answering these questions, it is necessary to make the two basic predicates of Levinas's reading explicit and to focus on its overall teleology.

After situating the peculiarity of Blanchot's writing, Levinas claims that "Blanchot determines writing as a quasi mad structure in the general economy of being, by which being is no longer an economy, as it no longer possesses, when approached through writing, any *abode*—no longer has any *interiority* (*aucune habitation, ne comporte aucune intériorité*)" (SMB 17/ PN 133, my emphasis). This statement expresses an ambiguous assessment of writing. On the one hand, writing exceeds the restricted economy of being and is conceived as something radically strange. On the other, writing does not entail inwardness and a dwelling, the two crucial concepts that for Levinas constitute the possibility of the face-to-face with the other.[25] We must recall that this essay was published in 1956, at the time Levinas was writing *Totality and Infinity* and that, consequently, the principles guiding his reading are those he outlined in "Reality and Its Shadow" and in some of the essays that make up the basic argument of *Totality and Infinity*.[26] Let's look closely at how Levinas determines the singularity of Blanchot's writing:

It is literary space, that is, absolute exteriority: the exteriority of absolute exile. . . . Modern art speaks of nothing but the adventure of art itself. . . . No doubt the critical and philosophical work, relating that adventure, is far below art, which is the voyage into the end of the night itself, and not merely the travel narrative. And yet Blanchot's research *brings to the philosopher a "category" and a new "way of knowing" that I would like to clarify, independently of the philosophy of art proper*. (SMB 18/PN 133, my emphasis)

At first, Levinas recognizes that writing exceeds the frames of "the general economy of being" as well as philosophical discourse, since no discourse operating under the law of the same would be able to approach its specificity or absolute exteriority. There is therefore agreement between Levinas and Blanchot on the question of writing. Yet in spite of all the precautions Levinas takes, such as his use of quotation marks to signal the impropriety of certain philosophical concepts within this context, he ultimately recuperates what exceeds or resists philosophical conceptuality. He does so by a double movement whose necessity is systematic.

The first turn of this appropriating movement is marked by a lexical slippage; Levinas begins by referring to writing (*écriture*) and concludes in the realm of *art*. As soon as he conflates writing and *art*, he activates the legitimacy of a philosophical approach to art (even if Levinas's clarification functions "independently of the philosophy of art proper").[27] The second turn in this movement consists of a reduction and final appropriation of what by Levinas's own definition seems to resist appropriation. The appropriated excess is put to work against philosophy itself (Heidegger), but this confrontation takes place within philosophy's economy, as could not be otherwise: Blanchot's search is thus profitable for the philosopher. If in "Reality and Its Shadow" the work of art had no claim whatsoever on knowledge since it "[let] go of the prey for the shadow" (CPP 12), Blanchot's writing now provides the philosopher with a *new way of knowing.*"

At stake for Levinas is the function he assigns to art/*writing*, according to the oscillation noted in his own account: "Does Blanchot not attribute to art the function of uprooting the Heideggerian universe? Does not the poet, before the 'eternal streaming of the outside,' hear the voices that call away from the Heideggerian world?" (SMB 25/PN 139) Levinas's *telos* (Blanchot as a way out of Heidegger) determines his reading and dilutes the complexity of Blanchot's relationship to Heidegger.[28] In Levinas's thinking Blanchot is a writer who evolves from an early Hegelian phenomenological position in the 1940s to a late Heideggerian in the 1950s and finally leaves Heidegger behind. Blanchot thus marks an escape from the thinking of Being, and although Levinas draws the outline of his own trajectory through Blanchot, it is still not clear whether this escape leads to an ethical thought understood as "first philosophy" (SMB 22/PN 137).[29]

Levinas attenuates the complexity of Blanchot's relation to Heidegger, which cannot be interpreted simply as carrying out a transformation of the "thinking of Being" into *ethics*.[30] Since *Being and Time* there is in Heidegger a thread where the other is thought not simply in terms of difference, but also of nearness (*nähe*). Such thinking intensifies with the so-called *Kehre* and, above all, with the thinking of the "neighborness" of *Denken* and *Dichtung*. This thinking produces the reconfiguration of the former in terms of another reading of *lógos* and elicits other forms of rationality beyond the logocentric tradition and instrumental reason proper to *Ge-Stell*, the essence of technology. This reconfiguration reaches its peak in *On the Way to Language*, in which a collision between the thought of difference and the thought of nearness (*nähe*) can be detected. This tension indicates that in the "differend" between identity and difference, the pressure of an "element" that allows the play of difference is "felt" without necessarily unfolding in it. In other words, in the last Heidegger it is possible to read the protosyntax of an alterity that transforms the economy of being into a secondary dimension.

Levinas's elaboration of ethics as "first philosophy" includes a strong critique of Heidegger's thinking that obfuscates the complexity of the German philosopher's thinking on nearness and conceals Levinas's own debt to him.[31] No less important in questioning Levinas's account is the fact that, as we will see below, Blanchot will find the term *ethics* to be an inappropriate concept to refer to the "rapport tout autre."[32] Blanchot, in fact, tries to separate his elaboration of the question of the other from Levinas's, and this move will not only activate the whole graphics of Heidegger's *Ent-fernung*, but also exploit the question of the ontological difference that takes him to a radical exploration of language.

It is possible to detect a shift in Levinas from the use of descriptive language to a more evaluative one when he attempts to specify Blanchot's understanding of writing:

To write is to return to essential language, which consists in moving things aside in words, and echoing being. . . . To be is to speak, but in the absence of any interlocutor. An impersonal speech without "you," without address, without vocative, and yet distinct from the "coherent discourse" which manifests a Universal Reason belonging to the order of the Day. (SMB 15/PN 130–31)

Although Levinas acknowledges that writing does not fully belong to totality, he juxtaposes writing and speech by characterizing writing as a speech that occurs in the interlocutor's absence and thus asserts the non-ethical nature of writing. Levinas reinforces this view when he adds that the two basic modalities of ethical speech—interpellation and the vocative—do not belong to writing. In other words, Levinas evaluates Blanchot's writing from the perspective of the conceptuality elaborated in *Totality and Infinity*.

Levinas returns to Blanchot ten years later in "The Servant and His Master" (1966), which includes a reading of Blanchot's *L'Attente, l'oubli* and marks a major shift in conceptuality.[33] Levinas's understanding of language and poetic writing in *Otherwise than Being* are crucial to his reassessment.[34] Blanchot's text challenges Hegelian dialectics, says Levinas:

L'Attente l'oubli denies the philosophical language of interpretation, which "speaks incessantly," the dignity of being and ultimate language. To seek—beyond the poetic discourse that expresses, dispersedly, the impossible escape from discourse—the *lógos* that gathers, is to block the opening through which the circularity of coherent discourse announces (but also denounces, and in so doing transcends) itself. Could one not venture further, and think what speech wants to say? *And perhaps we are wrong in using the designation art and poetry for that exceptional event, that sovereign forgetting that liberates language with respect to the structures in which the said maintains itself.* Perhaps Hegel was right as far as art is concerned. What counts—*whether it be called poetry or what you will*—is that a meaning be able to proffer itself beyond the closed discourse of Hegel; that a meaning that forgets the presuppositions of that discourse becomes *fable.* (SMB 33/PN 143, my emphasis)

Levinas situates Blanchot's text "after Hegel" and, more importantly, announces that his writing no longer belongs to the space of "art." In spite of Levinas's lack of specificity regarding the status of that space, this statement marks a distance from "The Poet's Vision," where he conflated the space of art with that of writing (*écriture*) and without assessing their difference in Blanchot.

What is traditionally called art or poetry becomes an "exceptional event" in which saying (*le dire*) exceeds the propositional dimension of language (*le dit*) and no longer amounts to a "return to essential language, which consists in moving things aside in words, and echoing being." As we saw in the previous chapter, in *Otherwise than Being* Levinas elucidates the preontological (ethical) "essence" of language, referred to as the saying (*le dire*). This saying is understood as the "one-for-the-other" or proximity (exposition of the one to the other) and, fundamentally, as "*exception* from being." However, this exception can only take place in a said (*le dit*), a propositional utterance that synchronizes and thematizes the irreducibility of saying to the other. In this sense, the saying is translated and, therefore, betrayed by and in its said. This betrayal must show itself in the said for Levinas, since it amounts to an indication of the excess of saying over manifestation, of the play of (un)-veiling (*alêtheia*) that characterizes Heidegger's understanding of the essence of language.

The excess of language over its own apophantic dimension takes the form of a noncorrelation between the saying and the said in what Levinas calls the saying's diachrony, "a signification in which what is signified is not a 'something' identified in the theme of the said" (AE 30/OB 15). But how can a language that, as Levinas affirms, uses and abuses the verb *to be*, as in *Otherwise than Being*, show the excess of this enclosure of language, even while betraying it? The solution to what appears to be an impasse lies in a movement of reduction that will "show the saying's proper signification independently of the said's thematization" (AE 34/OB 19).

In spite of the Husserlian provenance of this concept, the reduction does not take place at once. Levinas's reduction is a generalized and not a discrete occurrence since its interruptive force must "insist" on the recurrence of the ethical saying. In this sense it is linked to the return of skepticism, even after its refutation: "[reduction] must keep, under the modes of diachronic expression, that Said of which the Saying is, at the same time, affirmation and retraction. It is a question of a reduction that feeds the ethical interruption of essence"(AE 35/OB 20) with its energy. As I showed in the previous chapter, the "return of skepticism," the figure of the irreducible nature of reduction, is framed by an allusion to Blanchot's literary writing.

This reduction is also not simply a methodological movement, but an operation of writing. Therefore it is not sufficient to expose the reduction of the saying to the said through a said (a description regulated by discursive presentation). The reduction has "to take place," has to be marked and remarked in order to "welcome" the excess of ontology, in spite of its being written in and by the language of ontology: "philosophical saying that betrays in its Said the proximity that it translates before us remains inasmuch as Saying, as proximity and responsibility. This is said to the other who is outside a theme. This return that resists the present constitutes the invincible force of skepticism" (AE 260–61/OB 168–69). In this context, skepticism is a figure for diachrony, the immemorial and anarchic temporality of an irreducible, unassimilable and unsynchronisable "double speech."

It is within the context of reading Blanchot that Levinas considers "poetic" writing an ethical event whose features are comparable to those of the ethical saying. Poetic language now "signals to us, without the sign's bearing a meaning by giving up meaning" (PN 147).[35] In a footnote that still shows a certain reticence toward the poetic and precludes him from making this claim explicitly, Levinas clarifies what he understands by "poetry":

I have already said above, that the word poetry, to me, means the rupture of the immanence to which language is condemned, imprisoning itself. I do not think that *this rupture is a purely esthetic event*. But the word poetry does not, after all, designate a species, the genus of which would be art. Inseparable from the verb, it overflows with *prophetic meaning*. (SMB 79 n. 3/PN 185 n. 4, my emphasis)

Poetic writing produces an interruption of totality exceeding the realm of aesthetics because "poetry" no longer names an artistic genre, but rather something endowed with "prophetic significations." We must remember that in *Otherwise than Being* the term *prophetic* defines the "reverting in which the perception of an order coincides with the signification of this order given to him that obeys him" (AE 232/OB 149). The term *prophetic* is, strictly speaking, an ethical term since it refers to the other in the same or ethical signification. It is precisely this ethical dimension that, according to Levinas, Blanchot's writing liberates by disrupting the work of assimilation proper to culture (totality). Blanchot's poetic saying "preserves this movement that is located between seeing and saying. . . . a language going from one singularity to the other without having anything in common, a language without words that beckons before signifying anything" (SMB 41/PN 148).

In 1975 Levinas devotes an essay to Blanchot's *The Madness of the Day* that provides an enlarged version of what was earlier just a discrete allusion. Does Levinas wish to make up for the allusion's ingratitude and to acknowledge the pivotal role that Blanchot's writing plays in *Otherwise than Being*? This is a tempting explanation given that only one year separates the allusion and the essay, except that ingratitude is precisely the concept that organizes the latter. As we will see, something decisive concerning the "possibility (*vertu*) of poetic language" unfolds in this final confrontation with Blanchot, which will also allow us to evaluate retroactively what took place in *Otherwise than Being*. By referring to Blanchot's text as a "texte déjà ancient," Levinas indicates that he is not writing a chronicle, review, or note and that his reading of the *Madness of the Day* is extemporaneous.[36] However, one should not overlook that in 1974 Blanchot publishes a series of fragments under the title "Discours sur la patience," devoted to two key concepts in *Otherwise than Being*, passivity and responsibility.[37]

"Discours sur la patience" and "Exercises sur *La Folie du jour*" may be read as a diptych, as some critics have done, in which Levinas reciprocates Blanchot's gesture, but only if their "infinite conversation" is figured as an exchange rather than a friendship, which supposes asymmetry and lack of reciprocity. Levinas's notion of work (*œuvre*) also stresses nonreciprocity and asymmetry: "[it] demands a radical generosity from the Same who, in the work, goes toward the Other. The work demands the Other's ingratitude. Gratitude would precisely mean the movement's return to its point of origin" (EDEHH 191).[38] Levinas questions, not unlike Blanchot, the circular economy of the same by opposing the story of Ulysses' return to the safety of Ithaca to the dispersal and exile condensed in the figure of Abraham.[39] What remains to be seen is whether Levinas preserves the ingratitude that the work demands or if a more complex gesture takes place.

Ingratitude is a movement that interrupts the return to the point of origin; it alters and therefore accomplishes a series of reversals that allows one to substitute "discourse" for "exercises." There are good reasons for this substitution since Blanchot's fragments not only bear little resemblance to "continuous speech," but also propose a reflection on patience and passivity that puts the order of discourse in disarray. Levinas's essay, meanwhile, where a "translation" of a poetic text into prose (ethical language) takes place, seems to operate under the order of discourse. However, it would be a mistake to overlook the fact that Levinas's essay also functions under the exigency of a double law and performs a series of displacements on Blanchot's text.

What relationship can we establish between the allusion and the essay? Can one simply read the latter as expanding the former and making explicit what was said elliptically? Does it "do justice" to Blanchot's text if "ingratitude" is the principle of the work (*œuvre*)? In *Otherwise than Being* the allusion to *The Madness of the Day* enables Levinas to condense several threads of his argument (diachrony, substitution, saying, and skepticsism) and thus come to a strategic point: just before the determination of the "outside," which is also a crucial "concept" in Blanchot's writing. Since only one year separates *Otherwise than Being* from the "Exercises," it is valid to expect that the basic premises of the essay would also be those of the book. Indeed, in the essay the "quasi hagiographical style" that dominates *Otherwise than Being* energizes the deployment of some of its crucial figures. It is as if its rhythm were marking the pace of a double set of operations; on the one hand, the interpretation of Blanchot's text, on the other hand, a rewriting of "Reality and Its Shadow," in which a reassessment of the ethical "potentialities" of poetic language is at stake.

The essay is made up of two different sets of premises that juxtapose each other: those of *Otherwise than Being* and those of "Reality and Its Shadow" that the "linguistic turn" of the former should have superseded. It is necessary to isolate these two different sets of premises and to see the kind of figure they compose when responding to *The Madness of the Day*. I will then determine whether there are differences or displacements between Levinas's allusion to this text in *Otherwise than Being* and what he explicitly affirms in the "Exercises."

Levinas opens his essay with a section titled "From Poetry to Prose," where he defines expression as "sens inspiré" (SMB 55/PN 156),[40] according to the principles of *Otherwise than Being*. At the same time, he performs a reduction, a "translation" of the text's musicality (poetry) into prose reminiscent of "Reality and Its Shadow." This "translation" removes the text from the jurisdiction of "artistic criticism" in order to place it within that of "philosophical criticism." It is this movement "from poetry to prose" that allows the "Exercises" to operate as discourse, even if *Otherwise than Being* simply *alludes* to the interruption of discourse in Blanchot's text. In addition, this movement goes hand in hand with establishing a distance between a "philosophical criticism" and an "artistic criticism" that does not "interrogate [the] figures [of Blanchot's text] indiscreetly, as if a code were applicable to them by which their poetry could be translated into prose. All back away from such presumption, such profanation or treason" (SMB 57/PN 157). Levinas situates his reading at a level removed from those interpretations that preserve the text in its own "musicality"; to this "preliminary criticism" he opposes, as he did in "Reality and Its Shadow," a "philosophical criticism." However, as in "La Transcendance des mots" Levinas introduces "the perspective of the other." Levinas's ethical reading of *The Madness of the Day* translates the "musicality" of Blanchot's text into "prose," a philosophical statement according to which the *récit* is "a *fable* about the closure of being" (SMB 57/PN 158). He also condenses the reading's *telos* in the syntagm "relation to the other—a last way out" (*rapport avec autrui—dernière issue*) (SMB 68/ PN 165) that organizes the last part of the essay.

What is at stake in Levinas's commentary is the very possibility of reading the opening of being's closure as the approach of the other. It is for this reason that he appeals to the notion of intelligibility, to the space of the Book:

The reading proposed here of a short and no longer recent text of Blanchot's touches upon a few points of its texture as if they had been singled out solely for their *symbolic power*. A hesitant pedantry? Lèse-poetry? Indeed so, but it is also one of the possible lives of that work, even if you reject the idea behind my *deciphering*: the idea that the irreducible (*inspired*) exoticism of poetry refers back to (*en appelle à*) a saying *properly so-called* (*a dire proprement dit*), a saying that thematizes, even if it may be obliged to unsay (*dédire*) itself in order to avoid disfiguring the secret it exposes. (SMB 56/PN 156–57, my emphasis)

Levinas anchors his interpretation in the "symbolic power" of certain textual elements. This term seems out of place within the context of reading someone who had systematically put into question all the values of plenitude associated with the symbol. Although Levinas's "symbolic" ought to be understood in a broad sense, it is not clear whether the figures or sequences he analyzes are endowed with the same "symbolic power." Levinas first isolates an "optical focus" (*foyer optique*), the madness of the day, which unfolds in a temporal figure he calls "hell" and associates to the name of Auschwitz. Second, Levinas takes into account the lacerating and transparent opening of truth and, finally, the appearance of a baby carriage.[41] Do these textual elements belong to the same level of the story or of narration? Levinas refuses the presuppositions of a criticism that does not "touch" the materiality of the text, but deprives himself of the resources of a narratology that would allow him to delimit levels and form series, even if it is true that one cannot take them very far when it comes to Blanchot's *récits*. Although the first two textual elements that Levinas focuses on are sequences whose metonymic scope deploys a topology of essence and truth, the last one (the baby carriage) is a much more discrete element, and it is in the latter that he cyphers his reading. Levinas's exercises confine themselves to a semantics (expression, space of intelligibility, and the book are the dominant coordinates) underwritten by an archi-pragmatics: the ethical a priori saying that inhabits every historical language, according to the principles of *Otherwise than Being*.

The idea that an "irreducible exoticism" characterizes *The Madness of the Day* is a confirmation that some of the underlying principles of "Reality and Its Shadow" still shape the essay. We are familiar with the expression "irreducible exoticism" that, as in 1948, must be redirected to the "straightforwardness of prose." What remains of this "*irreducible* exoticism" once translated into "prose"? In addition, to the familiar expression "irreducible exoticism" Levinas adds a new term: the adjective *inspired* that in *Otherwise than Being* emigrated from the realm of aesthetics to that of ethics. It is for this reason that Levinas can claim that this "irreducible (inspired) exoticism" "en appelle au dire *proprement dit*." Does this mean that the said is equivalent to a saying as such (that the nominal verb *dire* is the subject of a nominal verbal phrase modified by an adverbial clause), or is it rather a said (*dit*) that, properly speaking, can only achieve its maximum level of "symbolic power"? Is the "irreducible (inspired) exoticism" a saying of "being otherwise" or of "the otherwise than being"? This is an important distinction given that Levinas reads Blanchot's *récit* as an *inspired* "fable about the *closure of being*," where the term *inspired* indicates that breaching of totality or the same has taken place.

Levinas's procedure is double; on the one hand, he channels poetry into prose, while on the other hand, in the very text on the closure of being, he localizes the possibility of an opening, of an "otherwise than being." However, this possibility is quickly transferred from the text to an act of reading that seeks to find some "breathing room":

the irresistible temptation of commentary attests to the fact that for this reader this text on *closure* is inspired—that in it the *other* of the Image and the Letter rend the *same* of the Said, according to a modality of awakening (*éveil*) and sobering up (*dégrisement*) and that this writing is Book. (SMB 58/PN 158).

Inspiration tears the texture of the same in the very heart of the fable that tells what the closure of being means. This means that for Levinas Blanchot's "writing is Book" (SMB 58/PN 158). It is here that the ingratitude of the commentary reveals itself. The interruption of the said is not a textual trope because no figure of writing can convey it, but rather an ethical trope that Levinas expresses by the figures of "awakening" (*réveil*) and "sobering up" (*dégrisement*). This gesture may be justified given that the same of the work (*œuvre*) goes in the direction of the other without a return to the point of origin or any hope for restitution. In addition, Levinas transfers these ethical tropes to the space of the Book, and it is in this space that the reader manages to find some "breathing room." Even if one agrees that restitution does not command ingratitude, how far can one go in establishing a "difference" separating the writer from the reader? Levinas goes as far as to restore Blanchot's writing to the order of the book, an order that Blanchot himself rejects since *The Infinite Conversation*.[42] Is this just ingratitude or is it a form of summoning Blanchot to operate within a space alien to his writing?

Levinas's commentary on *The Madness of the Day* is in line with the allusion he made to this text in *Otherwise than Being*. He deploys the text's *said* in terms of a philosophical proposition, the fable of the closure of Being, but he also inflects this proposition with an ethical torsion: the figure of an inspired exoticism that, in the end, belongs to the space of the book. Levinas's language has begun to hear the rumbling of the "double speech," and it is on this same but differential site that his language will also give Blanchot something to hear.

Blanchot with Levinas

The question of what exceeds philosophy's said (*le dit*) finds its way into *The Infinite Conversation*. This is one of Blanchot's most "systematic" treatments of "double speech," now called "plural speech or speech of writing" (*parole d'écriture*). Perhaps "systematic" is not the most appropriate word here since it refers to a way of thinking alien to Blanchot, but also because *The Infinite Conversation* is a heterogeneous text composed of expository pieces, *polylogues* and dialogues. The text's multiplicity defies the concept of unity as well as the whole economy of meaning underlying the concept of Book. Yet, the word *systematic* does come to mind, given that there is something "thorough" about Blanchot's investigation. The plurality of language is not simply the thesis of *The Infinite Conversation*, which is also a response to this "plural speech"; *The Infinite Conversation* exposes itself as a plural and multiple text and as a response to what defies unity, totality and closure. My reading of *The Infinite Conversation* first contextualizes Blanchot's reading of Levinas and then elucidates how he establishes the relationship between writing and the question of the other. This contextualization is necessary because Blanchot's reading of Levinas's *Totality and Infinity* marks a turning point in his conception of the neuter and in the relationship between writing and thinking.

Blanchot's trajectory can be divided into three periods. The first goes from *Faux Pas* (1943) to *The Space of Literature* (1955) and is dominated by a Hegelo-Kojèvian conceptuality and a Mallarmean understanding of language. Blanchot brings together the experience of the night with an excessive negativity that cannot be put at the service of comprehension. This nothing is, as in Mallarmé, constitutive of language and constitutive of the world, following Kojève's reading of Hegel. Blanchot associates this negative force with "two versions" of death. In the first, the negative is as mediation in the world and therefore a possibility, the working of the concept and language. In the second, "the other night," death resists dialectical sublation.[43] By naming things, language makes them appear but can only do so by substituting the thing for its absence (PF 46).

To Hegel's negativity as pure nothingness in *The Space of Literature* Blanchot grafts Heidegger's schema of ontological difference and his understanding of the nothing (*das Nichts*).[44] Hegel's negativity thus becomes, as in Heidegger, unveiling of truth, a concealed origin: the condition of all presence and truth which language is unable to gather, since in literary language the object gives way to its "disparition vibratoire" (PF 46). Things can only come into presence because language presupposes a constitutive absence and dissimulates the nothingness that is its very condition. Language's ambiguity lies in that, while bearing witness to a constitutive absence, it forbids access to what it cannot apprehend. By the same token, it invites a transgression of this limit because the writer desires the absence that makes language possible or what resists nomination. Orpheus's figure incarnates the ambiguity of literary language, and the "space of literature" is the region where the unnamable outside (*le dehors*) is deployed. *The Space of Literature* establishes a link between negativity and nothingness and shows that the outside attracts literary language from within. In the myth of Orpheus, as told by Blanchot, there is a shift from the night as object of thinking to what eludes thinking, the absence of meaning. The absence of meaning becomes Blanchot's main concern from then on.

In the second period, already announced in the final pages of *The Space of Literature*, but whose main insights unfold in *The Infinite Conversation* (1969), Blanchot submits Heidegger's nothing to a radical reduction and empties it of any form of presence. By grafting this Heideggerian matrix to excessive negativity, Blanchot elucidates a form of negativity called the *neuter* that belongs neither to presence nor to absence. The thinking/writing of the neuter can only take place by presupposing that the working of totality has already been accomplished (Hegel) and that the neuter does not constitute a form of opening (Heidegger). In the first part of *The Infinite Conversation* the neuter becomes the question of the "other than being" or "the most profound question." This turning point opens a third period, in which writing, understood as the question of the neuter, is also conceived as the question of the other in the ethical sense of the term. This period closes with *The Step Not Beyond* (1973) and *The Writing of the Disaster* (1980). The focus of my reading is the first part of *The Infinite Conversation* where Blanchot engages Levinas's ethics.

One can read the opening section "Thought and the Exigency of Discontinuity" as a microgenealogy of language's place in philosophical thinking. Two questions articulate this micronarrative: how should one speak in order for this speech (*parole*) to be essentially plural, and how should one write so that the continuity in *writing* allows both interruption and rupture to take place? The first permits Blanchot to elaborate the question of the other or neuter (*neutre*) and the second provides an access to the problematic of writing and its different configurations: *récit, polylogue, parole du fragment*. I will focus on the first question.

Philosophical discourse has systematically absorbed plurality, interruption and rupture, and Blanchot's exposition aims to reverse one of the most deeply rooted presuppositions of philosophical discourse, the idea that the "real" is continuous or a continuum. Blanchot also seeks to show

how philosophy, unlike literature, has always repressed the question of its own language. Consequently, he claims that the language philosophy tends to privilege is the effect of its institutionalization as teaching, which reinforces the apparently "natural" choice of a continuous language. Although Blanchot enumerates the anomalies (Pascal and Nietzsche) within this genealogy, his study revolves around two pivotal moments, Aristotle and Hegel. With the former "the language of continuity becomes the official language of philosophy"(EI 6/IC 7), while the latter develops the most powerful discursive device ever to saturate discontinuity, dialectics.

Blanchot strategically chooses the scene of teaching as the point from which to reverse the dominion of the continuous word. This reversion finally leads to the positing of a different type of relation. At this point in Blanchot's argument what appears to be a common conceptual ground with the Levinas of *Totality and Infinity* emerges. At first this common ground is the "intersubjective" scene of teaching: the teacher–disciple relation understood as a relation of speech. When referring to the scene of teaching Blanchot stresses those features that Levinas values: the nonlinear nature of the interrelational space, the use of figures of non-Euclidean geometry to refer to the relation to the other (a curved space for Levinas, a space analogous to Riemann's surface for Blanchot; in both cases there is an emphasis on an asymmetrical space or "relation of infinity").

Blanchot thinks the relation teacher–disciple as one of language where "the incommensurable becomes measure therein, and irrelation, relation"(EI 5/IC 6). However, the speech of teaching contains within itself a double asymmetry, and the *unknown* at play in this relationship makes it a "relation of infinity." This constitutive structure of philosophy has given origin to several forms of language based upon symmetry, reversibility and linearity, all dissimulating the constitutive discontinuity of the "relation of infinity." In other words, the language of philosophy cannot give an account of the basic structure that puts philosophy into language. More importantly, Blanchot separates the structure of the relation of speech from the foundational scene of the Socratic-humanist word that presupposes the preeminence of speech over writing. At the end of the essay, Blanchot supplements this separation with a rather elliptical statement that lacks any further development: "the exigency of speech that is in advance always already written" (*toujours déjà préalablement écrite*)"(EI 10/ IC 11). Before the constitution of the Socratic word, the language of philosophy is already an interrupted language. This interruption has an asymmetrical form: the "relation of infinity" in which the human being becomes a nonunitary possibility announcing a "totally otherwise relation." This in turn marks a limit to the conception of being as continuity and constitutes an opening outside of dialectics and ontology.

The common ground as well as the differences between Blanchot and Levinas surface in the first chapter, especially in the sections "Knowledge of the Unknown" and "The Relation of the Third Kind (Man without Horizon)."[45] I will make these differences explicit in order to elucidate what Blanchot accomplishes by introducing the question of the other in Levinasian terms and within the context of his own reflection on alterity and difference. At stake is whether Blanchot preserves the approach of the human being as the question of the other, or if a more complex gesture takes place.

After showing the weaknesses in a conception of language that depends on vision to give an account of the "totally otherwise relation" and in philosophy's inability to describe that relation, one of the voices of this dialogue asks: "—How can we discover the obscure without exposing it to view? What would this experience of the obscure, in which the obscure offered in its obscurity, be?" (EI 50/IC 5). While attempting to circumscribe a nonpower different from a negation of power, the reference to Levinas is unavoidable for Blanchot, although Levinas is greatly modified here. Blanchot stays close to the letter of *Totality and Infinity*, but he states Levinas's ideas in a different idiom and inscribes them in a different space. On the one hand, Blanchot notes:

We are led by the teaching of Levinas before a radical experience.
Autrui is entirely Other; the other is what exceeds me absolutely. The
relation with the other that is *autrui* is a transcendent relation, which
means that there is an infinite, and, in a sense, an impassable distance
between myself and the other, who belongs to the other shore, who
has no country in common with me, and who cannot in any way
assume equal rank in a same concept or a same whole, cannot be
counted together with the individual that I am. (EI 74/IC 52)

Throughout this dialogue, the different voices value Levinas's insights in a hyperbolic manner in order to stress what is unique in his description of the relation to the other and how Levinas's description functions as a real turning point from previous philosophies of the other.

Blanchot's hyperbolic reading of Levinas also amounts to a reinscription of some of the philosopher's concepts: "everything that can be affirmed of the relation of transcendence—the relation of God to creature—must be first (*for my part, I would say only*) understood on the level of the social relation. *The Most High would be autrui (le Très Haut ce serait Autrui)*" (EI 77/IC 54, my emphasis). Of this "totally otherwise relation" Blanchot stresses a series of features: the infinite distance between I and the other, their separation, the "exteriority" from which this other comes to affect the subject and the nonbelonging of the other to a dimension of manifestation or face.[46] However, this last feature is especialy crucial for Blanchot since manifestation is at issue and, therefore, a revision of its main determinations. As we saw in chapter 4, in *Totality and Infinity* Levinas defines the face as the modality in which the other presents itself by exceeding the idea of the other in me. Given that the face exceeds thematization the other does not present itself within the economy of representation; for Blanchot this means that the other speaks. The relation to the other is language: "in speech, it is the *outside* that speaks in giving rise to speech, and permitting me to speak" (EI 78/ IC 55). What speaks for Blanchot is not the trace of transcendence in the immanence of the sensible (the face), but rather a preexisting strangeness at the root of any dialogue, this strangeness being both the "cause" and the "object" of any speech. In this sense, there is language because of separation and not having anything in common. One would be wrong to suppose that a dialogue creates common ground or that it erases separation, as most dialogical philosophies would suggest; it is instead the testimony of this separation.

Although Blanchot recognizes that the face is speech, one cannot forget that for Levinas the trace of a nonthematizable face passes through discourse. If face points to the irreducibility of the other, it is because "manifestation *kath'autó* consists in the being telling itself to us independently of every position we would have taken in its regard, *expressing itself*. . . . Manifestation *kath'autó* is not disclosure but revelation, and the

latter supposes a 'coinciding of the expressed with him who expresses'"
(TeI 60/TI 66). While arguing that signification is the presence of exteriority, Levinas brings into play Plato's conception of speech, according to
which "he who manifests himself comes to his own assistance," as the
Phaedrus states. Levinas's reference to Plato takes place before noting that
revelation constitutes the inversion of objectifying cognition and before
criticizing Buber's use of the *tutoiement* as implying a reciprocal relation
between the other and I. For Levinas the essential relation of language is
interpellation (the vocative): "the interpellated one is called upon to
speak; his speech consists in 'coming to the assistance' of his word, in
being present. Speech, better than a simple sign, is essentially magisterial"
(TeI 65/TI 69–70).

As could not be otherwise, the reactivation of the scene of full speech
goes hand in hand with a denunciation of rhetoric as nondiscourse, as an
oblique way of approaching the other. It is only by renouncing rhetoric
that one can face the other, be "in a veritable conversation" (TI 94/95)
and institute justice. In this sense, "language lays the foundations for a
possession in common. The world in discourse is no longer what it is in
separation; it is what I give: the communicable, the thought, the universal" (TeI 92/TI 96). The presence of the other in language arrests the
terrifying precession of simulacra, given that speech "surmounts the dissimulation inevitable in every apparition"(TeI 97–98/TI 91–92).

Although Blanchot follows Levinas's analysis by modulating the peculiarity of the relation to the other in his own idiom, he also takes an
opportunity to stress some ambiguities in Levinas's exposition; for example, the privileging of speech:

The thought that recognizes in *Autrui* this dimension of radical exteriority with respect to the Self cannot at the same time ask of interiority
that it furnish a common denominator between the Self and *Autrui,*
any more that it can seek in the (subjective) presence of the "I" to his
speech what would make language a manifestation without peer. (EI
81/IC 57)

Here we find the mark of the *unerasable difference* in their elucidation of the
relation to the other. While Levinas's treatment seems to weaken the
inhuman aspect of its asymmetry through the economy of full speech,

Blanchot inscribes the graphics of *Ent-fernung* and thus privileges distancing and inaccessibility. For Blanchot, "la parole se souvient de cette séparation véritable par laquelle elle parle" (EI 83). This is the separation that murders the thing and dissimulates its absence (Hegel-Mallarmé), but also the separation that is at the very origin of language, the unnamable and impossible outside (Heidegger and beyond). This difference unfolds, in part, in a reading of the *Phaedrus*. This is a fundamental text that allows Levinas to articulate an understanding of language as expression. However, read through the poetic saying of René Char and the prophetic saying of Heraclitus, Blanchot's *Phaedrus* points in a different direction. It becomes the testimony of the philosopher's horror when faced with a strange and foreign language: "the written word: dead word, word of forgetting."[47]

Does this difference between Levinas and Blanchot simply imply a different way of reading the *Phaedrus*? The difference is not simply one of reading or interpretation, but is related to the space from which they are enacted. On the one hand, and from Blanchot's perspective, it is possible to say that *Totality and Infinity* operates within the space of the Book. Although it attempts to secure an ethical saying not absorbed by the economy of the same regulating the book, there is no decisive breach of its logic. If it is true that there are indications of an interruption, they are too weak and again become reabsorbed by the logic of the Book. The performative dimension of *Otherwise than Being* is clear evidence that this is the case. It is as if Levinas had felt a need to supplement the descriptive and deductive language of philosophy with a writing that not only thematizes, but also fundamentally faces the reader with an "ethical performative."[48]

It is only through writing and in writing that Levinas interrupts and marks the interruptions of ontology. In spite of this interruption, as we saw above, the figure of the Book returns in "Exercises on *The Madness of the Day*" as the guarantor of intelligibility. On the other hand, Blanchot's *The Infinite Conversation* inscribes, from its very opening, a margin of the book, a border that ruins its economy. This is a margin that grafts a fictional beginning (a beginning which is already a repetition), distinctively distinguished from the rest of the text by typographical signs and format, and affecting the whole scene of knowledge or theory. "Fiction" supplements theory and ruins the nostalgia for unity and totality that the Book presupposes (EI 620–36/IC 422–34).

Blanchot approaches the human not as the horizon of a "first philosophy" or ethics, but in order to highlight the other as such that circulates among human beings. For Blanchot, "[the] human relation is terrible" (EI 84/IC 59) since it no longer passes through being and is without measure or mediation. The human being ceases to be the measure of all things; its presence (a presence that ceases to be self-presence and is no longer governed by the present) becomes the measure of what is strange, other. Yet, the human being is both totally strange and unknown and *at the same time* "immediate presence" (EI 72/IC 5), although not the presence of one "coming to the assistance" of someone else's saying. It is instead the mark of the human beings's inaccessibility; "the inaccessible is in a sense the immediate. . . . This encounter is terrible" (EI 85/IC 60). Blanchot here unfolds the graphics of *Ent-fernung* that requires thinking both the infinite interval as the immediate and the immediate as the most unfamiliar and strange. Blanchot calls this configuration "the thinking of essential speech" (EI 84/IC 59). This thinking thinks and writes both the force of the poetic word, as well as the quasi-ethical dimension of a "disastrous responsibility."[49]

To the question of how the notion of immediacy comes to be intertwined with that of the interval, distance and infinite separation, Blanchot responds, "immediate presence is presence of what could not be present, presence of the nonaccessible, presence excluding or exceeding any present"(EI 54/IC 38). One is tempted to assimilate these concepts to Levinas's face, whose immediacy overflows presence. There is a decisive difference, though. In Levinas the face (*visage*) organizes the field of intelligibility and, for this reason, possesses a horizon: could Blanchot be suggesting, as Levinas did with Heidegger, that Levinas does not fully break with vision? The relation to the other or "relation of the third kind" in Blanchot, however, supposes a notion of "human being without horizon," as well as a severing of vision from speech:

True strangeness, if it comes to me from man, comes to me from this Other that man would be. . . . *The Other: not only does he not fall within my horizon, he is himself without horizon.*

Man without horizon, and not affirming itself on the basis of a horizon . . . he is what comes to me as speech when to speak is not to see. The Other speaks to me and is only this exigency of speech. And when the Other speaks to me, *speech* is the relation of that which remains radically separate, *the relation of the third kind affirming a relation without unity, without equality.* (EI 98/IC 69, my emphasis)

The "relation of the third type" puts into question both immediacy and transcendence and operates under a double and asymmetrical exigency: "to *name* the possible, to *respond* to the impossible"(EI 92/IC 65). If in *Totality and Infinity* Levinas produces a "crossing out" of the empirical and the transcendental, a coimplication whose simultaneity defies any continuity and idenity, Blanchot posits their relation in a more stringent fashion.

It is time to assess the status of Levinas's conceptuality once it is grafted to the region of the neuter, as well as the metamorphosis it undergoes. As we have seen, for Blanchot literary language gives access to the regions of the neuter. This access takes several forms: the "experience of the *other* night" and the ambiguity of the image, which is the ambiguity of language itself. In addition, literary language affirms that this ambiguity is at the very heart of discourse and that philosophy represses this dimension of fascination and absence of the other as such. Blanchot conceives the question of the other as the question of language and the neuter as what differs from being. For him, other names a "trait" that can only unfold in language. However, the "relation of the third type" opens up this general "structure" of alterity to the relationship—the distance—between human beings. The hinge between the two configurations is language, which allows Blanchot to preserve alterity in general and to treat it as the space in which human language takes place since, according to Levinas, the other (*autrui*) is at the origin of signification. As soon as Blanchot grafts the ethical relation to the other (*autrui*) onto the neuter, the former suffers considerable displacements. As we saw above, when Blanchot affirms that the "wholly other" is the other human being, he cancels out the height of transcendence Levinas located in the other's face and transforms *autrui* into "the relation of the third kind" or neuter.[50] By the same token, the infinity of the face-à-face becomes the "very extent of the Outside" (EI 98/IC 69).

Although Blanchot introduces the term *autrui*, it does not have a privileged value: "perhaps, also, it is time to withdraw this term *autrui*, while retaining what it has to say to us: that the Other is always what *calls* upon 'man' (even if only to put him between parentheses or between quotation marks), not the other as God or other as nature but, as 'man,' more Other than all that is other" (EI 102/IC 72, my emphasis). Blanchot reduces *autrui* to an "essentially *neuter* name figure," and this move allows him to preserve the structure of the call, "the responsibility of attending to the neuter . . . to which we open when we seek to receive the speech of the Outside" (EI 102/IC 72). *Autrui* is not a final term, but the knot of an intrigue through which the neuter passes and which only refers to it as the unnamable "origin" that summons language. The ethical "structure" that Levinas isolates in the face-à-face is part of a larger "structure" since now it has an antecedent as old or older than Levinas's diachrony: the Outside (*Dehors*).

In Blanchot's elaboration of the (non)access to what is immediate, a realm emerges where power is no longer the ruling principle: "the thought (of) the impossible" (EI 110/IC 80) is the otherwise than power. Through a different strategy, Blanchot is again affecting dialectics. In this particular case his analysis passes through a description of *suffering* as an experience providing us with a means to approach "the thought (of) the impossible."

What is decisive about suffering is that it is a strange experience, not because of its exceptional character but rather because of its familiarity. Suffering is an uncanny experience that allows Blanchot to conceive another type of temporality that affects our way of interpreting and constructing the notion of present: "the present of suffering is the abyss of the present" (EI 92/IC 63).[51] Because of this abyssal falling in suffering we are exposed to a time deprived of its possibility of overcoming. In other words, one cannot transform suffering into a possibility of nonsuffering or salvation; suffering is not part of an economy of sacrifice. Because of this interruption, the time of suffering is a time without event, project or possibility; a time of impossibility or dying (*mourir*) (and not of a death that can be put to work at the service of life), a dispersion of the present and an inability to conclude:

We perceive here the point at which time and space would rejoin in an original disjunction: "presence" is as much the intimacy of instancy as the dispersal of the Outside, *the exterior that becomes an intrusion that stifles, and the reversal of both the one and the other; what we have called "the vertigo of spacing."* (EI 65–66/IC 46, my emphasis)

The expression "the vertigo of spacing" (*vertige de l'espacement*) alerts us to the peculiar status of "experience" in Blanchot. It also calls our attention to how writing is central to the approach of the other or, rather, how writing "is" the approach *of* the other. What is here called "experience" cannot be assimilated to something empirical, but instead must be related to the "immediate presence or presence as Outside (*Dehors*)" because this "other experience is always more intial than the affirmation that names being" (EI 65/IC 46).

If for Levinas poetry (*poïesis*) belongs to the realm of culture and, therefore, works under the ruling power of the one,[52] for Blanchot poetry (*poïesis, la parole poetique*) "says in responding" and thus responds to the impossible: "Every beginning speech begins by responding; a response to what is not yet heard, an attentive response in which the impatient waiting for the unknown and the desiring hope for presence are affirmed" (EI 69/IC 48).

The poetic nature of "double speech" determines writing as a responsive and responsible task. This is not a dialogic response, however, if by response one understands the linguistic conduct leading to an agreement between two alter egos. This response does not synchronize the lapse and interval between the question and its answer in a dialectical *après coup*. No common ground can be established between the response, that to which it responds or to which it is obliged to respond. Moreover, the response is a resaying; a saying entangled in an anarchic temporality that will alter both the time and the space of its saying:

Such then would be my task: to respond to this speech that surpasses my hearing, to respond to it without having really understood it, and to respond to it in repeating it, in making it speak.

This response, this speech that begins by responding and that in this beginning says over again the question that comes to it from the Unknown and the Stranger—here is what lies at the basis of the responsibility that is subsequently expressed in the hard language of exigency: one must speak. (EI 92/IC 65)

If Blanchot hesitates to employ the term "ethics" in order to refer to this "other relation," it is due to what he considers ethics' secondary and derivative determinations. Nevertheless, Blanchot has no hesitation in tying responsive speech and poetic language. Although for Blanchot an "ethical response" responds only to the possible, this is only half of the problem. Blanchot's poetics of obligation exceeds responsibility and faces the impossible.

Postface

Not unlike Levinas, Blanchot employs the term *intrigue* to refer to the "relation of the third type" and to the "exigency of speech" when faced with the strangeness of language. Intrigue is not only a descriptive term, but also what unfolds in and as *"le moment voulu."* *Intrigue* names the temporalizing of the other's approach, as well as the temporality of writing as "responsive speech." *Au Moment voulu* allowed me to read intrigue as a "passion of time," as the exploration of a passivity older than interiority and intention which opens language up "from within." However, this "passion of time" that the narrative mode of the intrigue brings into play can only unfold once the grip of both being and the negative are loosened. Blanchot's rewriting of Nietzsche's eternal return beyond or on the hither side of Heidegger's fundamental ontology clears the ground for Levinas's confrontation with Heidegger's thinking. But it also provides us with a syntax from which to read language's responsive, ethical, dimension.

Throughout Levinas's work it is possible to distinguish two different conceptions of language that have decisive implications for his thinking on the other. They are speech as the plenitude of discourse and language as "amphibology" or ambiguity. The first conception is implicit in *Existence and Existents*, "Reality and Its Shadow," and *The Time of the Other*. However, it is not until *Totality and Infinity*, where ethical language becomes pure immediacy, that this conception reaches its justification and grounding. The face (*visage*) of the other faces me, concerns me (*me regarde*) without mediation. It exceeds the grasp of representation and overflows form but gives form to my answer: the face is discourse. Levinas conceives the sincerity or straightforwardness of discourse in opposition to rhetoric and other forms of representation, including those of artistic works. The speaking of the face is, for Levinas, the "primordial essence of language."

The presence of the other in language arrests the terrifying procession of simulacra, given that speech "surmounts the dissimulation inevitable in every apparition" (TI 97–98). While aiming to shield the other from the violence of ontology, Levinas employs all of its resources, and thus some presuppositions regarding writing go unquestioned. The absence of such an explicit reflection goes hand in hand with the form of exposition—the ontological plot—that fails to secure a "welcoming of the other." A set of binary oppositions (infinity/totality, straightforwardness of prose/fascinating hold of rhythm) articulates the plot that holds together the story of a joyous ego that, after a harmonious fusion with the feminine other (a familiar alterity), confronts a more demanding alterity.

In *Otherwise than Being* Levinas deploys the concept of trace as a way of thinking an ethical language that is no longer primarily determined by the plenitude of speech nor falls prey to ontological categories. The distinction between the said (*le dit*) (writing, synchrony, essence, history) and saying (*le dire*) (face, diachrony, passivity, testimony) permits Levinas to elucidate the ethical saying as an original presemiotic dimension inhabiting each historical language. In this second conception of language an immemorial trace haunts language and bears witness to "the glory of the infinite," or the proximity of the other to the same. In order to manifest itself, this preoriginal saying is destined to fix itself in a said or predicative proposition. It thus becomes a theme or the object of a narrative and is subordinated to a linguistic system woven by ontological categories. However, for Levinas the said's enunciative peripetia or plot is derivative and secondary and presupposes the gravity of a responsibility incommensurate to being and to the language in which it is uttered.

Within the context of Levinas's first conception of language, art, literature, and writing are neither philosophy's other nor the types of others able to interrupt the working of totality. At times, they are "fake" others easily assimilated by totality; at other times they lay bare language's possibility to exceed the order of discourse. This oscillation permeates Levinas's thinking and his conception of literary writing, which is visible at the level of judgment (critique), as well as at the most basic determination of the ethical relation. The proximity of ethics and aesthetics presents Levinas with a series of challenges that will go unresolved until he finds a place for the "there is" (*il y a*) within the larger context of the "otherwise than being," and when he attenuates his critique of Heidegger's thinking. These shifts will enable a reassessment of language and the deployment of a type of writing whose effects are broader than even Levinas himself acknowledges. It is possible to claim that "the question of writing" (Blanchot) is the hinge between ethics and aesthetics. Although this is precisely the question that Levinas never addresses explicitly, it will produce a profound mutation in his thinking.

The conception of language developed in *Totality and Infinity* grounds Levinas's indictment of art. Although "Reality and Its Shadow," the main focus of chapter 5, predates *Totality and Infinity*, the main characteristics of the ethical relation and language are already in place in this essay. Levinas defines his thinking as a "humanism of the other man," but there is no traditional humanistic use of art here; the work of art entails a relapse into destiny and not the loftiness that humanism tends to value. However, although Levinas refuses a humanistic use of art, he does not subscribe to a post-humanist discourse, as in the so-called post-structuralist thinkers.

In "Reality and Its Shadow" Levinas takes issue with the function that Heidegger's fundamental ontology reserves for the work of art, a point usually overlooked by Levinas criticism. Heidegger defines essential language as poetry (*Dichtung*) and conceives it as the working of truth, the ecstatic bringing forth of truth in which *Dasein* can found its dwelling. The goal of Heidegger's reflection on art and poetry is to secure a more essential dwelling, a more originary ethics in which man could preserve being as a whole (*phusis*) and respond to the call of being. *Poíesis* thus names a more originary unveiling of being than "challenging reserve," that is, the essential determination of technology. In an age threatened by the departure of the gods and the danger of technology, only poetic language can safeguard the traces of the sacred.

Through the assessment of the ontological use of the work of art, I claim that in "Reality and Its Shadow" Levinas stages a critique of Heidegger's immanent (political) ontology which explains only in part the virulent condemnation of art. Levinas severs art from ethics by circumscribing it to the space of pure being (*il y a*) from which the subject cannot fully break unless the other faces him. In the work of art, the *il y a* filters through the human order, bringing with it the worst: a mythical rootedness in a place that grounds the distinction between an autochthonous people and strangers. At one level, Levinas's indictment of art denounces the co-belonging of myth and art and the concomitant violence of aesthetic manifestations. Levinas endows the work of art with exoticism and alterity and these compete with ethical otherness, since the plastic hold of the image or rhythm occupies the subject with a façade, instead of having him preoccupied with the other's face. Equating the spatio-temporal schema of art with paganism, Levinas unfolds the matrix of his essay "Philosophy of Hitlerism" and highlights the complicity between aesthetics and ontology's totalitarian order, which Levinas still detects in liberal philosophies of freedom, such as Sartre's.

"Reality and Its Shadow" not only argues against Heidegger's sacralization of the work of art, but also against Sartre's notion of commitment. For Levinas, the work of art does not belong to the sphere of knowledge, since it does not concern truth but a non-truth (the "shadow") that belongs to the inhuman and pre-human dimension of the *il y a* and from which the subject must escape. The work of art is "mute," and only by introducing the perspective of the other can "philosophical criticism" reintegrate it into the human order. The task of "philosophical criticism" is to make "the position an image occupies between two times and their ambiguity" (RS 13) explicit, and it can only do so by introducing the perspective of the other, which Levinas himself refrains from doing in this essay. However, this decisive element is already in place in *Existence and Existents* and in *Time of the Other*; what is truly lacking in "Reality and

Its Shadow" is a conception of language and writing capable of dealing with the image's negative dimension in a positive way. It is this absence, together with the critique of Heidegger's ontological use of art, which explains Levinas's virulent indictment of the work of art.

Otherwise than Being writes a "clandestine *intrigue*" that bears witness to an "allegiance to the other." It thus secures an ethical writing by leaving behind the ontological plot and by recasting a metaphysical conception of language in terms of "amphibology" or duality. Here Levinas no longer abides by binary categories and develops a method different from that of transcendental philosophy. In *Otherwise than Being* it is no longer a question of grounding concepts but of forcefully transforming them. This transformation comes about through two tropes, emphasis and hyperbole, as well as by a "linguistic turn" whose impact can be measured in the very structure of the book.

Otherwise than Being not only writes the *intrigue* of the other but is itself this *intrigue*. The book lacks a linear and progressive narrative organization and moves in "a spiraling movement." Instead of being assembled according to the logic of conceptual exposition, the chapters function as appositions that break with conceptual binary hierarchies. This structure produces the emphatic transformation or hyperbolic rewriting of the "argument" or plot, which is transformed into an *intrigue* or *ex-position*. However, the nature of this *ex-position* differs both from transcendental philosophy and fundamental ontology. It escapes the frame of the present and, therefore, supposes a reassessment of temporality and spatiality where the subject is no longer the source and guarantor of experience.

Although Levinas does not explicitly elaborate a positive concept of writing, like Blanchot or even Derrida, *Otherwise than Being*'s crucial ethical reduction of the said takes place within the context of a literary allusion to Maurice Blanchot's *récit*, *The Madness of the Day*. Levinas's ambiguity regarding the ethical relevance of the work of art has not diminished. Without fully distinguishing between a traditional (aesthetic) category of art and a "post-aesthetic" understanding of writing (as Blanchot does), he reserves for the latter some potentialities that exceed the grasp of discourse. This allusion to the potentialities of literary language goes hand in hand with the deployment of a series of textual tropes that make the ethical reduction of constative utterances possible.

Levinas invokes the *poetic said* at the very moment that he determines language as skepticism. Critical readings of *Otherwise than Being* tend to stress Levinas's reference to "the return of skepticism" as the trope of the two-times (*contre-temps*) or diachrony of ethical writing (the interruptions of discourse and the maintaining of the knots of the interruptions). However, by reading this trope within a larger sequence that opens with the allusion to Blanchot's literary text, I show that "literary language" is already skepticism. Levinas ethical reduction is energized by the partially unacknowledged "positivity" of literary language. Levinas implicitly puts into play a dimension of literary writing that he explicitly acknowledges as potentiality; in the textual fabric of *Otherwise than Being*, however, this potentiality is everywhere at work.

The allusion to Blanchot is discreet; it mentions neither the author's name nor the text's title and attenuates literary writing's ability to interrupt the order of discourse, since Levinas still envisions literary language as a "said"—a constative or thematizing utterance. Yet the allusion evinces a philosophical compromise when faced with writing; it acknowledges, but at the same time suppresses, that the unnarrative ethical modality Levinas calls *intrigue* has a Blanchotian provenance.

It is as if a certain substitution (the master trope of Levinas's ethics) were taking place between philosophical exposition and literary writing. Does Levinas acknowledge that poetic language finally manages to unsaid the said and allows the inscription of the saying to take place? Is it possible to mark a passage from an ethical writing to an ethics of writing? Everything hinges on this possible passage or reversal. The features that characterize the relation to the other (asymmetry, lack of reciprocity, impossibility of reappropriation, one-way movement without return to a dwelling place or inwardness) are at play in the encounter between Levinas and Blanchot. *Intrigue* thus becomes a matter of reading, the modality under which this encounter takes place. No conventional approach based on questions of influence, priority, or misunderstanding can provide an accurate account of it. On Levinas's side, the *intrigue* unfolds under two crucial terms, "work" and "ingratitude"; on Blanchot's side, it unfolds under the term "friendship."

Within the context of this *intrigue*, philosophy and literature become two limit concepts that mark the site of their encounter. Levinas refuses ontology's theoretical hegemony as well as its aesthetic complicity and thus conceives of ethical writing as the underside of discourse. Blanchot not only refuses philosophy's inability to let the other come into language, but also any aesthetic determination of writing. In spite of these similarities, what is at stake in this chapter is what keeps Levinas and Blanchot apart, or in Blanchot's words, "the *fundamental separation* on the basis of which *what separates becomes relation*" (F 29).[1] Levinas's essays on Blanchot and Blanchot's meditation on Levinas's *Totality and Infinity* make the relation between these two thinkers explicit.

What Blanchot gives Levinas, as a question of thinking, is the other that (literary) writing liberates in a modality that is not manifestation, but rather the night, the neuter, the outside, and the disaster. And although writing is a concept for which Levinas reserves no decisive place in his philosophy, the question of literary writing constantly surfaces in his thinking. How does Levinas finally deal with this question?

What Levinas gives to Blanchot is the question of the other as ethics, which manifests itself in the face of the other human being, bearer of the trace of transcendence. It is true that the question of the other as the approach of the other human being is not crucial for Blanchot, although its ethical force imposes itself in *The Infinite Conversation*. This book marks an important turning point in how Blanchot conceives writing's otherness and the task of thinking. How does Blanchot treat the human dimension of Levinasian ethics?

Levinas's reading of Blanchot's texts provides an ideal opportunity to investigate these issues because both writers share the exigency of interrupting the work of totality and of thinking the other on the hither side of representation. The case of Blanchot interests me because his project forces Levinas to think the materiality of writing without the assistance of traditional aesthetic categories. The encounter between Levinas and Blanchot thus offers me an opportunity to elucidate Levinas's shifting position regarding literature, as well as to redirect the *intrigue* into a different space. But this encounter also compels Blanchot to undergo an "ethical turn." By grafting the question of the other as the approach of the other human being to the question of writing, he gives way to an ethics of writing in which language is primarily conceived as "responsive speech."

NOTES

INTRODUCTION

1. Martin Heidegger, "A Letter on Humanism," in *Martin Heidegger: Basic Writings*, ed. David F. Krell (New York: Harper & Row: 1982), 232–33. Hereafter, "A Letter on Humanism" will be cited in the text by the abbreviation LH. The *Basic Writings* will be cited by the abbreviation BW.

2. Martin Heidegger, *Being and Time*, trans. John Macquarrie and Edward Robinson (New York: Harper & Row, 1962.) Hereafter, this work is cited in the text by the abbreviation BT.

3. Martin Heidegger, *Poetry, Language, Thought*, trans. Alfred Hofstadter (New York: Harper & Row, 1977). Hereafter, this work is cited in the text by the abbreviation PLT.

4. Martin Heidegger, *Heraklit 2. Logik: Heraklit Lehre vom Logos. Gesamtausgabe* 55. (Frankfurt: Klosterman, 1977). Hereafter, this work is cited in the text by the abbreviation GA 55.

5. Martin Heidegger, *Elucidations of Hölderlin's Poetry*, trans. Keith Hoeller (Amherst, N.Y.: Humanity Books, 2000). Hereafter, this work is cited in the text by the abbreviation EHP.

6. Maurice Blanchot, "Le 'Discourse Philosophique,'" *L'Arc* 46 (1971): 1–4. Hereafter, this work is cited in the text by the abbreviation DP.

7. Maurice Blanchot, *The Writing of the Disaster*, trans. Ann Smock (Lincoln: University of Nebraska Press, 1986). Hereafter, this work is cited in the text by the abbreviation WD.

8. See Gayatri Chakravorty Spivak, *In Other Worlds: Essays in Cultural Politics* (New York: Routledge, 1987); Homi K. Bhabha, *The Location of Culture* (London: Routledge, 1994); Judith Butler, *Gender Trouble: Feminism and the Subversion of Identity* (London: Routledge, 1990); and A. Arteaga, ed., *An Other Tongue: Nation and Ethnicity in the Linguistic Borderland* (Durham: Duke University Press, 1994).

9. I am thinking here about feminist readings of Levinas in which the question of an ethical subjectivization is at stake. See Catherine Chalier, *Figures du féminine: Lecture d'Emmanuel Lévinas* (Paris: Verdier, 1982); Tina Chanter, ed., *Feminist Interpretations of Levinas* (University Park: Pennsylvania State University Press, 2001) and Tina Chanter, *Time, Death, and the Feminine: Levinas with Heidegger* (Stanford: Stanford University Press, 2001).

10. I am alluding to an expression found in Michel Foucault, "The Writing of the Outside," in *Foucault/Blanchot* (New York: Zone Books, 1987).

11. For these contemporary approaches to the other, see Edith Wyschogrod, *Saints and Postmoderns* (Chicago: University of Chicago Press, 1990); and John D. Caputo, *Against Ethics* (Bloomington and Indianapolis: Indiana University Press, 1993), 56–68.

12. This distinction is authorized by *Totality and Infinity*, since *Otherwise than Being* and *Of God Who Comes to Mind* will unsettle the very structure of ontotheology and of modern conceptions of transcendence. Two excellent essays that focus on the tension between morality and ethical transcendental philosophy are Hent de Vries, "Adieu, à-dieu, à-Dieu," in *Ethics as First Philosophy*, ed. Adriaan T. Peperzak (London: Routledge, 1995), 211–20; and Theodore de Boer, "An Ethical Transcendental Philosophy," in *Face to Face with Levinas*, ed. Richard A. Cohen (Albany: State University of New York Press, 1986), 83–115.

13. Emmanuel Levinas, *Totality and Infinity: An Essay on Exteriority*, trans. Alphonso Lingis (Pittsburgh: Duquesne University Press, 1969). Originally published as *Totalité et infini: Essai sur l'extériorité* (The Hague: Martinus Nijhoff, 1961). Hereafter, the English work is cited in the text by the abbreviation TI, and the original French by the abbreviation TeI.

14. Emmanuel Levinas, *Otherwise than Being: or, Beyond Essence*, trans. Alphonso Lingis (Pittsburgh: Duquesne University Press, 1998). Hereafter, this work is cited in the text by the abbreviation OB.

15. For a distinction between an inventory of the other and the invention of the other in the sense of *invenire* or "letting the other come," see Jacques Derrida, *Psychè: Inventions de l'autre* (Paris: Gallimard, 1987). Hereafter, this work is cited in the text by the abbreviation PSY.

16. See Emile Littré, *Dictionnaire de la langue française en un volume* (Paris: Hachette, 2000); *Le Grand Dictionnaire Hachette* (Paris: Hachette, 1991); and the *Oxford English Dictionary* (Oxford: Oxford University Press, 1976). The meanings of "intrigue" and "plot" belong to the same semantic field in French and English to the point that the OED defines intrigue as "the plot of a play, novel or romance." As we will see in chapter 6, in *Otherwise than Being* Levinas implicitly distinguishes plot from *intrigue*, reserving the latter for the un-narrative modality of ethical writing.

17. Maurice Blanchot, *Faux Pas* (Paris: Gallimard, 1943). Hereafter, this work is cited in the text by the abbreviation FP.

18. Maurice Blanchot, *The Space of Literature*, trans. Ann Smock (Lincoln: University of Nebraska Press, 1992). Hereafter, this work is cited in the text by the abbreviation SL.

19. Maurice Blanchot, *La Part du feu* (Paris: Gallimard, 1949). Hereafter, this work is cited in the text by the abbreviation PF.

20. Maurice Blanchot, *The Infinite Conversation*, trans. Susan Hanson (Minneapolis: University of Minnesota Press, 1993). Hereafter, this work is cited in the text by the abbreviation IC.

21. Maurice Blanchot, *The Step Not Beyond*, trans. Lycette Nelson (Albany: State University of New York Press, 1992). Originally published as *Le Pas au-delà* (Paris: Gallimard, 1971). Hereafter, the English work is cited in the text by the abbreviation SNB, and the original French by the abbreviation PAD.

22. Maurice Blanchot, "The Song of the Sirens," in *The Station Hill Blanchot Reader*, ed. George Quasha (Barrytown, N.Y.: Station Hill Press, 1998), 450. Hereafter, this work is cited in the text by the abbreviation SH.

23. The bibliography on narratology is extensive and I will refer only to those books that present an overview of the field: Robert Scholes, *Structuralism and Literature* (New Haven: Yale University Press, 1974); Seymour Chatman, *Story and Discourse* (Ithaca: Cornell University Press, 1979); Gerald Prince, *Narratology: The Form and Functioning of Narrative* (The Hague: Mouton, 1982); and Peter Brooks, *Reading for the Plot: Design and Intention in Narrative* (Cambridge: Harvard University Press, 1984).

24. Paul Ricoeur, *Time and Narrative* (Chicago: University of Chicago Press, 1988).

25. Walter Benjamin, "The Storyteller," in *Illuminations* (New York: Schocken Books, 1969), 83–109.

CHAPTER 1. THE PASSION OF TIME: *AU MOMENT VOULU* (NIETZSCHE-HEIDEGGER-BLANCHOT)

1. I will discuss these terms in more detail in chapters 3 and 6.

2. Maurice Blanchot, *Au moment voulu* (Paris: Gallimard, 1951). Hereafter, this work is cited in the text by the abbreviation AMV.

3. A section of *Au moment voulu* was originally published as "Le Retour" in *Botteghe Oscure* 7 (1951): 416–14. "Le Régard d'Orphée" appeared in *Cahiers de l'Art* 28, no. 1 (June 1953): 73–75; "Le Chant de sirènes" was published in *Nouvelle Revue Française* 19 (July 1954): 95–104. "L'Étrange et l'étranger" appeared in *Nouvelle Revue Française* 70 (October 1958), 673–83. The essays on Nietzsche, later included in *The Infinite Conversation*, appeared in *Nouvelle Revue Française* between 1958 and 1960.

4. Jean-Luc Nancy, *Being Singular Plural*, trans. Robert D. Richardson and Anne E. O'Byrne (Stanford: Stanford University Press, 2000), 4.

5. "Last witness, end of history, close of a period, turning point, crisis—or, end of (metaphysical philosophy). . . . Why does writing—when we understand this movement as the change from one era to a different one, and when we think of it as the experience (the inexperience) of the disaster—always imply the words inscribed at the beginning of this 'fragment,' which, however, it revokes? It revokes them even if what they announce is announced as something new which has always already taken place, *a radical change* from which the present is excluded. . . . To write in the ignorance of the philosophical horizon—or refusing to acknowledge the punctuation, the groupings or separations determined by the words that mark this horizon—is necessarily to write with facile complacency (the literature of elegance and good taste). Hölderlin, Mallarmé, so many others, do not permit this" (WD 102–3).

6. Leslie Hill, *Maurice Blanchot: Extreme Contemporary* (London: Routledge, 1997).

7. Gerald L. Bruns, *Maurice Blanchot: The Refusal of Philosophy* (Baltimore: Johns Hopkins University Press, 1998), and Hill, *Maurice Blanchot*.

8. Martin Heidegger, *Nietzsche*, vol. 1, trans. David F. Krell (New York: Harper Collins, 1991), 15. Hereafter, this work is cited in the text by the abbreviation N.

9. As C. Fynsk notes, this claim applies only to the texts collected in the first volume of Nietzsche lectures; the style becomes confrontational and critical in the rest of the lectures. See Chrystopher Fynsk, "Nietzsche's Testimony," in *Heidegger: Thought and Historicity* (Ithaca: Cornell University Press, 1986).

10. Martin Heidegger, *Sein und Zeit* (Tübingen: Max Niemeyer, 1984). Hereafter, this work is cited in the text by the abbreviation SZ.

11. I am concerned here neither with a detailed analysis of temporality in Heidegger's *Being and Time*, nor with his reassessment of temporality in his late work. For these two problematics, the reader can consult David F. Krell, *Intimations of Mortality: Time, Truth, and Finitude in Heidegger's Thinking of Being* (University Park: Pennsylvania State University Press, 1986); Françoise Dastur, *Heidegger and the Question of Time* (Atlantic Highlands, N.J.: Humanities Press, 1998); Jean-Michel Salanskis, *Heidegger* (Paris: Les Belles Letres, 1997), 90–8; and my "Abyssal Grounds: Heidegger and Lacan on Truth," *Qui parle?* 9, no. 2 (1996): 51–76.

12. "When resolute, *Dasein* has brought itself back from falling, and has done so precisely in order to be more authentically 'there' in the 'moment of *vision*' (*Augenblink*) as regards the Situation which has been disclosed" (BT 65, 376).

13. "L'événement nous atteint en bouleversant le fond du monde où nous avons notre ancrage et l'horizon de monde sous lequel nous nous signifions." Henry Maldiney, "L'Irreductible," *Epokhè* 3 (1993): 11–49.

14. Claude Romano, *L'Événement et le temps* (Paris: PUF, 1999).

15. Maurice Blanchot, *L'Instant de ma mort* (Montpellier: Fata Morgana, 1994).

16. Maurice Blanchot, *L'Entretien infini* (Paris: Gallimard, 1969). Hereafter, this work is cited in the text by the abbreviation EL.

17. This reading can be placed within the context of the confrontation Heidegger-Nietzsche and includes: Pierre Klossowsky, *Nietzsche et le circle vicieux*; Gilles Deleuze, *Nietzsche et la philosophie*; Jacques Derrida, *Eperons*; Eugen Fynk, *La Philosophie de Nietzsche*; and Krell and Wood, *Exceedingly Nietzsche*. For an assessment of Nietzsche's impact on contemporary French thinking, see Alan Schrift, *Nietzsche's French Legacy: A Genealogy of Poststructuralism* (London: Routledge, 1995).

18. See "When the Time Comes," in *Station Hill Blanchot Reader*, 255. Hereafter, this work is cited in the text by the abbreviation SH.

19. I use the word "dimension" to refer to the peculiar temporalizing of the event, since the relation of the other is not a fact and, thus, supposes an absence of horizon. For the distinction between horizon and dimension (*dimensionnel*), see Claudio Romano, *L'Événement et le temps* (Paris: PUF, 1999.)

20. Heidegger, *Nietzsche*, vol. 1.

21. See Maurice Blanchot, "Le Chant des sirènes," in *Le Livre à venir* (Paris: Gallimard, 1976). Hereafter, this work is cited in the text by the abbreviation LV.

22. And that are referred to with regularity and according to their intensity as scene: "the scene of hair-combing" (84–85), and "Nescio vos" (115–17); event: "the shock" (87–88) and "the figure of the outside" (92–93); incident: "the upheaval of Claudia and the narrator-character" (47–48) and "Claudia's prodigious cry" (106); image: "Judith's portrait" (64); situation: "the gay force" (123–26); gesture: "Claudia's pressing of the narrator-character's cold hands on her throat"; ceremony: "on Claudia's singing" (69).

23. Jacques Derrida, *Parages* (Paris: Galilée, 1980), 15. Hereafter, this work is cited in the text by the abbreviation P.

24. "The text of the aporia (*aporetique*) intensifies the antagonism between illusion and reading. By positing the inadequacy of language to 'express,' it stands at the dead-end where the failure of logic and the signifying machinery has pushed it. . . . The aporia's disturbances postpone an illusion that finally returns under the species of the phantasm, of what is unnamable or surreal. The conflictive radicalization gives no respite to the vertigo of the illusionist art that the novel is." Mireille Calle-Gruber, *L'Effet-fiction: De l'illusion romanesque* (Paris: Nizet, 1989): 26–27.

25. See Blanchot's "Two Versions of the Imaginary," in *The Space of Literature*.

26. Maurice Blanchot, *L'Écriture du désastre* (Paris: Gallimard, 1980). Hereafter, this work is cited in the text by the abbreviation ED.

27. For a systematic development of the logic of "sans" in Blanchot, see Derrida, in *Parages*, and "The *Sans* of the Pure Cut," in *The Truth in Painting*. For

Derrida "sans" ruins the working of the negative since it is neither an operator of contradiction nor of negation.

28. See Steven Shaviro, *Passion and Excess: Blanchot, Bataille, and Literary Theory* (Tallahassee: Florida State University Press, 1990), especially chapters 6 and 7.

29. Georg Lukács, *Soul and Form*, trans. Anna Bostock (Cambridge: MIT Press, 1974).

30. ". . . but what I had perhaps let fall as a grammatical fact was being thrown back at me" (AMV 137/SH 250).

31. "The [work] reaches, in that instant, its point of extreme uncertainty. That is why it resists so often and so strongly that which inspires it. That is also why it protects itself by saying to Orpheus: You will keep me only if you keep from looking at her (*Tu ne me garderas que si tu ne* la *regardes pas*)" (EL 229/ SL 174).

32. Eurydice is not "turned into a kind of embodiment of artistic raw material." First, because in Blanchot, contrary to what Karen Jacobs claims, negation does not become "a means for transcendence," a claim which would make Blanchot a dialectician. More importantly, Blanchot's gaze is not shaped "in conformity to an ideology of visual violence that takes place over and through a woman's body." It would be necessary to compare Sartre's *L'Imaginaire* and *L'Être et le néant* with Blanchot's "Two Versions of the Imaginary" here. In chapter 5 I show how Blanchot reverses Sartre's concept of fascination by inscribing it within a register where power and the autonomy of consciousness are no longer operative. For these two reasons, Jacobs's assimilation of Blanchot to Sartre's scopophilic "appropriative enjoyment" in *L'Être et le néant* amounts to more than optical violence. See Karen Jacobs, "Two Mirrors Facing: Freud, Blanchot, and the Logic of Invisibility," in *Qui parle?* 4, no. 1 (fall 1990): 23–31.

33. "Nonexperience" because it is not a lived event and puts the present out of play. However, the negative prefix does not indicate a diminishing of intensity or danger. The modality of "experience as nonexperience" is that of an excess over itself and this excess is the a-thematizable theme of *Au moment voulu*.

34. "At night, in the South, when I get up, I know that it isn't a question of proximity, or of distance, or of an event belonging to me, or of a truth capable of speaking, this is not a scene, or the beginning of something. An image, but a futile one, an instant, but a sterile one, someone for whom I am nothing and who is nothing to me—without bonds, without beginning, without end—a point, and outside this point, nothing in the world, that is not foreign to me. A face? But one deprived of a name, without a biography, one that is rejected by memory, that does not want to be recounted, that does not want to survive; present, but she is not there; absent, and yet in no way elsewhere, here; true? Altogether outside of what is true. If someone says, she is bound to the night, I

deny it; the night doesn't know her. If someone asks me, but what are you talking about? I answer, well, there is no one to ask me that" (AMV 151–52/SH 255). On *quelqu'un* see both Giorgio Agamben's *The Coming Community*, trans. Michael Hardt (Minneapolis: University of Minnesota Press, 1993) and Jean-Luc Nancy's *The Sense of the World*, trans. Jeffrey Librett (Minneapolis: University of Minnesota Press, 1997).

CHAPTER 2. DWELLING: BETWEEN *POIÉSIS* AND *TECHNÉ*

1. See Blanchot, "La Parole 'sacrée' de Hölderlin," in *La Part du feu*, 115–32; Beda Alleman, *Hölderlin und Heidegger* (Zürich and Freiburg: Atlantis Verlag, 1956), and "Hölderlin zwischen Antike und Moderne," in *Hölderlin-Jahrbuch* 24 (1984–85): 29–62; Theodor W. Adorno, "Parataxis: On Hölderlin's Late Poetry," in *Notes to Literature*, trans. Shierry Weber Nicholsen (New York: Columbia University Press, 1992), 2:109–49; Paul de Man, "Heidegger's Exegesis of Hölderlin," in *Blindness and Insight* (Minneapolis: University of Minnesota Press, 1971), 246–66, and "The Image of Rousseau in Hölderlin," in *The Rhetoric of Romanticism* (New York: Columbia University Press, 1984), 19–46; *Romanticism and Contemporary Criticism*, ed. Kevin Newmark, Andrzej Warminski, and E. S. Burt (Baltimore: Johns Hopkins University Press, 1993), 55–56, 65; Annemarie Gethmann-Siefert, "Heidegger and Hölderlin: The Over-Usage of 'Poets in an Impoverished Time,'" *Research and Phenomenology* 19 (1989): 59–88; John D. Caputo, "Heidegger's Poets," in *Demythologizing Heidegger* (Bloomington: Indiana University Press, 1992), 148–68; Véronique Fóti, *Heidegger and the Poets: Poiésis, Sophia, Techné* (Atlantic Highlands, N.J.: Humanities Press International, 1992).

2. Although there is consensus that Heidegger's turn to Hölderlin should be read as the result of his political withdrawal, a more complex picture of this move emerges by inserting Heidegger's conferences and courses on Hölderlin within the series of the four courses on logic, that is, within Heidegger's attempt to think the articulation of being, language and truth: *Logik: Die Frage nach der Wahrheit* (GA 21, 1925–26); *Metaphysische Anfangsgründe der Logik im Ausgang von Leibniz* (GA 26, 1928); *Logik als die Frage nacht dem Wesen der Sprache* (GA 38, 1934, unpublished); *Heraklit 2. Logik: Heraklit Lehre vom Logos* (GA 55, 1944). That a course on Hölderlin is part of this sequence is indicative that "logic" in Heidegger names something else than a regional discipline that deals with the rules for thinking correctly. The "turn" names the transition from metaphysics to a nonmetaphysical thinking. See Werner Marx, *Heidegger and the Tradition*, trans. Theodore Kiesel and Murray Greene (Evanston, Ill.: Northwestern University Press, 1971), 173–79, and James Risser, ed., *Heidegger toward the Turn: Essays on the Work of the 1930s* (Albany: State University of New York Press, 1999).

3. Martin Heidegger, *Kant and the Problem of Metaphysics,* trans. Richard Taft (Bloomington: Indiana University Press, 1990). Hereafter, this work is cited in the text by the abbreviation KPM.

4. In addition to the authors mentioned in note 1, see Robert Bernasconi, *The Question of Language in Heidegger's History of Being* (Atlantic Highlands, N.J.: Humanities Press International, 1985); Christopher Fynsk, *Language and Relation* (Stanford: Stanford University Press, 1996); Gerald L. Bruns, *Heidegger's Estrangements: Language, Truth and Poetry in the Later Writings* (New Haven: Yale University Press, 1989); Michael Roth, *The Poetics of Resistance: Heidegger's Line* (Evanston, Ill.: Northwestern University Press, 1996); David Halliburton, *Poetic Thinking: An Approach to Heidegger* (Chicago: University of Chicago Press, 1981); and Marc Froment-Meurice, *That Is to Say: Heidegger's Poetics,* trans. Jan Plug (Stanford: Stanford University Press, 1998).

5. Martin Heidegger, "Letter on Humanism," in *Pathmarks,* ed. William McNeill (Cambridge: Cambridge University Press, 1998). Hereafter, this work is cited in the text by the abbreviation LH. *Pathmarks* will be cited by the abbreviation PATH.

6. See Werner Marx, *Towards a Phenomenological Ethics: Ethos and the Life-World* (Albany: SUNY Press, 1992); Johanna Hodge, *Heidegger and Ethics* (New York: Routledge, 1995); Frank Schalow, "Language and the Tragic Side of Ethics," in *International Studies in Philosophy* 27, no. 11 (1996): 49–63; Frederick Olafson, *Heidegger and the Grounds of Ethics* (Cambridge: Cambridge University Press, 1998); Michel Haar, *The Song of the Earth: Heidegger and the Grounds of the History of Being,* trans. Reginald Lilly (Bloomington: Indiana University Press, 1993).

7. Heidegger, "The Origin of the Work of Art," in *Poetry, Language, Thought.*

8. Heidegger, *Hölderlin's Hymn "The Ister,"* trans. William McNeill and Julia Davis (Bloomington: Indiana University Press, 1994). Hereafter, this work is cited in the text by the abbreviation HHI.

9. The relation between the familiar and the unfamiliar has several configurations in Heidegger, but is most visible in his interpretation of Hölderlin's poem "Andenken," in *Elucidations of Hölderlin's Poetry,* 101–73; in the interpretation of Sophocles's "deinon deinotaton," in *An Introduction to Metaphysics,* 146–64; and in *Hölderlin's Hymn "The Ister,"* 51–73. I have dealt with the question of the ground in my "Abyssal Grounds: Lacan and Heidegger on Truth," *Qui parle?* 9, no. 2 (spring/summer 1997): 51–76.

10. Martin Heidegger, *An Introduction to Metaphysics,* trans. Ralph Mannheim (New Haven: Yale University Press, 1959). Originally published as *Einführung in die Metaphysik* (Tübingen: Niemeyer, 1953). Hereafter, the English work is cited in the text by the abbreviation IM and the original German by the abbreviation EM. For a distinction between commencement, the inaugural, or inception (*Anfang*) and beginning (*Beggin*), see Rainer Schürmann, *Heidegger on Being and Acting:*

From Principles to Anarchy, trans. Christine Marie Gros (Bloomington: Indiana University Press, 1987), 120–25.

11. "Daß es diesem seienden, in seinem *um* dieses sein selbst geht" (SZ 12).

12. Martin Heidegger, *On the Way to Language*, trans. Peter Hertz (New York: Harper & Row, 1971). Hereafter, this work is cited in the text by the abbreviation OWL.

13. See Martin Heidegger, *The Principle of Reason*, trans. Reginald Lilly (Bloomington: Indiana University Press, 1996).

14. It is also true that Heidegger listens to this language in the proximity of mystics such as Meister Eckhart and Angelus Silesius. See John D. Caputo, *The Mystical Element in Heidegger's Thought* (New York: Fordham University Press, 1987). Heidegger's visible and at times militant Greco-Germanism should not make one lose sight of his "debt" to other traditions, principally Jewish and Asian traditions. For the former, see Marlène Zarader, *La Dette impensée: Heidegger et l'héritage hébraïque* (Paris: Éditions du Seuil, 1990). For the latter see Carlo Saviani, *L'Orienti di Heidegger* (Genova: Il Melangolo, 1998).

15. "What is meant by the talk about the end of philosophy (*Ende der Philosophie*)? We understand the end of something all too easily in the negative sense as a mere stopping, as the lack of a continuation, perhaps even as decline and impotence. In contrast, what we say about the end of philosophy means the completion of metaphysics (*die Vollendung der Metaphysik*)," in Martin Heidegger, *The End of Philosophy*, trans. Joan Stambaugh (New York: Harper & Row, 1973), 84.

16. Schürmann, *Heidegger on Being and Acting*, 197. According to Schürmann one can approach this "history of being" in three different ways: by a prospective reading, that is, from the viewpoint of the pre-Socratic commencement; by a retrospective reading, which means from the perspective of the modern exhaustion of metaphysics; and finally, through a series of *categories of transition* that enabled Heidegger to go in the direction of a post-metaphysical thinking. However, "transitional" may be a misleading term when applied to Heidegger's most idiosyncratic categories, as one may lose sight of the true stakes at play in thinking the "topology of being" not only at the "end of metaphysics," but also and fundamentally beyond "the history of being" and of its epochal sendings.

17. Martin Heidegger, "The Question Concerning Technology," in *The Question Concerning Technology and Other Essays*, trans. William Lovit (New York: Harper & Row, 1977). Hereafter, this work is cited in the text by the abbreviation QCT.

18. Martin Heidegger, *On the Way to Language*, trans. Peter Hertz (New York, Harper & Row, 1971).

19. Heidegger formulates the idea of a dialogue between thinking and poetry for the first time in the 1929 essay "What Is Metaphysics?" in *Pathmarks*. Hereafter, this essay is cited in the text by the abbreviation WM.

20. Alain Badiou, "L'Âge de poètes," in *La Politique des poètes: Pourquoi des poètes en temps de détresse?* ed. Jacques Rancière, Bibliothéque du Collége International de Philosophie (Paris: Albin Michel, 1992), 21–38; *Manifesto for Philosophy*, trans. Norman Madarasz (Albany: State University of New York Press, 1999), 47–52 and 69–77; *Petit Manuel d'inesthétique* (Paris: Éditions du Seuil, 1988), 9–48; and *Court Traité d'ontologie transitoire* (Paris: Éditions du Seuil, 1998), 9–24.

21. The answer for Levinas, as we will see in the next chapters, is no.

22. See Derrida, "L'Oreille de Heidegger: Philopolémologie (*Geschlecht IV*)," in *Politiques de l'amitié* (Paris: Galilée, 1994), 343–403; and Philippe Lacoue-Labarthe, *Heidegger: La Politique du poème* (Paris: Galilée, 2002). Hereafter, *Politiques de l'amitié* will be cited in the text by the abbreviation PolA.

23. For Heidegger's politics, see Otto Pöggeler, *Martin Heidegger's Path of Thinking*, trans. Daniel Magurshak and Sigmund Barber (Atlantic Highlands, N.J.: Humanities Press International, 1987), 16; Rüdiger Safranski, *Martin Heidegger: Between Good and Evil*, trans. Ewald Osers (Cambridge: Harvard University Press, 1998); Richard Wolin, ed., *The Heidegger Controversy* (Cambridge: MIT Press, 1993); Philippe Lacoue-Labarthe, *Heidegger, Art and Politics*, trans. Chris Turner (Oxford: Basil Blackwell, 1990); Jacques Derrida, *Of Spirit: Heidegger and the Question*, trans. Rachel Bowlby and Geoffrey Bennington (Chicago: University of Chicago Press, 1991), and Jacques Derrida, "L'Oreille de Heidegger: Philopolémologie (*Geschlecht IV*)," in *Politiques de l'amitié*; Gregory Fried, *Heidegger's Polemos: From Being to Politics* (New Haven: Yale University Press, 2000); and Miguel de Beistegui, *Heidegger and Politics: Dystopias* (London: Routledge, 1998).

24. Hölderlin is fundamentally the poet in whom Heidegger ciphers the possibility of the foundation of the German people. He will gradually speak in terms of the poet as the one who secures a dwelling on earth, who preserves the "memory" of the holy and thus points to the possibility of salvation in a "time of distress," and finally as the one who opens up the time-space within which a being homely is possible. George is the figure of the poet who accompanies the thinker in his "experience with language" and who teaches about the resignation of mastery over language as the true saying of being. See OWL, 139–56.

25. If one excludes the Rectoral Address, most commentators agree that Heidegger's turn to poetry amounts to a withdrawal from politics. See Otto Pöggeler, *Philosophie und Politik bei Heidegger* (Freiburg: Niemeyer, 1972) and "Den Führer führen? Heidegger und keine Ende," *Philosophische Rundschau* 32 (1985).

Philippe Lacoue-Labarthe has shown that Heidegger's poetic meditations are political through and through; they are a continuation of politics. Although I do agree with the latter view, I think it is worthwhile to emphasize the counter-politics at stake in Heidegger's effort to extricate himself from National Socialism, even if he does not fully succeed. *An Introduction to Metaphysics* bears witness to this, especially when Heidegger speaks of the "inner truth and greatness of [the NS] movement" (IM 166/EM 152). Fred Dallmayr argues along these lines in *The Other Heidegger* (Ithaca: Cornell University Press, 1993), although I prefer Jean-François Lyotard's cautionary remark that "one cannot be satisfied with simply acknowledging the coexistence of the two faces of Heidegger, one venerable, the other ignoble, and diagnose a split between the two," in *Heidegger and "the Jews,"* trans. Andreas Michel and Mark Roberts (Minneapolis: University of Minnesota Press, 1995), 52.

26. According to Adorno, Heidegger sought in Hölderlin the justification of his dangerous ideology, an ontological radicalism that is the reflection of a political radicalism. See Adorno, "Parataxis," in *Notes to Literature*.

27. Martin Heidegger, *Gesamtausgabe* 39: Hölderlins Hymnen "Germanien" und "Der Rhein" (Frankfurt: Klostermann, 1980). Hereafter, this work is cited in the text by the abbreviation GA 39. See also HHI.

28. "Die φύσις ist das Sein selbst, kraft dessen das Seiende erst beobachtbar wird und bleibt," Martin Heidegger, *Einführung in die Metaphysik* (Tübingen: Niemeyer, 1953), 11. See also GA 55, 205, and *Vorträge und Aufsätze* (Pfullingen: Neske, 1954).

29. "Overcoming of Aesthetics in the Question of Art" was the title of a seminar that Heidegger organized in Freiburg in 1935 and which was the occasion for the first version of "The Origin of the Work of Art." See Martin Heidegger, "Vom Ursprung des Kunstwerks, Erste Ausarbeitung," *Heidegger Studies* 14 (1998): 6–22; *Der Ursprung des Kunstwerkes* (Stuttgart: Reclam, 1960); and "Der Ursprung des Kunstwerks," *Holzwege* (Frankfurt: Klostermann, 1950).

30. Martin Heidegger, *Contributions to Philosophy (From Enowning)*, trans. Parvis Emad and Kenneth Maly (Bloomington: Indiana University Press, 1999). Hereafter, this work is cited in the text by the abbreviation CP.

31. See David Krell, *Daimon Life: Heidegger and Life-Philosophy* (Bloomington: Indiana University Press, 1992).

32. See Martin Heidegger, "*Alêtheia* (Heraclitus, Fragment B 16)," in *Early Greek Thinking*, trans. David Farrell Krell and Frank A. Capuzzi (New York: Harper & Row, 1975), 102–24. We will see below how this *pólemos* unfolds as the working of the work of art. Hereafter, this work is cited in the text by the abbreviation EGT.

33. "Nur das Gewährte währt. Das anfänglich aus der Frühe wahrende ist das Gewährende."

34. Heidegger determines Hölderlin's holy or the divine in terms of the question of being, suppressing the subjective dimension of his poetics, as well as what goes by the name of life, its ungraspable nature. These are all questions that go beyond the scope of this chapter, but that have been addressed by

Stanley Corngold, *The Fate of the Self: German Writers and French Theory* (Durham, N.C.: Duke University Press, 1994); Hans-Jost Frey, *Studies in Poetic Discourse: Mallarmé, Baudelaire, Rimbaud, Hölderlin*, trans. William Whobrey (Stanford: Stanford University Press, 1996); and Thomas Pfau, "Critical Introduction," in *Hölderlin's Essays and Letters on Theory* (Albany: State University of New York Press, 1988).

35. Martin Heidegger, *Was heißt Denken?* (Tübingen: Max Niemeyer, 1984). Hereafter, this work is cited in the text by the abbreviation WHD. This is the version (*versant*) of essential language that Blanchot privileges in Heidegger, which he thinks in terms of unworking (*desœuvrement*) and plots by reinterpreting Orpheus's myth. See SL.

36. Martin Heidegger, "Vom Ursprung des Kunstwerks, Erste Ausarbeitung" *Heidegger Studies* 14 (1998): 6–22.

37. For the relationship between Nietzsche's and Heidegger's conceptions of art, see Christopher Fynsk, *Heidegger: Thought and Historicity* (Ithaca: Cornell University Press, 1986), 131–37; John Caputo, "Three Transgressions: Nietzsche, Heidegger, Derrida," *Research in Phenomenology* 15 (1985): 61–78; Johanna Hodge, *Heidegger and Ethics* (New York: Routledge, 1997), 122–33; and Gerald L. Bruns, *Heidegger's Estrangements: Language, Truth, and Poetry in the Later Writings* (New Haven: Yale University Press, 1984).

38. "The debate with Nietzsche's metaphysics is a debate with nihilism, as it manifests itself with increased clarity under the political form of fascism," Martin Heidegger, "Letter to Rector of Freiburg University, November 4, 1945," in *The Heidegger Controversy*, ed. Richard Wolin (Cambridge: MIT Press, 1992), 61–67.

39. Heidegger has Alfred Baumler's *Nietzsche der Philosoph un Politiker* (1931) in mind. See Philippe Lacoue-Labarthe and Jean-Luc Nancy, *Le Mythe nazie*; Philippe Lacoue-Labarthe, *Heidegger, Art and Politics*; and Miguel de Beistegui, *Heidegger and the Political: Dystopias*. I take the expression "philosophy of Hitlerism" from Levinas's essay, which I will discuss in chapter 5.

40. To anticipate what I will develop more fully in the following chapters: Levinas's point of departure is not distress, but enjoyment, and instead of being the caretaker of being, subjectivity becomes the caretaker of the other human being. Levinas replaces the traumatism of the god's flight with the traumatism of separation that infinity enacts, and later on, with the structure of the-other-in-the-same in which the self is hostage to the other.

CHAPTER 3. THE ENIGMA OF MANIFESTATION (FIGURATION IN HEIDEGGER)

1. Heidegger, "The Origin of the Work of Art," in *Poetry, Language, Thought*.
2. See Jean-François Courtine, "La Voix étrangere de l'ami: Appel et/ou dialogue," in *Heidegger et la phénoménologie* (Paris: Vrin, 1990), 327–54; Paul Ricoeur,

Soi-même comme un autre, 213–20; and Jacques Derrida, *Politics of Friendship*, trans. George Collins (London: Verso, 1977).

3. I will discuss Levinas's radical questioning of Heidegger's structure of being-with in the next chapter.

4. Martin Heidegger, *Unterwegs sur Sprache* (Pfullingen: Günter Neske, 1959). Hereafter, this work is cited in the text by the abbreviation US.

5. See TI and Jean-Paul Sartre, *Being and Nothingness* (New York: Philosophical Library, 1948).

6. Heidegger, *Gesamtausgabe* 39.

7. The first example Heidegger mentions is being's revelation as a burden, which indicates that affection has an ontological power of revelation more fundamental than understanding. In Heidegger's example then there is a coimplication of *Stimmung* and *Befindlichkeit*. If the question is "*Y* être ou ne pas *y* être" (Charcosset), Levinas will think the evasion out of pure being (il *y* a), since for Heidegger "in having a mood (*Stimmung*), *Dasein* is always disclosed moodwise as that entity to which it has been delivered over to the Being which, in existing, it has to be" (BT 173/135). See Leo Spitzer, *Classical and Christian Ideas of World Harmony: Prolegomena to an Interpretation of the Word "Stimmung"* (Baltimore: Johns Hopkins University Press, 1963); Jean-Pierre Charcosset, "*Y*. Notes sur la Stimmung," *Exercises de la patience* 3–4 (1982): 46–93; Henri Maldiney, *Regard, parole, espace* (Lausanne: L'Âge d'homme, 1973); Michel Haar, "La Pensée et le moi chez Heidegger: Le Dons et les épreuves de l'être," *Revue de métaphysique et morale* 4 (1975): 456–83; and Françoise Dastur, *Heidegger et la question anthropologique* (Louvain-Paris: Éditions Peters, 2003).

8. In the *Grundbegriffe* (1929–30) Heidegger stresses the musical dimension of the *Stimmung*. It is not the subject's interiority that would be apprehended in itself as feeling (*Gefühl*) but the world's tone which from the start places *Dasein* within the whole of beings. See Martin Heidegger, *Die Grundbegriffe der Métaphysik* (Frankfurt: Vittorio Klosterman, 1981), 101. Hereafter, this work is cited in the text by the abbreviation GA 30.

9. See Martin Heidegger, "Moira," in *Early Greek Thinkers*, trans. David Farrell Krell and John D. Capuzzi (New York: Harper & Row, 1975), 79–101.

10. Friedrich Hölderlin, *Poems and Fragments*, trans. Michael Hamburger (London: Anvil Press Poetry, 1994), 32.

11. Friedrich Hölderlin, "Brot und wine," in *Poems and Fragments*, trans. Michael Hamburger (London: Anvil Press Poetry, 1994), 46.

12. Martin Heidegger, *Holzwege* (Frankfurt: Klostermann, 1950). Hereafter, this work is cited in the text by the abbreviation HW.

13. Friedrich Hölderlin, "On Religion," in *Hölderlin's Essays and Letters on Theory*, trans. Thomas Pfau (Albany: State University of New York Press, 1988), 120–27.

14. Martin Heidegger, *Vorträge und Aufsätze* (Pfullingen: Günter Neske, 1954). Hereafter, this work is cited in the text by the abbreviation VA.

15. Heidegger reinscribes the Kantian distinction of the beautiful and the sublime.

16. For the economy of restitution, see Jacques Derrida, "Restitutions," in *The Truth in Painting*, trans. Geoff Bennington and Ian McLeod (Chicago: University of Chicago Press, 1985), 255–382.

17. Bruns reads the "late Heidegger" in terms of "estrangement," which he places under the heading of *Gelassenheit*, Heidegger's final word. See Gerald L. Bruns, *Heidegger's Estrangements: Language, Truth, and Poetry in the Later Writings* (New Haven: Yale University Press).

18. For a reading that focuses on the presence of Hegel, see Jacques Taminiaux, *Poetics, Speculation and Judgment: The Shadow of the Work of Art from Kant to Phenomenology*, trans. Michael Gendre (Albany: State University of New York Press, 1993), 127–70. For the problematic of the hermeneutic circle in Hegel and Heidegger, see Jacques Derrida, *The Truth in Painting*, 17–34. For comprehensive studies on Heidegger's "conception of art," see Friedrich-Wilhelm von Herrmann, *Heideggers Philosophie der Kunst: Eine systematische Interpretation der Holzwege-Abhandlung "Der Ursprung des Kunstwerkes"* (Frankfurt: Klostermann, 1980); Joseph Kockelmans, *Heidegger on Art and Art Works* (Dordrecht: Martinus Nijhoff, 1985); Julian Young, *Heidegger's Philosophy of Art* (Cambridge: Cambridge University Press, 2004).

19. Martin Heidegger, *Being and Time*, 96–97 and ¶17–18. For Heidegger the world appears as everything that indicates. From an ontological point of view, the first function of the structure of assignment or reference is to allow an orientation among the things we come across in our everyday dealings. Heidegger's typology of signs corresponds to this concern with orientation. The structure of assignment or reference implies a *Bewandtnis*, an involvement, a "this is so," but without a teleological finality. The system of all the assignments or references is a figure of the world: *signifying* (*Bedeutsamkeit*, BT 120/87), the condition of possibility of signification and of language. *Signifying* brings a world into place and the whole of these places constitutes a region (*Gegend*): "In that significance with which *Dasein* is familiar, lies the essential co-disclosedness of space" (BT 145 / 111).

20. For the complex configuration of this *pólemos*, its onto-political stakes, see Jacques Derrida, *Politiques de l'amitié* (Paris: Galilée, 1994), 391–419. Hereafter, this work of Derrida is cited in the text by the abbreviation PolA.

21. For a different reading of the "that it be" (*Dass es sei*), see Marc Froment-Meurice, *That Is to Say: Heidegger's Poetics*, trans. Jan Plug (Stanford: Stanford University Press, 1998).

22. I borrow the expression from Philippe Lacoue-Labarthe and Jean-Luc Nancy, *Le Mythe nazie* (La Tour d'Aigues: Editions de l'Aube, 1991).

23. The standard translations of *Ereignis* are *event, appropriation, event of appropriation,* and *befitting,* although the translators of *Contributions to Philosophy* (From En-owning) renders it *enowning,* where the prefix *en-* carries the sense of enabling, bringing into condition of, welling up of. What this translation manages to capture is the movement of "a going all the way into and through" without *possessing.* At stake in *Ereignis* is the enabling power as an ongoing movement that does not rest in a "property" or "possession." See Heidegger, "Translator's Foreword," in CP, 15–44.

24. One cannot help but notice that "The Origin of the Work of Art" was a conference and that Heidegger may have felt the need to introduce more familiar examples for a German audience: Mercedes, Volkswagen, and the heroic German peasant woman. See Jacques Derrida, "Restitutions," in *The Truth in Painting,* trans. Geoff Bennington and Ian McLeod (Chicago: University of Chicago Press, 1987), 318–21.

25. This is the crux of Levinas's critique of Heidegger's ontology of art, as we will see in the next two chapters.

26. For an analysis of the semantic network of *Stellen,* see Philippe Lacoue-Labarthe, *Typography,* trans. Christopher Fynsk (Stanford: Stanford University Press, 1989), 43–138.

27. For a detailed reading of the *Riss* and the logic of the remarking (*retrait*), see Derrida, "Le Retrait de la métaphore," in *Psyché: Inventions de l'autre,* 63–93.

CHAPTER 4. PLOT AND INTRIGUE: FROM BEING'S OTHER TO THE ''OTHERWISE THAN BEING'' (LANGUAGE, ETHICS, POETIC LANGUAGE IN LEVINAS)

1. "Plot" and "intrigue" are often defined synonymously, which explains why in *Otherwise than Being* Alphonso Lingis translates "intrigue diachronique" by "diachronic plot." Levinas is careful to distinguish between them according to the axis ontology/ethics. However rigorous this distinction may be, the contamination of plot (peripeteia, fable) and *intrigue* is unavoidable. Anticipating my analysis of the ways in which the ethical saying of the "otherwise than being" betrays itself in the said of ontology, it is possible to affirm that its *intrigue* is also betrayed by the plot of being or by "the peripetias of the said"; these are derivative with regard to the intrigue of the other.

2. Emmanuel Levinas, *Autrement qu'être, ou, Au-delà de l'essence* (Paris: Kluwer Academics, 1978). Hereafter, this work is cited in the text by the abbreviation AE.

3. Emmanuel Levinas, *De Dieu qui vient à l'idée* (Paris: Vrin, 1982.) Hereafter, this work is cited in the text by the abbreviation DQV.

4. I will go back to this example and to the rhetoric of exasperation in chapter 6. Levinas gives some indication of his way of understanding ethical

writing in an essay devoted to Michel Leiris's *Biffures*, "La Transcendance des mots: A propos de biffures," that predates *Otherwise than Being*. That the protocols for writing the "otherwise than being" are presented in an essay that deals precisely with poetic language is very telling, especially for a thinker like Levinas whose views on art are generally harsh. I will discuss this essay in more detail in the next chapter.

5. As Derrida claims in "Violence and Metaphysics," in Levinas philosophical conceptuality has only one function. Although Levinas employs all the resources of the Greek *logos*, his aim is to express what exceeds it. This is precisely what Derrida calls "écriture clôtural." For a detailed analysis of the question of closure in Levinas, see Simon Critchley, *The Ethics of Deconstruction: Derrida and Levinas* (London: Blackwell, 1992).

6. Robert Eaglestone, *Ethical Criticism: Reading after Levinas* (Edinburgh: Edinburgh University Press, 1997); Thomas Docherty, *Alterities: Criticism, History, Representation* (Oxford: Clarendon Press, 1996); Andrew Gibson, *Postmodernity, Ethics and the Novel: From Leavis to Levinas* (London: Routledge, 1999); and Simon Critchley, *Very Little . . . Almost Nothing: Death, Philosophy and Literature* (London: Routledge, 1997).

7. See LH, 232–33.

8. For two different readings of Levinas's ethics organized around the question of subjectivity as traumatism, see Michel Haar, "L'Obsession de l'autre: L'Éthique comme traumatisme," in *Emmanuel Lévinas*, eds. Cathérine Chalier and M. Abensour (Paris: Éditions de l'Herne, 1991); and Simon Critchley, "The Original Traumatism: Levinas and Psychoanalysis," in *Ethics, Politics and Subjectivity* (London: Verso, 1999).

9. For Levinas's ethics as welcoming or hospitality, see Jacques Derrida, *Adieu to Emmanuel Lévinas*, trans. Pascale-Anne Brault and Michael Naas (Stanford: Stanford University Press, 1999). Hereafter, this work is cited in the text by the abbreviation AEL.

10. For a detailed study on Levinas and Kant, see Cathérine Chalier, *Pour une morale au-delà du savoir* (Paris: Albin Michel, 1998).

11. Or at least this is what the Levinas of *Totality and Infinity* attempted to formulate, a type of "relation" between an I and a you preserved from the violence of intersubjectivity. Nevertheless, as Derrida has shown, there are some "inconsistencies" in Levinas's analysis. Although Levinas refuses to treat the other as an alter ego, but rather as the "wholly other *(tout autre)*," the other is determined as "origin" of the self; that is, as an alter ego. This contradiction leads Derrida to conclude that what Levinas describes as alterity is what Husserl calls intersubjectivity. See Jacques Derrida, "Violence and Metaphysics," in *Writing and Difference*, trans. Alan Bass (Chicago: University of Chicago Press, 1978). Hereafter, this work is cited in the text by the abbreviation WAD.

12. In this sense, Levinas moves away from the "inconsistencies" of *Totality and Infinity*.

13. See Marjorie Garber, ed., *The Turn to Ethics* (London: Routledge, 2000).

14. For Levinas's understanding of language, see Adriaan T. Peperzak, "From Intentionality to Responsibility: On Levinas's Philosophy of Language," in *The Question of the Other: Essays in Contemporary Continental Philosophy*, eds. Arleen Dallery and Charles Scott (Albany: SUNY Press, 1989), 3–22.

15. Here I will follow the periodization of Levinas's work proposed by Silvano Petrosino and Jacques Rolland according to which "a first period would link together *On Evasion* to *Existence and Existents* and to the contemporary conferences on *Time and the Other*. A second period, crowned by *Totality and Infinity*, would have started with the set of preparatory essays to this major work: 'Is Ontology Fundamental?' (1951), 'Freedom and Command' (1953), 'The Ego and the Totality' (1954), 'Philosophy and the Idea of Infinity' (1957). A third period would begin with the essays that immediately followed the publication of *Totality and Infinity* and were included in the second part of *En découvrant l'existance* (2ᵉ ed., 1967) and would end with *Otherwise than Being*. . . . One could, although more problematically, see a fourth period taking shape . . . in which certains themes such as 'wakefulness' ('From Consciousness to Wakefulness,' 1974) and bad consciousness ('The Bad Conscience and the Inexorable,' 1981) have been more fully developed in texts included in *Of God Who Comes to Mind*." Silvano Petrosino and Jacques Rolland, *La Vérité nomade: Introduction à Emmanuel Lévinas* (Paris: La Découverte, 1984), 154, n. 29.

16. Levinas, *Autrement qu'être*.

17. Levinas, *De Dieu qui vient à l'idée*.

18. Levinas, *Entre nous: Essais sur le penser-à-l'autre* (Paris: Grasset, 1991). Hereafter, this work is cited in the text by the abbreviation EN.

19. For a critique of Heidegger's analytic of the self, see Paul Ricoeur, *Oneself as Another* (Chicago: University of Chicago Press, 1992).

20. See John Llewelyn's comments on Levinas's "absolute empiricism" in *Emmanuel Levinas: The Genealogy of Ethics* (London: Routledge, 1995), 112–15. Robert Bernasconi focuses on the irreducibility of the transcendental and the empirical in "Rereading *Totality and Infinity*," in Dallery and Scott, eds., *The Question of the Other*, 23–34.

21. For the nondialectical relation between I and other, see Adriaan T. Peperzak, *To the Other: An Introduction to the Philosophy of Emmanuel Levinas* (West Lafayette, Ind.: Purdue University Press, 1993).

22. For Levinas, it is not a question of elaborating a Jewish theology, since God "signifie de façon invraisemblable—c'est à dire—sans analogie avec une idée exposé à la sommation de se montrer vraie ou fausse—l'au-delà de l'être, la transcendance" (DQV 94–95). With Maimonides, Levinas shares the impossibility of elaborating a positive discourse on God, but he refuses to follow the

via negativa, as it is still too dependent on the positivity of being, thus ending up in a discourse on the ineffable. From this tradition, however, Levinas retains the need to unsay the theological said, as a way of escaping the grip of theology. See Marc Faessler, "Dieu, Autrement," in *Emmanuel Lévinas,* eds. Catherine Chalier and Miguel Abensour (Paris: Editions de L'Herne, 1991), 477–91; Catherine Chalier, *La Trace de l'infini: Emmanuel Lévinas et la source hébraïque* (Paris: Les Editions du Cerf, 2002); and Jacques Derrida, "Comment n'est pas parler: Dénegations," in *Psyché: Inventions de l'autre* (Paris: Galilée, 1988), 535–96.

23. The source of Levinas's concept of the face is Maimonides' *panim,* "the presence of a person in the place where he stands," that he defines through the notion of "face to face," the presence of one person to another other without any mediation. Maimonides quotes Dt 4:12: "you heard a voice speaking, but you saw no figure; there was only a voice" and states, "this is what is called a face-to-face." Maimonides also refers to the ethical use of the term *panin* in the Torah to express regard, care and attention toward another person. Finally, he also isolates two adverbial uses, one that suggests a temporal aspect, "before," and another that suggests a spatial aspect "in front." Levinas's formulation of the face as the other that precedes me from an anteriority that is not that of a past present, obliging me for all eternity, is contained in these lines. See Moshe Maimonides, "Laws of Repentance," in *Mishneh Torah: The Book of Knowledge,* ed. Moses Hyamson (Jerusalem: Henry Regnery, 1952); *The Guide of the Perplexed,* trans. Shlomo Pines (Chicago: University of Chicago Press, 1963). On Maimonides, see Moshe Idel, *Maïmonide et la mystique juive* (Paris: Cerf, 1991); Shlomo Pines, *La Liberté de philosopher: De Maïmonide à Spinoza* (Paris: Desclée de Brouwer, 1997); Leo Strauss, *Maïmonide* (Paris: Desclée de Brouwer, 1988); and Gérard Haddad, *Maïmonide* (Paris: Les Belles Lettres, 1998).

24. As we will see in the next chapter in our discussion of the *il y a* or pure being, Levinas reads *das Nicht* as nonbeing, that is, as an irrecuperable difference, the *in-* of the infinite, the invisible, or as the *un-* of the undefined. In the *in-*fini (the *eyn-sof,* the "there is no end"), one goes from God's infinity to the finite creation through the *in- (il n'y a pas).* In God's withdrawal creation takes place. But the risk consists in confusing God's withdrawal *(tsim-tsum)* that enables creatures to exist at a distance from him with nonexistence or pure being. A long tradition that includes Maimonides sees pure being or nonbeing as the source of evil. See M. Faessler, "L'Intrigue du tout autre: Dieu dans la pensée d'Emmanuel Lévinas," in *Emmanuel Lévinas,* Les Cahiers de La Nuit surveillée, no. 3, ed. Jacques Rolland (Lagrasse: Verdier, 1984), 119–47.

25. As in Kierkegaard, whose point of departure is the critique of Socratic maïeutics, the teacher delivers and frees the self from itself. See Søren Kierkegaard, *Philosophical Fragments,* trans. Howard V. Hong and Edna H. Hong (Princeton: Princeton University Press, 1985), 9–36.

26. While in *Totality and Infinity* Levinas uses the term *height* to privilege the transcendence and infinity of the ethical relation, in *Otherwise than Being* he shifts to the language of *proximity*, as he understands that *"height"* is still caught up in the syntax of a positive theology and that, consequently, it fails to render the meaning of ethical transcendence. See Levinas, "L'Idée de Dieu," in *De Dieu qui vient à l'idée*, 91–189.

27. In the final chapter I will discuss teaching as an asymmetrical relation in more detail since it is the crux of the *differend* between Levinas and Blanchot.

28. See Robert Gibbs, "Jewish Dimensions of Radical Ethics," in *Ethics as First Philosophy*, ed. Adriaan Peperzak (New York: Routledge, 1995), 12–23.

29. For an interpretation of Levinas's position on transcendence, see Peperzak, "Transcendence," in *Ethics as First Philosophy*, 185–92.

30. Emmanuel Levinas, *Hors sujet* (Montpellier: Fata Morgana, 1987), 183–94. Hereafter, this work is cited in the text by the abbreviation HS.

31. I will discuss this point in more detail in the next chapter.

32. For Levinas, the exposition of entities is only one dimension of signification for which he reserves the term *said (dit)*. However, "behind being and its monstration, there is now already heard the resonance of other significations forgotten in ontology" (AE 66–67/OB 38), for which Levinas reserves the term *saying (dire)*. I discuss these two terms in more detail below.

33. In other words, in Levinas art's relation to thinking cannot be equated with the treatment of this question in Foucault, Derrida, Lyotard and Badiou, to name just a few.

34. "The philosophical speaking that betrays in its said the proximity it conveys before us still remains, as a saying, a proximity and a responsibility" (AE 262 / OB 168).

35. In *Existence and Existents* (1947) and "Reality and Its Shadow" (1948).

36. Emmanuel Levinas, "Reality and Its Shadow," in *Collected Philosophical Papers*, trans. Alphonso Lingis (Pittsburgh: Duquesne University Press, 1998), 1–13. The essay was originally published in *Les Temps Modernes* 38 (1948): 771–89. Future reference to this essay will be made with the abbreviation RS.

37. See Levinas, "Détermination philosophique de l'idée de culture," in EN.

38. Levinas, *Hors sujet* (Montpellier: Fata Morgana, 1987.) (I discuss this essay more fully in the next chapter.)

39. Levinas, "Quelques réflexions sur la philosophie de l'hitlerisme," in *Les Imprévus de l'histoire* (Paris: Fata Morgana, 1974). Hereafter, this work will be cited in the text by the abbreviation RPH. The essay was originally published in *Esprit* 26 (1934): 199–208.

40. Levinas, "Heidegger, Gagarin et nous," in *Difficile Liberté: Essais sur le Judaïsme* (Paris: Albin Michel, 1976). Future reference to this essay, which was originally published in 1961, will be made with the abbreviation HGN.

41. Levinas, *Existence and Existents*, trans. Alphonso Lingis (The Hague: Martinus Nijhoff, 1978.) Hereafter, this work is cited in the text by the abbreviation EE.

42. The French original reads "caractère désertique, obsédant et horrible et [de] son inhumanité."

43. In this sense Levinas anticipates sociological readings of Heidegger's politics. See Pierre Bourdieu, "L'Ontologie politique de Martin Heidegger," in *Actes de la recherche en sciences sociales* 5–6 (1975), later expanded in *L'Ontologie politique de Martin Heidegger* (Paris: Èditions de Minuit, 1988); and Victor Farías, *Heidegger and Nazism* (Philadelphia: Temple University Press, 1989).

44. Unlike Blanchot, who gives a more positive treatment of the ambiguity of writing in a seminal essay in which he contests both Sartre's and Heiddeger's conceptions of art. See Blanchot, "La Littérature et le droit à la mort," in *La Part du feu*. This essay was originally published in two parts as "Le Règne animal de l'esprit," *Critique* 18 (November 1947): 387–405, and "La Littérature et le droit à la mort," *Critique* 20 (January 1948): 30–47.

45. Emmanuel Levinas, *De l'oblitération: Entretien avec Françoise Armengaud à propos de l'œuvre de Sosno* (Paris: Éditions de la Différence, 1990), 28. Hereafter, this work is cited in the text by the abbreviation O. But even in *De l'obliteration*, Levinas expresses some reservations regarding the concept of an "art of obliteration." While subscribing to F. Armengaud's idea that "obliteration interrupts the image's silence and obliges one to speak," Levinas claims that "it is the word that counts as mediation, since it bears witness to the relation with someone."

CHAPTER 5. ART'S INHUMANITY: ''REALITY AND ITS SHADOW''

1. In *Existence and Existents* and in *Time and the Other* Levinas calls the movement by which a being snatches its existence from pure being *hypostasis*. This is an act without transcendence, the positing of a being that comes into existence and opposes itself to the *il y a*. In *Time and the Other* "the indissoluble unity between the existent and its existing" (54) is called *solitude*. Solitude as "a category of being" (40) does not derive its tragic character from nothingness, but from the "privation of the other." Two important readings of the concept of evasion are Jacques Rolland, "Sortir de l'être par une nouvelle voie," in Emmanuel Levinas, *De l'évasion* (Paris: Fata Morgana, 1982), 10–87; and Hent de Vries, "Levinas," in Simon Critchley and William Schroeder, eds., *A Companion to Continental Philosophy* (London: Blackwell, 1999), 245–55.

2. Levinas's analysis was first published as "Il y a" in *Deucalion* 1 (1946): 141–54. In a footnote he credits Blanchot's *Thomas l' Obscure* with providing a description of the *il y a* (EE 103 / 63). In "Literature and the Right to Death" Blanchot credits Levinas for having elucidated the experience of the *il y a*.

3. Heidegger, *Being and Time*, 228–35, and "What Is Metaphysics?" in *Pathmarks*.

4. "When I am alone, I am not alone, but, in this present, I am already returning to myself in the form of Someone (*quelqu'un*). Someone is there, where I am alone. . . . Where I am alone, I am not there; no one is there, but the impersonal is: the outside, as that which prevents, precedes, and dissolves the possibility of any personal relation with Someone (*quelqu'un*). Someone is what is still present when there is no one. When I am alone, the light of day is only the loss of a dwelling place. It is intimacy with the outside that has no location and affords no rest. Coming here makes the one who comes belong to dispersal, to the fissure where the exterior is the intrusion that stifles, but is also nakedness, the chill of the enclosure that leaves one utterly exposed. Here the only space is vertiginous separation (*vertige de l'espacement*). Here fascination reigns" (EL 27–8/SL 31).

5. It is necessary to stress that in *Otherwise than Being* the "reversal of ontological difference" is followed by its reinscription and displacement. This is a precondition for writing the "otherwise than being," as Levinas explicitly states in the preface to the second edition of *De l'existence à l'existant* (1977) and in part as a response to Jean-Luc Marion's objections in *L'Idole et la distance*. Levinas's treatment of Heidegger's ontological difference is a contentious issue, as evidenced in Derrida's "Violence and Metaphysics." For an assessment of this problematic, see Silvano Petrosino, "D'un livre à l'autre: *Totalité et infini* et *L'Autrement q'être*," in *Emmanuel Lévinas*, ed. Jacques Rolland (Lagrosse: Verdier, 1984); and Silvano Petrosino and Jacques Rolland, *La Vérité nomade: Introduction à Emmanuel Lévinas* (Paris: La Decouverte, 1984).

6. The genealogy of this concept, according to which in the altering being of things a naked type of inwardness takes place, is Husserl's irreflexive consciousness. See Edmund Husserl, *The Idea of Phenomenology: A Translation of "Die idee der Phaënomenologie," Husserliana II*, trans. Lee Hardy (Dordrecht and Boston: Kluwer Academic, 1999). This concept is akin to Merleau-Ponty's *entre-deux*. See Maurice Merleau-Ponty, "La Philosophie et son ombre," in *Signes* (Paris: Gallimard, 1962), 201–28. Hereafter the work by Husserl will be cited in the text by the abbreviation IP.

7. This type of exoticism is once again condemned in *Totality and Infinity*, where the allusion to Rimbaud's "je est un autre" can be read as a synecdoche for a critique of modern aesthetics from premises not very different from those of "Reality and Its Shadow."

8. I must stress the "as if," since Levinas does not specify this deformalization in a positive way. The concept of obliteration that he sketches in an occasional dialogue on the work of Sosno may be the closest he comes. See Levinas, *De l'oblitération*.

9. See Heidegger, "The Origin of the Work of Art."

10. For other readings of "Reality and Its Shadow," see Françoise Armengaud, "Éthique et esthétique: De l'ombre à l'obliteration," in *Emmanuel Lévinas*, eds. Catherine Chalier and Miguel Abensour (Paris: Editions de l'Herne, 1991), 605–19; Robert Eagleston, "Cold Splendor: Levinas's Suspicion of Art," in *Ethical Criticism: Reading after Levinas* (Edinburgh: Edinburgh University Press, 1997); Jill Robbins, "Aesthetic Totality and Ethical Infinity," in *Altered Reading: Levinas and Literature* (Chicago: University of Chicago Press, 1999), 75–90; and Thomas C. Wall, "The Allegory of Being," in *Radical Passivity: Levinas, Blanchot and Agamben* (Albany: State University of New York Press, 1999), 13–30.

11. See Jean-Paul Sartre, "Qu'est-ce que la littérature?" in *Situations II* (Paris: Gallimard, 1964) and Heidegger, "The Origin of the Work of Art." Hereafter the Sartre work will cited in the text by the abbreviation QL.

12. Emmanuel Levinas, "Realité et son ombre," *Les Temps Modernes* 25 (1948). Malka attributes the note's authorship to Maurice Merleau-Ponty. See Salomon Malka, *Lire Lévinas* (Paris: Cerf, 1984), 32. The French reads: "Les ideés de Sartre sur l'engagement de la littérature n'on été examinées qu'à moitié."

13. See Eugen Fink, "Vergegenwärtigung und Bild: Beiträge zur Phänomenologie der Unwirklichkeit," in *Studien zur Phänomenologie, 1930–39* (The Hague: M. Nijhoff, 1966), 71–72. This essay was originally written in 1927.

14. Emmanuel Levinas, *Collected Philosophical Papers*. trans. Alphonso Lingis (Pittsburgh: Duquesne University Press, 1998). Hereafter, this work is cited in the text by the abbreviation CPP.

15. See chapter 3.

16. Levinas's aesthetic conceptuality belongs to a French literary and philosophical tradition whose points of origin are Alain and Paul Valéry. It is Sartre who popularizes this tradition. Some of the main tenets of this tradition are: the clear distinction of color and sound from words, the distinction between sound and image, the opaque nature of sensation, and the placing of art on the hither side of form's material values.

17. For an argument that develops the possibilities of an ethical face-to-face in writing, see A. Ponzio, *Sujet et alterité sur Emmanuel Lévinas* (Paris: L'Harmattan, 1996), 28.

18. Levinas's critique of classic art generally follows Rosenzweig's analysis of pagan art and the anti-iconic Jewish tradition that issues from Maimonides.

19. Emile Benveniste, "La Notion de 'rythme' dans son expression linguistique," in *Problèmes de linguistique générale* 1 (Paris: Gallimard, 1966), 327–35.

20. Henri Meschonic, *Critique du rythme* (Paris: Verdier, 1990).

21. R. Court, "Rythme, tempo, mésure," *Revue d'esthétique* 2 (1974): 148–50.

22. Court, "Rythme, tempo, mésure," 148.

23. For the conceptual solidarity of the language of *Totality and Infinity* with a metaphysics of presence, see Derrida, "Violence and Metaphysics," in WAD. For the performative dimension of *Otherwise than Being*, see Thomas Wiemer, "Das Unsagbare sagen," in *Levinas* eds. M. Mayer and M. Hentschel, Parabel 12 (Giessen: Focus Verlag, 1990), 21; and Derrida, "En ce moment même dans cette ouvrage me voici," in PSY.

24. I am here following Edith Wyschogrod's "The Art in Ethics," in Adriaan Peperzak, ed., *Ethics as First Philosophy* (New York: Routledge, 1995), 137–50.

25. Edmund Husserl, *Cartesian Meditations* (Dordrecht and Boston: Kluwer, 1995); Jean-Paul Sartre, *L'Imaginaire* (Paris: Gallimard, 1940), which was translated as *The Psychology of the Imagination* (London: Routledge, 1995). Hereafter, the Husserl work will be cited by the abbreviation CM, the English version of Sartre's work by PI, and the original French by I.

26. "The unreal is produced outside the world by a consciousness which stays in the world and it is because he is transcendentally free that man can imagine" (I 248/PI 216).

27. In a 1984 essay, "Interdit de la représentation et droits de l'homme," Levinas questions the representational horizon of a phenomenology that takes the body as its point of departure in its appresentation of the other and asks if "sous la méfiance recommandée par le monothéisme juif relativement aux représentations et aux images d'être, ne se dénonce pas, dans les sructures de la signifiance et du sensé, un certain prévaloir de la représentation sur des autres modalités possibles de la pensée." Levinas is here questioning the privilege representation enjoys in phenomenology, in its determination of intentionality, even in the case of a phenomenology of perception like Merleau-Ponty's. Levinas claims that "l'interdit de la représentation suggérerait au contraire dans le sensé une transcendance par rapport à laquelle celle de l'intentionnalité n'aura été qu'un enfermement dans une conscience de soi." See Levinas, *Altérité et transcendance* (Montpellier: Fata Morgana, 1995), 130; 133. Hereafter, this work is cited in the text by the abbreviation AT.

28. See Catherine Chalier, "The Philosophy of Emmanuel Levinas and the Hebraic Tradition," Robert Gibbs, "Height and Nearness: Jewish Dimensions of Radical Ethics," and Charles Scott, "A People's Witness beyond Politics," in Peperzak, ed., *Ethics as First Philosophy*, 3–38; Charles Mopsik, "La Pensée d'Emmanuel Lévinas et la Cabbale," in *Emmanuel Lévinas*, eds. Catherine Chalier and Miguel Abensour (Paris: Éditions de l'Herne, 1991), 428–41; *Idoles: Données et débats*, Actes du XXIVᵉ Colloque des Intellectuels Juifs de Langue Française (Paris: Denoël, 1985); Catherine Chalier, "L'Interdit de la représentation," *La Trace de l'infini: Emmanuel Levinas et la source hébraïque* (Paris: Cerf, 2002), 253–67.

29. Chalier's discussion of the different positions in the debate on the prohibition of images in the Jewish tradition seems to indicate an oscillation between

a complete condemnation, especially when the object of representation is the human face, and the position that sees in the use of the image a tentative orientation in the direction of the invisible so as to better celebrate it and for which art becomes a form of praying. See "L'Interdit de la représentation," 256–57.

30. For the question of "saturated phenomena" and the approach to the invisible beyond being, see Jean-Luc Marion, *L'Idole et la distance* (Paris: Grasset, 1977); *Étant donné: La Croisée du visible* (Paris: Éditions de la Différence, 1996); *God Without Being* (Chicago: University of Chicago Press, 1991), 25–52; and *In Excess: Studies of Saturated Phenomena*, trans. Robyn Horner and Vincent Berraud (New York: Fordham University Press, 2002).

31. See Franz Rosenzweig, *The Star of Redemption*, trans. Barbara E. Galli (Madison: University of Wisconsin Press, 2005), 117–18. Here he defines the language of art as the language of the "before-world." For a comparative study of Levinas see Robert Gibbs, *Correlations in Rosenzweig and Levinas* (Princeton: Princeton University Press, 1992).

32. See also Levinas, "Lévy-Bruhl et la philosophie contemporaine" in *Entre nous.* According to Jill Robbins, participation "describes primitive mentality's mystic belief in the unseen, supernatural forces, its emotional and affective relation to collective representations, which are perceived as having a transitive influence. . . . Participation [is] a way of thinking indifferent to the law of contradiction." See Jill Robbins, *Altered Readings* (Chicago: University of Chicago Press, 1999), 86–89.

33. For a comprehensive study of Heidegger's ontology of the world, see Michel Haar, *The Song of the Earth: Heidegger and the Grounds of the History of Being*, trans. Reginald Lilly (Bloomington: Indiana University Press, 1993).

34. There are several signs of this appeasement: Levinas's explicit recognition of his debt to Heidegger's thinking in *Otherwise than Being*; his way of rethinking the place of being in the general economy of the "otherwise than being"; as well as his reassessment of technology's value in "Idéologie et idéalisme" (1972), published in *Of God Who Comes to Mind* and of the work of art in *Otherwise than Being*. See Levinas, *Of God Who Comes to Mind*, trans. Bettina Bergo (Stanford: Stanford University Press, 1998). Hereafter, this work is cited in the text by the abbreviation GCM.

35. See "Preface à la deuxieme edition," in *De l'existance à l'existant* (Paris: Vrin, 1963), 11–12. This preface dates from 1981 and is not included in the English translation. Hereafter the French version is cited in the text by the abbreviation DEE.

36. Emmanuel Levinas, *Hors sujet* (Montpellier: Fata Morgana, 1972). Hereafter, this work is cited in the text by the abbreviation HS.

37. Levinas, *Noms propres* (Montpellier: Fata Morgana, 1976). Hereafter, this work is cited in the text by the abbreviation NP.

38. The most in-depth study of figuration in Levinas is John Llewelyn, *Emmanuel Levinas: The Genealogy of Ethics* (London: Routledge, 1995), 162–96.

39. In chapter 6 we will see that the introduction of a human dimension at the heart of difference takes place in Blanchot's reading of Levinas's *Totality and Infinity*.

40. "In the image, the object again touches something it had mastered in order to be an object, something against which it had built and defined itself, but now that its value, its signification, is suspended, now that the world is abandoning it to worklessness (*désœuvrement*) and putting it to one side, the truth in it withdraws, the elemental claims it, which is the impoverishment, the enrichment that consecrates it as image" (EL 343–4/SH 419).

CHAPTER 6. "THE WRITING OF THE OUTSIDE,"
BLANCHOT WITH LEVINAS, OR THE "POTENTIALITY"
OF POETIC LANGUAGE IN *OTHERWISE THAN BEING*

1. This expression refers to Foucault's formula for Blanchot's writing. See Michel Foucault, "La Pensée du dehors," in *Dits et écrits I, 1954–1975* (Paris: Gallimard, 1994), 546–67. Hereafter, this work is cited in the text by the abbreviation PD.

2. I focus here only partially on this *rapprochement* and devote the next chapter to a more detailed analysis of how Levinas's and Blanchot's thinking intersect and radically diverge.

3. Alphonso Lingis translates "autrement dit" as "in other words," although the French expression does not contain a nominal form. What is at stake is not the possibility of deploying different ways of naming, but rather the very modality of "l'autrement," the adverbial character of "the otherwise than being." The expression "in other words" still carries the weight of nouns, while "autrement dit" deposes the imperialism of nouns by an adverbial locution that introduces the resounding of the other in the proposition (*dit*). What counts here is the "how" of the coming of the other, which is neither that of a being nor of an entity.

4. Blanchot, "Qui parle?," in *Le Livre à venir*.

5. "A word is a nomination, as much as a denomination, a consecrating of the 'this as this' or 'this as that' by a saying which is also understanding and listening, absorbed in the said. It is an obedience in the midst of the will ('I hear this or that said'), a *kérygma* at the bottom of a fiat" (AE 64/OB 36).

6. See chapter 7 for a more detailed discussion of Levinas's reading of this text.

7. "In all the compunction of Heidegger's magical language and the impressionism of his play of lights and shadows . . . does poetry succeed in reducing rhetoric? Everything that claims to come from elsewhere, even the marvels of which essence is itself capable, even the surprising possibilities of renewal by technology and magic . . . —all this does not deaden the heartrending bustling

of the there is (*il y a*) recommencing behind every negation. There is no break in the business carried by essence . . ." (AE 280/OB 182–83).

8. For a reading more attuned to the dimension of the saying exceeding the grasp of the said, see Derrida, "La Loi du genre," in *Parages*, 231–66.

9. Derrida coins the term *seriature* (*série + rature*) in order to refer to the complex structure of Levinas's text. Derrida describes this structure as "an interrupted series of interlaced interruptions, a series of hiatuses . . . that I shall henceforth call, in order to formalize in economical fashion and so as not to dissociate what is no longer dissociable within this fabric, *sériature.*" See Derrida, "En ce moment même dans cet ouvrage me voici," in *Psychè: Inventions de l'autre*.

10. Emmanuel Levinas, "Exercises on *The Madness of the Day*," in *Proper Names*, trans. Michael Smith (Stanford: Stanford University Press, 1996). The essay was originally published as part of *Sur Maurice Blanchot* (Paris: Fata Morgana, 1975). Hereafter these works will be cited in the text by the abbreviations PN and SM respectively.

CHAPTER 7. THE UNERASABLE DIFFERENCE (LEVINAS IN BLANCHOT)

1. During the 1930s the young Blanchot collaborated with a series of publications from the French extreme right. He became the chief editor of *Journal des débats*, where he published a series of essays on foreign policy characterized by an antidemocratic, antiparliamentary, and anticapitalist rhetoric. Although these publications were anti-Semitic, Blanchot was a close friend of Emmanuel Levinas and Paul Lévy and shared in their struggle against the rising tide of Hitlerism: their denunciation of the camps, and their critique of totalitarianism and the myth of an organic community. Blanchot soon broke ties with anti-Semitic and collaborationist circles. Emmanuel Levinas, a Jew of Lithuanian origin, came to France in the 1930s. During the war he was drafted and was captured by the Germans in 1940. He became a war prisoner and was transferred to a camp near Hanover, where he remained until 1945. In November 1940 Blanchot and his sister saved Paul Lévy from imminent arrest by the Petain regime. After Levinas's capture, his daughter Simone was sent to the countryside to stay with Blanchot's friends, but returned to Paris. Blanchot hid Levinas's wife, Raïssa, and his daughter for several weeks in his Paris apartment, until he was able to secure (through the contacts he had with the Resistance) a safe haven for them in a convent near Orleans. For more details, see Paul Lévy, *Journal d'un exilé* (Paris: Grasset, 1949); Claude Roy, *Moi je* (Paris: Gallimard, 1969); Marie-Anne Lescourret, *Emmanuel Levinas* (Paris: Flammarion, 1994), 64–68; Christof Biden, *Maurice Blanchot: Partenaire invisible* (Paris: Champ Vallon, 1998), 38–42. For Blanchot's own account of his encounter with Levinas, see *Exercise de la patience* 1 (1980): 67; "N'oubliez pas," *L'Arche* 373 (May 1988): 68; "Ce qu'il nous a appris,"

L'Arche 459 (February 1996): 68; and *Pour l'amitié* (Paris: Fourbis, 1996), 35. For Levinas's account, see François Poirié, *Emmanuel Lévinas* (Paris: La Manufacture, 1992), 59–60; Salomon Malka, *Emmanuel Lévinas: La Vie et la trace* (Paris: JC Lattès, 2002).

2. Maurice Blanchot, *Friendship*, trans. Elizabeth Rottenberg (Stanford: Stanford University Press, 1997). Originally published as *L'Amitié* (Paris: Gallimard, 1971). Hereafter, the English translation will be cited in the text by the abbreviation F and the original French will be cited by the abbreviation A.

3. See "Literature and the Right to Death," in *The Station Hill Blanchot Reader*, 359–400; originally published as "La Littérature et le droit à la mort," in *Faux Pas* in 1942, and in *The Space of Literature*.

4. Brian Fitch, *Lire les récits de Maurice Blanchot* (Atlanta: Rodopi, 1992), 9; my emphasis. Hereafter this work is cited in the text by the abbreviation LR.

5. For this reductive view of Blanchot, see Tzvetan Todorov, *Critique de la critique: Un roman d'apprentissage* (Paris: Seuil, 1984).

6. Blanchot, *The Step Not Beyond*, 18.

7. An early essay by Blanchot bears witness to this preoccupation with the other: "Poetry is an encounter, in language, of what is strange, an encounter that preserves it and keeps it in the absolute distance of separation. Poetry is this encounter . . . and thus seems to refer to something that would be anterior, but poetry is this anteriority itself, the affirmation that precedes itself in order to subtract itself from the meaning of what it affirms." "L'Étrange et l'étranger," *La Nouvelle Revue Française* 70 (1958): 753–83.

8. Gerald Bruns, *Maurice Blanchot: The Refusal of Philosophy* (Baltimore: Johns Hopkins University Press, 1999).

9. Bruns's provocative labeling of Blanchot has the merit of manifesting how Blanchot escapes labels, as well as being a painstaking "philological" reading.

10. Françoise Collin, *Maurice Blanchot et la question de l'écriture* (Paris: Gallimord, 1971).

11. Maurice Blanchot, *Le Pas au-delà* (Paris: Gallimard, 1971). Hereafter, this work is cited in the text by the abbreviation PAD.

12. This fragment should be read alongside the essay "Literature and the Right to Death," where "literature" names the very *ambiguity* of language. See Rodolphe Gasché, "The Felicities of Paradox: Blanchot on the Null Space of Literature" and Christopher Fynsk, "Crossing the Threshold: On 'Literature and the Right to Death,'" in *Maurice Blanchot: The Demand of Writing*, ed. Carolyn Bayley Gill (London: Routledge, 1996); and Andrzej Warminski, *Readings in Interpretation: Hölderlin, Hegel, Heidegger* (Minneapolis: University of Minnesota Press, 1987).

13. For Blanchot's reading of Odysseus as a conceptual personae of the man of power, see "Le Chant des sirénes," in *Le Livre à venir*. Odysseus's figure has to

be opposed to Orpheus's, the poet whose infidelity is toward both the realm of action and power, and the realm of the artwork. But Orpheus's infidelity is necessarily double, as we saw in chapter 1.

14. Blanchot, DP, 1–4.

15. In *The Infinite Conversation* the question of philosophy's language will be rephrased as the repressed question of philosophy.

16. Leslie Hill, *Maurice Blanchot: Extreme Contemporary* (London: Routledge, 1999). See chapter 3, "Writing the Neuter," for a thorough discussion of the neuter in Blanchot. This analysis revolves around the second version of the essay "René Char et la pensée du neutre," written two years before "Le 'Discourse Philosophique,'" and later included in *The Infinite Conversation*.

17. Leslie Hill, *Maurice Blanchot: Extreme Contemporary*.

18. In *The Writing of Disaster* we read: "thus there are not two discourses: there is discourse—and then there would be dis-course, were it not that of it we 'know' practically nothing. We 'know' that it escapes systems, order, possibility, including the possibility of language, and that writing, perhaps—writing, where totality has let itself be exceeded—puts it in play" (204/134).

19. Maurice Blanchot, *Le Dernier Homme* (Paris: Gallimard, 1975). Hereafter, this work is cited in the text by the abbreviation DH.

20. Emmanuel Levinas, *Sur Maurice Blanchot* (Montpellier: Fata Morgana, 1975). Hereafter, this work is cited in the text by the abbreviation SMB.

21. Joseph Libertson, *Proximity: Levinas, Blanchot, Bataille and Communication* (The Hague: Nijhoff, 1982).

22. Emmanuel Levinas, *Proper Names*, trans. Michael Smith (Stanford: Stanford University Press, 1996). Hereafter, this work will be cited in the text by the abbreviation PN.

23. See Martin Heidegger, *On the Way to Language*; Timothy Clark, *Derrida, Heidegger, Blanchot*; and Veronique Foti, *Heidegger and the Poets* (Atlantic Highlands, N.J.: Humanities Press, 1992).

24. *For* here signals the giving of a dimension that cannot be absorbed by a philosophical discourse. Therefore, *for* should not be read as "for-philosophy," as a substance philosophy will digest and be nourished by, but instead as a gift that interrupts the logic of assimilation, of the reduction of the other to the same.

25. See "Interiority and Economy," in *Totality and Infinity*, 109–21.

26. "Is Ontology Fundamental?"; "Freedom and Command" (1953); "The Ego and the Totality" (1954); and "Philosophy and the Idea of Infinity" (1957).

27. This distinction has never been overlooked by Blanchot; witness this highly economic formulation: "Writing, without placing itself above art, supposes that one not prefer art, but efface art as writing effaces itself" (ED 89/ WD 53).

28. Blanchot's relationship to Heidegger's thinking merits a study in itself. Although it is true that during the forties Blanchot subscribes to many of Heidegger's theses on art, as early as "La Parole 'sacrée' de Hölderlin," he begins to question some of Heidegger's premises. For a detailed reading of this essay and of the relationship between Blanchot's and Heidegger's conception of the work of art, see Leslie Hill, *Maurice Blanchot: Extreme Contemporary.*

29. A trajectory that is more complex than this critical account would like to suggest, since in key moments of his thinking, such as *Otherwise than Being* and *La Mort et le temps*, Levinas has to recognize his debt to Heidegger. The "profound need to leave behind the climate of Heideggerian philosophy" felt by some Levinasians cannot be easily dismissed.

30. Taking into account the different ways that Heidegger and Levinas understand this term. While for the former, ethics refers to an ontic or regional domain grounded in metaphysics ("Letter on Humanism"), for the latter, ethics refers to a breaching of ontology.

31. On Levinas's reading of Heidegger, see Derrida, "Violence and Metaphysics," in *Writing and Difference.*

32. Much like Heidegger, Blanchot is apprehensive regarding the term "ethics," but does not elude the force of the ethical injunction, as *The Writing of Disaster* and *The Step Not Beyond* clearly show.

33. "Le Servant et son maître" originally appeared in *Critique* 229 (1966).

34. These concepts are the trace, and the distinction between the said and saying, as well as the ethical reduction of the said to the saying that I study in detail in the previous chapter.

35. The French text reads: "fait signe sans que le signe soit porteur de une signification en se désaissant de la signification" (SMB 39).

36. *La Folie du jour* was originally published as "Un récit" in the journal *Empedocles* in 1948.

37. Maurice Blanchot, "Discours sur la patience," *Nouveau Commerce* 30–31 (1975): 19–44. These fragments became part of *The Writing of Disaster.*

38. Emmanuel Levinas, *En découvrant l'existence avec Husserl and Heidegger* (Paris: Vrin, 1967). Hereafter, this work will be cited in the text by the abbreviation EDEHH.

39. "The work . . . is a movement from the Same toward the Other that never returns to the Same. To the myth of Ulysses returning to Ithaca, we would like to oppose Abraham's story, leaving his homeland for good for a land yet unknown" (EDEHH 191).

40. The reader should note that the expression "sens inspiré" is deleted from the English translation, although it appears in the second paragraph within a less decisive context.

41. "Outdoors, I had a brief vision: a few steps away from me, just at the corner of the street I was about to leave, a woman with a baby carriage had

stopped, I could not see her very well, she was manoeuvering the carriage to get it through the outer door. At that moment a man whom I had not seen approaching went in through that door. He had already stepped across the sill when he moved backward and came out again. While he stood next to the door, the baby carriage, passing in front of him, lifted slightly to cross the sill, and the young woman, after raising her head to look at him, also disappeared inside" (SH 194).

42. To say *Book* supposes at least three configurations: empirical (a material volume that functions as the support of something ideal: revelation, ideas, feelings, the expression of a subjectivity); immaterial (the Book as the condition of possibility of any reading and writing); and, finally, a transcendental configuration (the Book understood as an absolute totality, the condition of any possible intelligibility). Common to all these forms is the idea that the Book entails a form of knowledge conceived as the presence of something virtually present, that with the help of a network of mediations becomes immediately accessible. In the Book there is something that presents itself when presenting it, something that the act of reading animates and reestablishes as a living presence: the presence of a content or a signified thing; the presence of a form, signifier or operation; or, finally, the presence of a system of virtual relations. In its leaves the Book both folds and unfolds time, which also means that it contains within itself this unfolding of time as the continuity of a presence in which the present, the past, and the future become actual. See Maurice Blanchot, "L'Absence de livre," in *L'Entretien infini* (Paris: Gallimard, 1969), 620–36.

43. Blanchot, *La Part du feu*, especially "Le mythe de Mallarmé," 35–48; "Le mystère dans les lettres," 49–65; "Le langage de la fiction," 66–78; and "La littérature et le droit à la mort," 291–331.

44. "The nothing is the complete negation of the totality of beings" that manifests itself in anxiety and that opens *Dasein* to Being. Heidegger, "What Is Metaphysics?" in *Pathmarks*.

45. The first version of this essay appeared in *Nouvelle Revue Française* in 1961, the same year that *Totality and Infinity* was published.

46. This is Levinas's articulation of "rapport tout autre": "The absolutely other is the Other (*l'absolument Autre, c'est autrui*). . . . The Stranger (*l'Étranger*) who disturbs the being at home with oneself (*le chez soi*). But stranger also means the free one: over him I have no power (*je ne peux pas pouvoir*). He is not wholly in my site. But I, who have no concept in common with the stranger, am, like him, without *genus*. We shall try to show that the relation between the same and the other is language; it is enacted in discourse, where the same gathered up in its ipseity as an 'I' leaves itself" (TI 55/39).

47. "Parole écrite: parole morte, parole de l'oubli" (12). This reading of the *Phaedrus*, which intersects many of the "motifs" of Derrida's *Of Grammatology*,

takes place in *La Bête de Lascaux* (Montpellier: Fata Morgana: 1982), a meditation on the origins of art, originally published in *Nouvelle Revue Française* 4 (1953). In the aftermath of Heidegger's deconstruction of the concept of the sign and as its most rigorous continuation, Derrida discusses the implications of the devalorization of writing in Western philosophy. Traditionally writing has been characterized by the repetition of a preexisting sensible content (the oral signifier) and the absence of an animating intention, which entails the risk of loss, death and ambiguity. However, speech would not be possible without these values, which explains why the relationship between speech and writing in the classical sense draw its possibilities from a more originary configuration Derrida calls "writing" or "archi-writing." As a more originary "structure" than the distinction speech/writing, "writing" infiltrates experience itself and affects expression, that is, the contiguity of consciouness' self-presence to itself (ideality). The structural necessity of repetition without which there would be no ideality undermines the privileging of presence. In this sense, writing is *différance*: the forces or the rhythm of differentiation, its delay (the possibility of reestablishing meaning after the event of its production), and the condition of possibility *and* impossibility of any conceptual distinction. *Différance* supposes a diachrony, a trace of otherness (absence) that makes any form of manifestation possible, but not without effacing itself. Derrida thinks the movement of *differánce* in terms of *trace*, by which he names the intrigue of the-other-in-the-same as a play of differences without any enrootedness in a transcendental signifier. See Jacques Derrida, "Plato's Pharmacy," in *Dissemination*, trans. Barbara Johnson (Chicago: University of Chicago Press, 1981), 61–171. Levinas's trace can be considered an antecedent of *différance*, and his "unsaying of the said" one way of undermining the classical contiguity of speech and writing still prevalent in *Totality and Infinity*. See Robert Bernasconi, "The Trace of Levinas in Derrida," in *Derrida and Différance*, eds. David Wood and Robert Bernasconi (Evanston, Ill.: Northwestern University Press, 1988), 13–29.

48. For the question of writing in *Otherwise than Being*, see Jacques Derrida, "En ce moment même me voici," in *Psychè: Les inventions de l'autre*. Derrida describes the series of interruptions and weaving as *seriature* ("serie + rature"), through an analysis of Levinas's textile metaphors. For an interesting reading of Derrida's way of approaching Levinas, see Simon Critchley, *The Ethics of Deconstruction* (Oxford: Blackwell, 1992)

49. "When the other (*autrui*) turns toward me, he, being essentially exterior to me, is as though infinitely diverted; and the other (*autrui*) is this movement of turning toward—there where detour reigns. The presence turned toward me is thus still a presence of separation, of what to me is presence even as I am separated from it, distant and turned away. And for me, to be facing the other (*autrui*) is always to be in the abrupt presence, without intermediary, of the one who turns toward me in the infinite approach of the detour"(EI 89/IC 62).

50. "The Other is in the neuter, even when it speaks to us as *Autrui*, then speaking by way of the strangeness that makes it impossible to situate and always exterior to whatever would identify it" (EI 456/IC 311).

51. Blanchot's interest in suffering does not entail an existentialist perspective. He is not interested in suffering as an experience that provides a more authentic dimension of existence. Through the experience of suffering Blanchot has access to a differential temporality. Chapters 1 and 6 focus on this temporality.

52. After the decisive developments of *Otherwise than Being*, in "Détermination philosophique de l'idée de culture"(1983), Levinas defines art as the expression of culture operating under the dependency of the one. See Levinas, *Entre nous.*

POSTFACE

1. Maurice Blanchot, *Friendship*, trans. Elizabeth Rottenberg (Stanford: Stanford University Press, 1997).

Adorno, Theodor W. *Notes to Literature*. Translated by Shierry Weber Nicholsen. New York: Columbia University Press, 1992.

Agamben, Giorgio. *The Coming Community*. Translated by Michael Hardt. Minneapolis: University of Minnesota Press, 1993.

—————. *Language and Death: The Place of Negativity*. Translated by Karen Pinkus and Michael Hardt. Minneapolis: University of Minnesota Press, 1991.

—————. *Stanzas: Word and Phantasm in Western Culture*. Translated by Ronald Martinez. Minneapolis: University of Minnesota Press, 1993.

Alleman, Beda. *Hölderlin und Heidegger*. Zürich and Freiburg: Atlantis Verlag, 1956.

—————. "Hölderlin zwischen Antike und Moderne." In *Hölderlin-Jahrbuch* 24 (1984–85): 29–62.

Aristotle. *The Complete Works of Aristotle*. Edited by Jonathan Barnes. Princeton: Princeton University Press, 1984.

—————. *The Poetics*. Translated and with commentary by Stephen Halliwell. Chapel Hill: University of North Carolina Press, 1987.

Arteaga, A., ed. *An Other Tongue: Nation and Ethnicity in the Linguistic Borderland*. Durham, N.C.: Duke University Press, 1994.

Badiou, Alain. *Court Traité d'ontologie transitoire*. Paris: Éditions du Seuil, 1998.

—————. *Ethics: An Essay on the Understanding of Evil*. Translated by Peter Hallward. London: Verso, 2001.

—————. *Manifesto for Philosophy*. Translated by Norman Madarasz. Albany: State University of New York Press, 1999.

—————. *Petit Manuel d'inesthétique*. Paris: Éditions du Seuil, 1988.

Bailey Gill, Carolyn, ed. *Maurice Blanchot: The Demand of Writing*. London: Routledge, 1996.

Benjamin, Walter. "The Storyteller." In *Illuminations*. Translated by Harry Zohn, 83–109. New York: Shocken Books, 1969.

Benveniste, Emile. *Problèmes de linguistique générale* 1. Paris: Gallimard, 1966.

Bernasconi, Robert. *The Question of Language in Heidegger's History of Being.* Atlantic Highlands, N.J.: Humanities Press International, 1985.

Bernasconi, Robert, and Simon Critchley, eds. *Re-reading Levinas.* Bloomington, Ind.: Indiana University Press, 1991.

Bernasconi, Robert, and David Wood, eds. *The Provocation of Levinas: Rethinking the Other.* London: Routledge, 1988.

———. "The Trace of Levinas in Derrida." In *Derrida and Différance,* eds. David Wood and Robert Bernasconi, 13–9. Evanston, Ill.: Northwestern University Press, 1988.

Bhabha, Homi K. *The Location of Culture.* London: Routledge, 1994.

Bident, Christophe. *Maurice Blanchot, partenaire invisible: Essai biographique.* Seyssel: Champ Vallon, 1998.

Blanchot, Maurice. *Au moment voulu.* Paris: Gallimard, 1951.

———. *La Bête de Lascaux.* Montpellier: Fata Morgana, 1982.

———. "Ce qu'il nous a appris." *L'Arche* 459 (February 1996).

———. *La Communauté inavouable.* Paris: Èditions de Minuit, 1984.

———. *Le Dernier Homme.* Paris: Gallimard, 1953.

———. "Le 'Discourse Philosophique.'" *L'Arc* 46 (1971).

———. "Discours sur la patience." *Nouveau Commerce* 30–1 (1975): 19–44.

———. *Écrits politiques, 1958–93.* Paris: Leo Scherer, 2003.

———. "L'Étrange et l'étranger." *La Nouvelle Revue Française* 70 (1958): 6753–83.

———. *Faux Pas.* Paris: Gallimard, 1943.

———. *La Folie du jour.* Paris: Fata Morgana, 1973.

———. *Friendship.* Translated by Elizabeth Rottenberg. Stanford: Stanford University Press, 1997. Originally published as *L'Amitié* (Paris: Gallimard, 1971).

———. *The Infinite Conversation.* Translated by Susan Hanson. Minneapolis: University of Minnesota Press, 1993. Originally published as *L'Entretien infini* (Paris: Gallimard, 1969).

———. *L'Instant de ma mort.* Montpellier: Fata Morgana, 1994.

———. *Lautréamont et Sade.* Paris: Èditions de Minuit, 1963.

———. *Le Livre à venir.* Paris: Èditions de Minuit, 1963.

———. "N'oubliez pas." *L'Arche* 373 (May 1988): 68.

———. *Pour l'amitié.* Paris: Fourbis, 1996.

———. *The Sirens' Song.* Translated by Gabriel Josipovici. Bloomington, Ind.: Indiana University Press, 1982.

———. *The Space of Literature.* Translated by Ann Smock. Lincoln: University of Nebraska Press, 1992. Originally published as *L'Espace littéraire* (Paris: Gallimard, 1955).

———. *The Station Hill Blanchot Reader.* Edited by George Quasha. Barrytown, N.Y.: Station Hill Press, 1998.

———. *The Step Not Beyond.* Translated by Lycette Nelson. Albany: State University of New York Press, 1992. Originally published as *Le Pas au-delà* (Paris: Gallimard, 1971).

————. *The Work of Fire.* Translated by Charlotte Mandell. Stanford: Stanford University Press, 1995. Originally published as *La Part du feu* (Paris: Gallimard, 1949).

————. *The Writing of the Disaster.* Translated by Ann Smock. Lincoln: University of Nebraska Press, 1986. Originally published as *L'Ecriture du désastre* (Paris: Gallimard, 1980).

Bourdieu, Pierre. "L'Ontologie politique de Martin Heidegger." *Actes de la recherche en sciences sociales* 5–6 (1975).

————. *L'Ontologie politique de Martin Heidegger.* Paris: Éditions de Minuit, 1988.

Brooks, Peter. *Reading for the Plot: Design and Intention in Narrative.* Cambridge: Harvard University Press, 1984.

Bruns, Gerald L. *Heidegger's Estrangements: Language, Truth, and Poetry in the Later Writings.* New Haven: Yale University Press, 1989.

————. *Maurice Blanchot: The Refusal of Philosophy.* Baltimore: Johns Hopkins University Press, 1997.

————. *Tragic Thoughts at the End of Philosophy: Language, Literature, and Ethical Theory.* Evanston, Ill.: Northwestern University Press, 1999.

Butler, Judith. *Gender Trouble: Feminism and the Subversion of Identity.* London: Routledge, 1990.

Calle-Gruber, Mireille. *L'Effet-fiction: De l'illusion romanesque.* Paris: Nizet, 1989.

Caputo, John D. *Against Ethics.* Bloomington, Ind.: Indiana University Press, 1993.

————. *Demythologizing Heidegger.* Bloomington, Ind.: Indiana University Press, 1992.

————. *The Mystical Element in Heidegger's Thought.* New York: Fordham University Press, 1987.

————. "Three Transgressions: Nietzsche, Heidegger, Derrida." *Research in Phenomenology* 15 (1985): 61–78.

Chalier, Catherine. *Figures du féminin: Lecture d'Emmanuel Lévinas.* La Nuit Surveillée. Paris: Verdier, 1982.

————. *Pour une morale au-délà du savoir: Kant et Lévinas.* Paris: Albin Michel, 1998.

————. *La Trace de l'infini: Emmanuel Lévinas et la source hebraïque.* Paris: Les Editions du Cerf, 2002.

Chalier, Catherine, and Miguel Abensour, eds. *Emmanuel Lévinas.* Paris: L'Herne, 1991.

Chanter, Tina. *Time, Death, and the Feminine: Levinas with Heidegger.* Stanford: Stanford University Press, 2001.

————, ed. *Feminist Interpretations of Levinas.* University Park: Pennsylvania State University Press, 2001.

Charcosset, Jean-Pierre. "*Y.* Notes sur la *Stimmung.*" *Exercises de la patience* 3–4 (1982): 46–93.

Chatman, Seymour. *Story and Discourse.* Ithaca: Cornell University Press, 1979.

Clark, Timothy. *Derrida, Heidegger, Blanchot: Sources of Derrida's Notion and Practice of Literature.* Cambridge: Cambridge University Press, 1992.

Cohen, Richard. *Ethics, Exegesis, and Philosophy: Interpretation After Levinas.* Cambridge: Cambridge University Press, 2001.

————, ed. *Face to Face with Levinas.* Albany: State University of New York Press, 1986.

Collin, Françoise. *Maurice Blanchot et la question de l'écriture.* Paris: Gallimard, 1971.

Corngold, Stanley. *The Fate of the Self: German Writers and French Theory.* Durham, N.C.: Duke University Press, 1994.

Court, R. "Rythme, tempo, mésure." *Revue d'esthétique* 2 (1974): 133–58.

Courtine, Jean-François. *Heidegger et la phenomenologie.* Paris: Vrin, 1990.

Critchley, Simon. *The Ehtics of Deconstruction: Derrida and Levinas.* Oxford: Blackwell, 1992.

————. *Ethics, Politics, and Subjectivity.* London: Verso, 1999.

————. *Very Little . . . Almost Nothing: Death, Philosophy, and Literature.* London: Routledge, 1997.

Critique (Paris). "Maurice Blanchot." Special issue, no. 229 (June 1996).

Dallery, Arleen, and Charles Scott, eds. *The Question of the Other: Essays in Contemporary Continental Philosophy.* Albany: State University of New York Press, 1989.

Dallmayr, Fred. *The Other Heidegger.* Ithaca: Cornell University Press, 1993.

Dastur, Françoise. *Heidegger and the Question of Time.* Atlantic Highlands, N.J.: Humanities Press, 1998.

————. *Heidegger et la question anthropologique.* Louvain-Paris: Éditions Peters, 2003.

de Beistegui, Miguel. *Heidegger and Politics: Dystopias.* London: Routledge, 1998.

de Man, Paul. *Allegories of Reading.* New Haven: Yale University Press, 1979.

————. *Blindness and Insight.* Minneapolis: University of Minnesota Press, 1971.

————. *The Rhetoric of Romanticism.* New York: Columbia University Press, 1984.

Deleuze, Gilles. *Difference and Repetition.* Translated by Paul Patton. New York: Columbia University Press, 1994.

Derrida, Jacques. *Adieu to Emmanuel Levinas.* Translated by Pascale-Anne Brault and Michael Naas. Stanford: Stanford University Press, 1995.

————. *La Carte postale.* Paris: Flammarion, 1980.

————. *Demeure: Maurice Blanchot.* Paris: Galilée, 1998.

————. *Dissemination.* Translated by Barbara Johnson. Chicago: University of Chicago Press, 1981.

————. *Of Grammatology.* Translated by Gayatri C. Spivak. Chicago: University of Chicago Press, 1976.

————. *Of Spirit: Heidegger and the Question.* Translated by Rachel Bowlby and Geoffrey Bennington. Chicago: University of Chicago Press, 1991.

————. *Parages.* Paris: Galilée, 1986.

————. *Politics of Friendship.* Translated by George Collins. London: Verso, 1997.

————. *Psychè: Inventions de l'autre.* Paris: Galilée, 1988.

————. *The Truth in Painting.* Translated by Geoff Bennington and Ian McLeod. Chicago: University of Chicago Press, 1987.

————. *Writing and Difference.* Translated by Alan Bass. Chicago: University of Chicago Press, 1978.

de Vries, Hent. "Levinas." In *A Companion to Continental Philosophy*, ed. Simon Critchley and William R. Schroeder. Oxford: Blackwell, 1998.

Docherty, Thomas. *Alterities: Criticism, Theory, and Representation.* Oxford: Clarendon Press, 1996.

Eaglestone, Robert. *Ethical Criticism: Reading after Levinas.* Edinburgh: Edinburgh University Press, 1997.

Esprit (Paris). "Lectures d'Emmanuel Lévinas." Special issue, no. 234 (1997): 112–72.

L'Esprit Créateur (Baton Rouge). "Maurice Blanchot: L'Éthique de la literature." Special issue, 24, no. 3 (fall 1984).

Exercises de la patience (Paris). "Blanchot." Special issue, no. 2 (winter 1981).

————. "Emmanuel Lévinas." Special issue, no. 1 (winter 1980).

Farías, Victor. *Heidegger and Nazism.* Philadelphia: Temple University Press, 1989.

Féron, E. *De l'idée de transcendance à la question du langage: L'Itinéraire philosophique d' Emmanuel Levinas.* Grenoble: Millon, 1982.

Fitch, Brian. *Lire les récits de Maurice Blanchot.* Amsterdam-Atlanta: Rodopi, 1992.

Foti, Veronique. *Heidegger and the Poets.* Atlantic Highlands, N.J.: Humanities Press, 1992.

Foucault, Michel. *Language, Counter-Memory, Practice.* Edited by Donald Bouchard. Ithaca: Cornell University Press, 1977.

————. *The Order of Things: An Archaeology of the Human Sciences.* New York: Vintage, 1973.

————. "La Pensée du dehors." In *Dits et écrits I, 1954–75,* 546–67. Paris: Gallimard, 1994.

Frey, Hans-Jost. *Studies in Poetic Discourse: Mallarmé, Baudelaire, Rimbaud, Hölderlin.* Translated by William Whobrey. Stanford: Stanford University Press, 1996.

Fried, John. *Heidegger's Polemos: From Being to Politics.* New Haven: Yale University Press, 2000.

Froment-Meurice, Marc. *That Is to Say: Heidegger's Poetics.* Translated by Jan Plug. Stanford: Stanford University Press, 1998.

Fynsk, Christopher. *Language and Relation: That There Is Language.* Stanford: Stanford University Press, 1996.

————. "Nietzsche's Testimony." In *Heidegger: Thought and Historicity,* 55–103. Ithaca: Cornell University Press, 1986.

Garber, Marjorie, ed. *The Turn to Ethics.* London: Routledge, 2000.

Gethmann-Siefert, Annemarie. "Heidegger and Hölderlin: The Over-Usage of 'Poets in an Impoverished Time.'" *Research and Phenomenology* 19 (1989): 59–88.

Gibson, Andrew. *Postmodernity, Ethics and the Novel: From Leavis to Levinas.* London: Routledge, 1999.

Gramma. "Lire Blanchot I." Special issue, nos. 3–4 (1976). (1976).

Gramma. "Lire Blanchot II." Special issue, no. 5 (1976). (1976).

Greisch, J, and J. Rolland, eds. "L' éthique comme philosophie première." In *Actes du Colloque de Cerisy-la-Salle.* Paris: Cerf, 1993.

Haar, Michel. "La Pensée et le moi chez Heidegger: Le Dons et les épreuves de l'être." *Revue de métaphysique et morale,* no. 4 (1975): 456–83.

———. *The Song of the Earth: Heidegger and the Grounds of the History of Being.* Translated by Reginald Lilly. Bloomington, Ind.: Indiana University Press, 1993.

Haddad, Gérard. *Maïmonide.* Paris: Les Belles Lettres, 1998.

Halliburton, David. *Poetic Thinking: An Approach to Heidegger.* Chicago: University of Chicago Press, 1981.

Harpham, Geoffrey Galt. *Shadows of Ethics: Criticism and the Just Society.* Durham, N.C.: Duke University Press, 1999.

Hegel, G. W. F. *Phenomenology of Spirit.* Translated by A. V. Miller. Oxford: Oxford University Press, 1988.

Heidegger, Martin. *Basic Writings.* Edited by David F. Krell. New York: Harper & Row, 1977.

———. *Being and Time.* Translated by John Macquarrie and Edward Robinson. New York: Harper & Row, 1962.

———. *Contributions to Philosophy (From Enowning).* Translated by Parvis Emad and Kenneth Maly. Bloomington, Ind.: Indiana University Press, 1999.

———. *Early Greek Thinking: The Dawn of Western Philosophy.* Translated by David Farrell Krell and Frank A. Capuzzi. New York: Harper & Row, 1975.

———. *Einführung in die Metaphysik.* Tübingen: Niemeyer, 1953.

———. *Elucidations of Hölderlin's Poetry.* Translated by Keith Hoeller. Amherst, New York: Humanity Books, 2000.

———. *Erläuterungen zu Hölderins Dichtung.* Frankfurt: Klostermann, 1951.

———. *Hölderlins Hymnen "Germanien" und "Der Rhein."* Gesamtausgabe 39. Frankfurt:: Klostermann, 1980.

———. *Hölderlin's Hymn "The Ister."* Translated by William McNeill and Julia Davis. Bloomington, Ind.: Indiana University Press, 1994.

———. *Holzwege.* Frankfurt: Klostermann, 1950.

———. *An Introduction to Metaphysics.* Translated by Ralph Manhein. New Haven: Yale University Press, 1959.

———. *Kant and the Problem of Metaphysics.* Translated by Richard Taft. Bloomington, Ind.: Indiana University Press, 1990.

———. *Nietzsche.* 4 vols. Translated by David F. Krell. New York: Harper Collins, 1991.

————. *On the Way to Language*. Translated by Peter Hertz. New York: Harper & Row, 1971.

————. *Pathmarks*. Edited by William McNeill. Cambridge: Cambridge University Press, 1998.

————. *Poetry, Language, Thought*. Translated by Alfred Hofstadter. New York: Harper & Row, 1971.

————. *The Question Concerning Technology and Other Essays*. Translated by William Lovit. New York: Harper & Row, 1977.

————. *Sein und Zeit*. Tübingen: Max Niemeyer, 1984.

————. *Sein und Zeit*. Textmit Randbemerkungen d. Auters aus d. Handexemplaren. *Gesamtausgabe* 2. Frankfurt: Klostermann, 1977.

————. *Die Technik und die Kehre*. Pfullingen: Ghünter Neske, 1962.

————. *Unterwegs sur Sprache*. Pfullingen: Günter Neske, 1959.

————. *Der Ursprung des Kunstwerkes*. Stuttgart: Reclam, 1960.

————. "Vom Ursprung des Kunstwerks, Erste Ausarbeitung." *Heidegger Studies* 14 (1998): 6–22.

————. *Vorträge und Aufsätze*. Pfullingen: Günter Neske, 1954.

————. *Was heißt Denken?* Pfullingen: Tübingen: Max Niemeyer, 1984.

————. *What is Called Thinking?* Translated by J. Glenn Gary. New York: Harper & Row, 1968.

Hill, Leslie. *Maurice Blanchot: Extreme Contemporary*. London: Routledge, 1997.

Hodge, Johanna. *Heidegger and Ethics*. New York: Routledge, 1995.

Hölderlin, Friedrich. *Hölderlin's Essays and Letters on Theory*. Translated by Thomas Pfau. Albany: State University of New York Press, 1988.

————. *Poems and Fragments*. Translated by Michael Hamburger. London: Anvil Press Poetry, 1994.

Husserl, Edmund. *Cartesian Meditations*. Dordrecht and Boston: Kluwer, 1995.

————. *The Idea of Phenomenology: A Translation of 'Die idee der Phaënomenologie,' Husserliana II*. Translated by Lee Hardy. Dordrech and Boston: Kluwer Academic, 1999.

Idel, Moshe. *Maïmonide et la mystique juive*. Paris: Cerf, 1991.

Idoles: Données et débats. Actes du XXIVe Colloque des Intellectuels Juifs de Langue Française. Paris: Denöel, 1985.

Kant, Immanuel. *Critique of Judgment*. Translated by Werner S. Pluhar. Indianapolis: Hackett, 1980.

Kierkegaard, Søren. *Fear and Trembling: Repetition*. Translated by Howard V. Hong and Edna H. Hong. Princeton: Princeton University Press, 1983.

————. *Philosophical Fragments*. Translated by Howard V. Hong and Edna H. Hong. Princeton: Princeton University Press, 1985.

Kockelmans, Joseph. *Heidegger on Art and Art Works*. Dordrecht: Martinus Nijhoff, 1985.

Kojève, Alexandre. *Introduction to the Reading of Hegel*. Translated by James Nichols Jr. Ithaca: Cornell University Press, 1980.

Krell, David F. *Daimon Life: Heidegger and Life-Philosophy*. Bloomington, Ind.: Indiana University Press, 1992.

————. *Intimations of Mortality: Time, Truth, and Finitude in Heidegger's Thinking of Being*. University Park: Pennsylvania State University Press, 1986.

Lacan, Jacques. *The Seminar of Jacques Lacan, Book 7: The Ethics of Psychoanalysis, 1959–60*. Translated by Dennis Porter. New York: Norton, 1997.

Lacoue-Labarthe, Philippe. *Heidegger, Art, and Politics: The Fiction of the Political*. Translated by Chris Turner. Oxford: Blackwell, 1990.

————. *Heidegger: La Politique du poème*. Paris: Galilée, 2002.

————. *Musica Ficta: Figures of Wagner*. Translated by Felicia McCarren. Stanford: Stanford University Press, 1994.

Lacoue-Labarthe, Philippe, and Jean-Luc Nancy. *Le Mythe nazie*. La Tour d'Aigues: Editions de l'Aube, 1991.

Laporte, Roger. *Maurice Blanchot: L'Ancien, l'effroyablement ancien*. Montpellier: Fata Morgana, 1987.

Laporte, Roger, and Noël Bernard. *Deux lectures de Maurice Blanchot*. Montpellier: Fata Morgana, 1973.

Laruelle, F., ed. *Textes pour Emmanuel Lévinas*. Paris: J. M. Place, 1980.

Lescourret, Marie-Anne. *Emmanuel Lévinas*. Paris: Flammarion, 1994.

Levinas, Emmanuel. *Altérité et transcendance*. Montpellier: Fata Morgana, 1995.

————. *Autrement que savoir*. Paris: Osiris, 1981.

————. *Autrement qu'être: ou, Au-delà de l'essence*. Paris: Kluwer Academic, 1978.

————. *Collected Philosophical Papers*. Translated by Alphonso Lingis. Pittsburgh: Duquesne University Press, 1998.

————. *De Dieu qui vient à l'idée*. Paris: Vrin, 1982.

————. *De l' Existence à l'existant*. Paris: Vrin, 1963.

————. *De l'oblitération: Entretien avec Françoise Armengaud à propos de l'œuvre de Sosno*. Paris: Éditions de la Différence, 1990.

————. *En dècouvrant l'existence avec Husserl et Heidegger*. Paris: Vrin, 1967.

————. *Entre nous: Essais sur le penser-à-l'autre*. Paris: Grasset, 1991.

————. *Éthique et infini*. Paris: Fayard, 1982.

————. *Existence and Existents*. Translated by Alphonso Lingis. The Hague: Martinus Nijhoff, 1978.

————. "Heidegger, Gagarin et nous." In *Difficile Liberté: Essais sur le Judaïsme*. Paris: Albin Michel, 1976.

————. *Hors sujet*. Montpellier: Fata Morgana, 1987.

————. *Humanisme de l'autre homme*. Montpellier: Fata Morgana, 1972.

————. *La Mort et le temps*. Paris: L'Herne, 1991.

————. *Of God Who Comes to Mind*. Translated by Bettina Bergo. Stanford. Stanford University Press, 1998.

————. *Otherwise than Being, or, Beyond Essence*. Translated by Alphonso Lingis. Pittsburgh: Duquesne University Press, 1998.

————. *Proper Names*. Translated by Michael Smith. Stanford: Stanford University Press, 1996. Originally published as *Noms propres* (Montpellier: Fata Morgana, 1976).

————. "Quelques réflexions sur la philosophie de l'hitlerisme." In *Les Imprévus de l'histoire*. Paris: Fata Morgana, 1974.

————. "Reality and Its Shadow," in *Collected Philosophical Papers*. Translated by Alphonso Lingis, 1–13. Pittsburgh: Duquesne University Press, 1998. The essay was originally published as "Réalité et son ombre" in *Les Temps Modernes* 38 (1948): 771–89.

————. *Sur Maurice Blanchot*. Paris: Fata Morgana, 1975.

————. *Time and the Other*. Translated by Richard Cohen. Pittsburgh: Duquesne University Press, 1987.

————. *Totalité et infini: Essai sur l'extériorité*. The Hague: Martinus Nijhoff, 1961.

————. *Totality and Infinity: An Essay on Exteriority*. Translated by Alphonso Lingis. Pittsburgh: Duquesne University Press, 1969.

Lévy, Paul. *Journal d'un exilé*. Paris: Grasset, 1949.

Libertson, J. *Proximity: Levinas, Blanchot, Bataille, and Communication*. The Hague: Nijhoff, 1982.

Lignes (Paris). "Maurice Blanchot." Special issue, no. 11 (September 1990).

Llewelyn, John. *Appositions of Jacques Derrida and Emmanuel Levinas*. Bloomington, Ind.: Indiana University Press, 2002.

————. *Emmanuel Levinas: The Genealogy of Ethics*. London: Routledge, 1995.

————. *The Hypocritical Imagination: Between Kant and Levinas*. London: Routledge, 2000.

Londyn, Evelyne. *Maurice Blanchot, romancier*. Paris: Nizet, 1976.

Lyotard, Jean-François. *Heidegger and "the Jews."* Translated by Andreas Michel and Mark Roberts. Minneapolis: University of Minnesota Press, 1995.

Madaule, Pierre. *Une tâche serieuse?* Paris: Gallimard, 1960.

Maimonides, Moshe. *Ethical Writings of Maimonides*. Edited by Raymond Weiss. New York: Dover, 1983.

————. *The Guide of the Perplexed*. Translated by Shlomo Pines. Chicago: University of Chicago Press, 1963.

————. "Laws of Repentance." In *Mishneh Torah: The Book of Knowledge*. Edited by E. Moses Hyamson. Jerusalem: Henry Regnery, 1952.

Maldiney, Henry. "L'Irreductible." *Epokhè* 3 (1993): 11–49.

————. *Regard, parole, espace*. Lausanne: L'âge de l'homme, 1973.

Mallarmé, Stéphane. *Mallarmé: Selected Prose Poems, Essays, Letters.* Translated by Bradford Cook. Baltimore: Johns Hopkins University Press, 1956.

————. *Œuvres complètes.* Paris: Gallimard, 1945.

Malka, Salomon. *Lire Lévinas.* Paris: Cerf, 1984.

Marion, Jean-Luc. *Étant donné: La Croisée du visible.* Paris: Èditions de la Différence, 1996.

————. *God Without Being: Hors-Texte.* Translated by Thomas A. Carlson. Chicago: University of Chicago Press, 1991.

————. *L'Idole et la distance.* Paris: Grasset, 1977.

————. *In Excess: Studies of Saturated Phenomena.* Translated by Robyn Horner and Vincent Berraud. New York: Fordham University Press, 2002.

————. *Reduction et donation: Recherches sur Hegel et la phénoménologie.* Paris: Presses Universitaires de France, 1989.

Marx, Werner. *Heidegger and the Tradition.* Translated by Theodore Kiesel and Murray Greene. Evanston, Ill.: Northwestern University Press, 1971.

————. *Towards a Phenomenological Ethics: Ethos and the Life-World.* Albany: State University of New York Press, 1992.

Merleau-Ponty, Maurice. *Eloge de la philosophie.* Paris: Gallimard, 1960.

————. *Signes.* Paris: Gallimard, 1960.

Meschonic, Henri. *Critique du rythme.* Paris: Verdier, 1990.

Mesnard, Philippe. *Maurice Blanchot: Le Sujet de l'engagement.* Paris: L'Harmattan, 1996.

Miller, J. Hillis. *The Ethics of Reading.* New York: Columbia University Press, 1987.

————. *Reading Narrative.* Norman: University of Oklahoma Press, 1998.

Nancy, Jean-Luc. *Being Singular Plural.* Translated by Robert D. Richardson and Anne W. O'Byrne. Stanford: Stanford University Press, 2000.

————. "L'"Ethique originaire' de Heidegger." In *La Penssée dérobée*, 85–113. Paris: Galilée, 2001.

————. *The Sense of the World.* Translated by Jeffrey Librett. Minneapolis: University of Minnesota Press, 1997.

Newmark, Kevin, Andrzej Warminski, and E. S. Burt, eds. *Romanticism and Contemporary Criticism.* Baltimore: Johns Hopkins University Press, 1993.

Nietzsche, Friedrich. *Beyond Good and Evil.* Translated by Walter Kaufmann. New York: Vintage, 1966.

————. *The Birth of Tragedy.* Translated by Walter Kaufmann. New York: Vintage, 1967.

————. *On the Genealogy of Morals.* Translated by Walter Kaufmann. New York: Vintage, 1967.

————. *Thus Spake Zarathustra.* Translated by Walter Kaufmann. London: Penguin, 1966.

————. *The Will to Power*. Translated by Walter Kaufmann and R. J. Hollingdale. New York: Vintage, 1968.

L'Œil-de-bœuf (Paris). "Maurice Blanchot." Special issue, 14–15 (May 1998).

Olafson, Frederick. *Heidegger and the Grounds of Ethics*. Cambridge: Cambridge University Press, 1998.

Peperzak, Adriaan T. *To the Other: An Introduction to the Philosophy of Emmanuel Levinas*. West Lafayette, Ind.: Purdue University Press, 1993.

————, ed. *Ethics as First Philosophy: The Significance of Emmanuel Levinas for Philosophy, Literature, and Religion*. New York: Routledge, 1995

Petrosino, Silvano. "D'un livre à l'autre: *Totalité et infini* et *L'Autrement qu'être*." In *Emmanuel Lévinas*, ed. Jacques Rolland. Le Cahiers de La Nuit surveillé, no. 3. Paris: Verdier, 1984.

Petrosino, S., and J. Rolland. *La Vérité nomade: Introduction à Emmanuel Lévinas*. Paris: La Découverte, 1984.

Pines, Shlomo. *La Liberté de philosopher: De Maïmonide à Spinoza*. Paris: Desclée de Brouwer, 1997.

Plato. *Phaedrus*. In *Euthyphro, Apology, Crito, Phaedo, Phaedrus*. Loeb Classical Library. 1915.

————. *The Republic*. 2 vols. Loeb Classical Library. 1930, 1935.

Pöggeler, Otto. "Den Führer führen? Heidegger und keine Ende." *Philosophische Rundschau* 32 (1985).

————. *Martin Heidegger's Path of Thinking*. Translated by Daniel Magurshak and Sigmund Barber. Atlantic Highlands, N.J.: Humanities Press International, 1987.

————. *Philosophie und Politik bei Heidegger*. Freiburg: Niemeyer, 1972.

Poirié, François. *Emmanuel Lévinas*. Paris: La Manufacture, 1992.

Ponzio, A. *Scrittura-Dialogo-Alterità tra Bachtin e Levinas*. Florence: La Nuova Italia, 1994.

————. *Sujet et alterité sur Emmanuel Lévinas*. Paris: L'Harmattan, 1996.

Préli, George. *La Force du dehors*. Fontenay-sous-Bois: Encres, 1977.

Prince, Gerald. *Narratology: The Form and Functioning of Narrative*. The Hague: Mouton, 1982.

Ralentir Travaux (Paris). "Maurice Blanchot." Special issue, no. 7 (1997).

Rancière, Jacques, ed. *La Politique des poètes: Pourquoi des poètes en temps de détresse?* Bibliothéque du Collége International de Philosophie. Paris: Albin Michel, 1992.

————. *Time and Narrative*. 3 vols. Translated by Kathleen McLaughlin and David Pellauer. Chicago: Chicago University Press, 1983.

————. *Oneself as Another*. Translated by Kathleen Blamey. Chicago: University of Chicago Press, 1992.

————. *Soi-même comme un autre*. Paris: Éditions du Seuil, 1990.

Ricoeur, Paul. *Autrement: Lecture d' "Autrement qu'être, ou, Au-delà de l'essence" d'Emmanuel Lévinas.* Paris: PUF, 1997.

Revue des Sciences Humaines (Lille). "Maurice Blanchot." Special issue, 1998.

Riera, Gabriel. "Abyssal Grounds: Heidegger and Lacan on Truth." *Qui parle?* 9, no. 2 (1997).

———. "For an Ethics of Mystery: Philosophy and the Poem." In *Alain Badiou: Philosophy and Its Conditions,* ed. Gabriel Riera. Albany: State University of New York Press, 2005.

———. " 'The Possibility of the Poetic Said' in *Otherwise than Being* (Allusion, or Blanchot in Lévinas I). *Diacritics* 34 no. 2 (summer 2004): 1–22.

———. " 'The Possibility of the Poetic Said': Between Allusion and Commentary (Ingratitude, or Blanchot in Levinas II). *Angelaki: Journal of the Theoretical Humanities* 9:3 (December 2004): 121–35.

Rimbaud, Arthur. *Œuvres complètes.* Paris: Gallimard, 1972.

Risser, James, ed. *Heidegger toward the Turn: Essays on the Work of the 1930s.* Albany: State University of New York Press, 1999.

Robbins, Jill. *Altered Reading: Levinas and Literature.* Chicago: University of Chicago Press, 1999.

Rolland, Jacques, ed. *Emmanuel Levinas.* Les Cahiers de La Nuit surveillée, 3. Lagrasse: Éditions Verdier, 1984.

Romano, Claude. *L'Événement et le temps.* Paris: Presses Universitaires de France, 1999.

Rosenzweig, Franz. *The Star of Redemption.* Translated by Barbara E. Galli. Madison: University of Wisconsin Press, 2005.

Roth, Michael. *The Poetics of Resistance: Heidegger's Line.* Evanston, Ill.: Northwestern University Press, 1996.

Roy, Claude. *Moi je.* Paris: Gallimard, 1969.

Rüdiger, Safranski. *Martin Heidegger: Between Good and Evil.* Translated by Ewald Osers. Cambridge: Harvard University Press, 1998.

Salanskis, Jean-Michel. *Heidegger.* Paris: Les Belles Lettres, 1997.

Sartre, Jean-Paul. *Being and Nothingness.* Translated by Hazel E. Barnes. New York: Philosophical Library, 1948.

———. *L'Être et le néant: Essaie d'ontologie phénomènologique.* Paris: Gallimard, 1943.

———. *L' Imaginaire.* Paris: Gallimard, 1940.

———. *The Psychology of the Imagination.* London: Routledge, 1995.

———. *Qu'est-ce que la littérature?* Paris: Gallimard, 1948.

———. *"What Is Literature?" and Other Essays.* Edited by Steven Ungar. Cambridge: Harvard University Press, 1998.

Schalow, Frank. "Language and the Tragic Side of Ethics." *International Studies in Philosophy* 27, no. 11 (1996): 49–63.

Scholes, Robert. *Structuralism and Literature.* New Haven: Yale University Press, 1974.

Schrift, Alan. *Nietzsche's French Legacy: A Genealogy of Poststructuralism.* London: Routledge, 1995.

Schulte Nordholt, Anne-Lise. *Maurice Blanchot: L'Écriture comme expérience du dehors.* Geneva: Droz, 1995.

Schürmann, Rainer. *Heidegger on Being and Acting: From Principles to Anarchy.* Translated by Christine Marie Gros. Bloomington, Ind.: Indiana University Press, 1987.

Shaviro, Steven. *Passion and Excess: Blanchot, Bataille, and Literary Theory.* Tallahassee: Florida State University Press, 1990.

Silesius, Angelus. *Cherubinischer Wandersmann.* Stuttgart: Reclam, 1984.

Spitzer, Leo. *Classical and Christian Ideas of World Harmony: Prolegomena to an Interpretation of the Word "Stimmung."* Baltimore: Johns Hopkins University Press, 1963.

Spivak, Gayatri Chakravorty. *In Other Worlds: Essays in Cultural Politics.* New York: Routledge, 1987.

Stoekl, Allan. *Politics, Writing, Mutilation.* Minneapolis: University of Minnesota Press, 1985.

Strauss, Leo. *Maïmonide.* Paris: Desclée de Brouwer, 1988.

SubStance. "Flying White. The Writings of Maurice Blanchot." Special issue, 14 (1976). Madison: University of Wisconsin Press, 1976.

Taminiaux, Jacques. *Poetics, Speculation and Judgment: The Shadow of the Work of Art from Kant to Phenomenology.* Translated by Michael Gendre. Albany: State University of New York Press, 1993.

————., ed. *Heidegger et la idée de la phénoménologie.* The Hague: Nijhoff, 1988.

Todorov, Tzvetan. *Critique de la critique: Un roman d'apprentissage.* Paris: Éditions du Seuil, 1984.

Ungar, Steven. *Scandal and Aftereffect.* Minneapolis: University of Minnesota Press: 1996.

Valèry, Paul. *Œuvres complètes.* Paris: Gallimard, 1965.

von Herrmann, Friedrich-Wilhelm. *Heideggers Philosophie der Kunst: Eine systematische Interpretation der Holzwege-Abhandlung "Der Ursprung des Kunstwerkes."* Frankfurt: Klostermann, 1980.

Wall, Thomas Carl. *Radical Passivity: Levinas, Blanchot, Agamben.* Albany: State University of New York Press, 1999.

Warminski, Andrzej. *Readings in Interpretation: Hölderlin, Hegel, Heidegger.* Minneapolis: University of Minnesota Press, 1987.

Wiemer, Thomas. "Das Unsagbare sagen." In *Levinas: Zur Möglichkeit einer prophetischen Philosophie,* eds. Michael Meyer and Markus Hentschel. Parabel, no. 12. Giessen: Focus Verlag, 1990.

Wilhem, Daniel. *Maurice Blanchot: La Voix narrative.* Paris: U.G.E, 1974.

Wolin, Richard, ed. *The Heidegger Controversy.* Cambridge: MIT Press, 1993.

Wyschogrod, E. *Emmanuel Levinas: The Problem of Ethical Metaphysics.* The Hague: Nijhoff, 1974.

————. *Saints and Postmoderns.* Chicago: University of Chicago Press, 1990.

Young, Julian. *Heidegger's Philosophy of Art.* Cambridge: Cambridge University Press, 2004.

Zarader, Marlène. *La Dette impensée: Heidegger et l'héritage hébraique.* Paris: Èditions du Seuil, 1990.

INDEX

243